Get the eBook FREE!

(PDF, ePub, Kindle, and liveBook all included)

We believe that once you buy a book from us, you should be able to read it in any format we have available. To get electronic versions of this book at no additional cost to you, purchase and then register this book at the Manning website.

Go to https://www.manning.com/freebook and follow the instructions to complete your pBook registration.

That's it!
Thanks from Manning!

Deep Learning with Structured Data

Deep Learning with
Structured Data

MARK RYAN

MANNING
SHELTER ISLAND

For online information and ordering of this and other Manning books, please visit www.manning.com. The publisher offers discounts on this book when ordered in quantity. For more information, please contact

Special Sales Department
Manning Publications Co.
20 Baldwin Road
PO Box 761
Shelter Island, NY 11964
Email: orders@manning.com

Manning Publications Co.
20 Baldwin Road
PO Box 761
Shelter Island, NY 11964

Development editor:	Christina Taylor
Technical development editor:	Al Krinker
Review editor:	Ivan Martinović
Production editor:	Lori Weidert
Copy editor:	Keir Simpson
Proofreader:	Melody Dolab
Technical proofreader:	Karsten Strobek
Typesetter:	Gordan Salinovic
Cover designer:	Marija Tudor

ISBN 9781617296727
Printed in the United States of America

To my daughter, Josephine,
who always reminds me that God is the Author.

brief contents

contents

preface

I believe that when people look back in 50 years and assess the first two decades of the century, deep learning will be at the top of the list of technical innovations. The theoretical foundations of deep learning were established in the 1950s, but it wasn't until 2012 that the potential of deep learning became evident to nonspecialists. Now, almost a decade later, deep learning pervades our lives, from smart speakers that are able to seamlessly convert our speech into text to systems that can beat any human in an ever-expanding range of games. This book examines an overlooked corner of the deep learning world: applying deep learning to structured, tabular data (that is, data organized in rows and columns).

If the conventional wisdom is to avoid using deep learning with structured data, and the marquee applications of deep learning (such as image recognition) deal with nonstructured data, why should you read a book about deep learning with structured data? First, as I argue in chapters 1 and 2, some of the objections to using deep learning to solve structured data problems (such as deep learning being too complex or structured datasets being too small) simply don't hold water today. When we are assessing which machine learning approach to apply to a structured data problem, we need to keep an open mind and consider deep learning as a potential solution. Second, although nontabular data underpins many topical application areas of deep learning (such as image recognition, speech to text, and machine translation), our lives as consumers, employees, and citizens are still largely defined by data in tables. Every bank transaction, every tax payment, every insurance claim, and hundreds more aspects of our daily existence flow through structured, tabular data. Whether you are a newcomer to deep learning or an experienced practitioner, you owe it to yourself to have deep learning in your toolbox when you tackle a problem that involves structured data.

By reading this book, you will learn what you need to know to apply deep learning to a wide variety of structured data problems. You will work through a full-blown application of deep learning to a real-world dataset, from preparing the data to training the deep learning model to deploying the trained model. The code examples that accompany the book are written in Python, the lingua franca of machine learning, and take advantage of the Keras/TensorFlow framework, the most common platform for deep learning in industry.

acknowledgments

I have many people to thank for their support and assistance over the year and a half that I wrote this book. First, I would like to thank the team at Manning Publications, particularly my editor, Christina Taylor, for their masterful direction. I would like to thank my former supervisors at IBM—in particular Jessica Rockwood, Michael Kwok, and Al Martin—for giving me the impetus to write this book. I would like to thank my current team at Intact for their support—in particular Simon Marchessault-Groleau, Dany Simard, and Nicolas Beaupré. My friends have given me consistent encouragement. I would like to particularly thank Dr. Laurence Mussio and Flavia Mussio, both of whom have been unalloyed and enthusiastic supporters of my writing. Jamie Roberts, Luc Chamberland, Alan Hall, Peter Moroney, Fred Gandolfi, and Alina Zhang have all provided encouragement. Finally, I would like to thank my family—Steve and Carol, John and Debby, and Nina—for their love. ("We're a literary family, thank God.")

To all the reviewers: Aditya Kaushik, Atul Saurav, Gary Bake, Gregory Matuszek, Guy Langston, Hao Liu, Ike Okonkwo, Irfan Ullah, Ishan Khurana, Jared Wadsworth, Jason Rendel, Jeff Hajewski, Jesús Manuel López Becerra, Joe Justesen, Juan Rufes, Julien Pohie, Kostas Passadis, Kunal Ghosh, Malgorzata Rodacka, Matthias Busch, Michael Jensen, Monica Guimaraes, Nicole Koenigstein, Rajkumar Palani, Raushan Jha, Sayak Paul, Sean T Booker, Stefano Ongarello, Tony Holdroyd, and Vlad Navitski, your suggestions helped make this a better book.

about this book

This book takes you through the full journey of applying deep learning to a tabular, structured dataset. By working through an extended, real-world example, you will learn how to clean up a messy dataset and use it to train a deep learning model by using the popular Keras framework. Then you will learn how to make your trained deep learning model available to the world through a web page or a chatbot in Facebook Messenger. Finally, you will learn how to extend and improve your deep learning model, as well as how to apply the approach shown in this book to other problems involving structured data.

Who should read this book

To get the most out of this book, you should be familiar with Python coding in the context of Jupyter Notebooks. You should also be familiar with some non-deep-learning machine learning approaches, such as logistic regression and support vector machines, and be familiar with the standard vocabulary of machine learning. Finally, if you regularly work with data that is organized in tables as rows and columns, you will find it easiest to apply the concepts in this book to your work.

How this book is organized: A roadmap

This book is made up of nine chapters and one appendix:

- Chapter 1 includes a quick review of the high-level concepts of deep learning and a summary of why (and why not) you would want to apply deep learning to structured data. It also explains what I mean by *structured data*.

- Chapter 2 explains the development environments you can use for the code example in this book. It also introduces the Python library for tabular, structured data (Pandas) and describes the major example used throughout the rest of the book: predicting delays on a light-rail transit system. This example is the streetcar delay prediction problem. Finally, chapter 2 previews the details that are coming in later chapters with a quick run through a simple example of training a deep learning model.

- Chapter 3 explores the dataset for the major example and describes how to deal with a set of problems in the dataset. It also examines the question of how much data is required to train a deep learning model.

- Chapter 4 covers how to address additional problems in the dataset and what to do with bad values that remain in the data after all the cleanup. It also shows how to prepare non-numeric data to train a deep learning model. Chapter 4 wraps up with a summary of the end-to-end code example.

- Chapter 5 describes the process of preparing and building the deep learning model for the streetcar delay prediction problem. It explains the problem of data leakage (training the model with data that won't be available when you want to make a prediction with the model) and how to avoid it. Then the chapter walks through the details of the code that makes up the deep learning model and shows you options for examining the structure of the model.

- Chapter 6 explains the end-to-end model training process, from selecting subsets of the input dataset to train and test the model, to conducting your first training run, to iterating through a set of experiments to improve the performance of the trained model.

- Chapter 7 expands on the model training techniques introduced in chapter 6 by conducting three more in-depth experiments. The first experiment proves that one of the cleanup steps from chapter 4 (removing records with invalid values) improves the performance of the model. The second experiment demonstrates the performance benefit of associating learned vectors (embeddings) with categorical columns. Finally, the third experiment compares the performance of the deep learning model with the performance of a popular non-deep learning approach, XGBoost.

- Chapter 8 provides details on how you can make your trained deep learning model useful to the outside world. First, it describes how to do a simple web deployment of a trained model. Then it describes how to deploy a trained model in Facebook Messenger by using the Rasa open source chatbot framework.

- Chapter 9 starts with a summary of what's been covered in the book. Then it describes additional data sources that could improve the performance of the model, including location and weather data. Next, it describes how to adapt the code accompanying the book to tackle a completely new problem in tabular, structured data. The chapter wraps up with a list of additional books, courses, and online resources for learning more about deep learning with structured data.

- The appendix describes how you can use the free Colab environment to run the code examples that accompany the book.

I suggest that you read this book sequentially, because each chapter builds on the content in the preceding chapters. You will get the most out of the book if you execute the code samples that accompany the book—in particular the code for the streetcar delay prediction problem. Finally, I strongly encourage you to exercise the experiments described in chapters 6 and 7 and to explore the additional enhancements described in chapter 9.

About the code

This book is accompanied by extensive code examples. In addition to the extended code example for the streetcar delay prediction problem in chapters 3–8, there are additional standalone code examples for chapter 2 (to demonstrate the Pandas library and the relationship between Pandas and SQL) and chapter 5 (to demonstrate the Keras sequential and functional APIs).

Chapter 2 describes the options you have for running the code examples, and the appendix has further details on one of the options, Google's Colab. Whichever environment you choose, you need to have Python (at least version 3.7) and key libraries including the following:

- Pandas
- Scikit-learn
- Keras/TensorFlow 2.x

As you run through the portions of the code, you may need to pip install additional libraries.

The deployment portion of the main streetcar delay prediction example has some additional requirements:

- Flask library for the web deployment
- Rasa chatbot framework and ngrok for the Facebook Messenger deployment

The source code is formatted in a `fixed-width font like this` to separate it from ordinary text. Sometimes code is also **in bold** to highlight code that has changed from previous steps in the chapter, such as when a new feature adds to an existing line of code.

In many cases, the original source code has been reformatted; we've added line breaks and reworked indentation to accommodate the available page space in the book. In rare cases, even this was not enough, and listings include line-continuation markers (➥). Additionally, comments in the source code have often been removed from the listings when the code is described in the text. Code annotations accompany many of the listings, highlighting important concepts.

You can find all the code examples for this book in the GitHub repo at http://mng.bz/v95x.

liveBook discussion forum

Purchase of *Deep Learning with Structured Data* includes free access to a private web forum run by Manning Publications where you can make comments about the book, ask technical questions, and receive help from the author and from other users. To access the forum, go to https://livebook.manning.com/#!/book/deep-learning-with-structured-data/discussion. You can also learn more about Manning's forums and the rules of conduct at https://livebook.manning.com/#!/discussion.

Manning's commitment to our readers is to provide a venue where a meaningful dialogue between individual readers and between readers and the author can take place. It is not a commitment to any specific amount of participation on the part of the author, whose contribution to the forum remains voluntary (and unpaid). We suggest you try asking the author some challenging questions lest his interest stray! The forum and the archives of previous discussions will be accessible from the publisher's website as long as the book is in print.

about the author

MARK RYAN is a data science manager at Intact Insurance in Toronto, Canada. Mark has a passion for sharing the benefits of machine learning, including delivering machine learning bootcamps to give participants a hands-on introduction to the world of machine learning. In addition to deep learning and its potential to unlock additional value in structured, tabular data, his interests include chatbots and the potential of autonomous vehicles. He has a bachelor of mathematics degree from the University of Waterloo and a master's degree in computer science from the University of Toronto.

about the cover illustration

The figure on the cover of *Deep Learning with Structured Data* is captioned "Homme de Navarre," or "A man from Navarre," a diverse northern region of northern Spain. The illustration is taken from a collection of dress costumes from various countries by Jacques Grasset de Saint-Sauveur (1757–1810), titled *Costumes de Différents Pays,* published in France in 1797. Each illustration is finely drawn and colored by hand. The rich variety of Grasset de Saint-Sauveur's collection reminds us vividly of how culturally apart the world's towns and regions were just 200 years ago. Isolated from each other, people spoke different dialects and languages. In the streets or in the countryside, it was easy to identify where they lived and what their trade or station in life was just by their dress.

The way we dress has changed since then and the diversity by region, so rich at the time, has faded away. It is now hard to tell apart the inhabitants of different continents, let alone different towns, regions, or countries. Perhaps we have traded cultural diversity for a more varied personal life—certainly for a more varied and fast-paced technological life.

At a time when it is hard to tell one computer book from another, Manning celebrates the inventiveness and initiative of the computer business with book covers based on the rich diversity of regional life of two centuries ago, brought back to life by Grasset de Saint-Sauveur's pictures.

Why deep learning
with structured data?

This chapter covers

- A high-level overview of deep learning
- Benefits and drawbacks of deep learning
- Introduction to the deep learning software stack
- Structured versus unstructured data
- Objections to deep learning with structured data
- Advantages of deep learning with structured data
- Introduction to the code accompanying this book

Since 2012, we have witnessed what can only be called a renaissance of artificial intelligence. A discipline that had lost its way in the late 1980s is important again. What happened?

In October 2012, a team of students working with Geoffrey Hinton (a leading academic proponent of deep learning based at the University of Toronto) announced a result in the ImageNet computer vision contest that achieved an error rate in identifying objects that was close to half that of the nearest competitor.

This result exploited deep learning and ushered in an explosion of interest in the topic. Since then, we have seen deep learning applications with world-class results in many domains, including image processing, audio to text, and machine translation. In the past couple of years, the tools and infrastructure for deep learning have reached a level of maturity and accessibility that make it possible for nonspecialists to take advantage of deep learning's benefits. This book shows how you can use deep learning to get insights into and make predictions about *structured data*: data organized as tables with rows and columns, as in a relational database. You will see the capability of deep learning by going step by step through a complete, end-to-end example of deep learning, from ingesting the raw input structured data to making the deep learning model available to end users. By applying deep learning to a problem with a real-world structured dataset, you will see the challenges and opportunities of deep learning with structured data.

1.1 *Overview of deep learning*

Before reviewing the high-level concepts of deep learning, let's introduce a simple example that we can use to explore these concepts: detection of credit card fraud. Chapter 2 introduces the real-world dataset and an extensive code example that prepares this dataset and uses it to train a deep learning model. For now, this basic fraud detection example is sufficient for a review of some of the concepts of deep learning.

Why would you want to exploit deep learning for fraud detection? There are several reasons:

- Fraudsters can find ways to work around the traditional rules-based approaches to fraud detection (http://mng.bz/emQw).
- A deep learning approach that is part of an industrial-strength pipeline—in which the model performance is frequently assessed and the model is automatically retrained if its performance drops below a given threshold—can adapt to changes in fraud patterns.
- A deep learning approach has the potential to provide near-real-time assessment of new transactions.

In summary, deep learning is worth considering for fraud detection because it can be the heart of a flexible, fast solution. Note that in addition to these advantages, there is a downside to using deep learning as a solution to the problem of fraud detection: compared with other approaches, deep learning is harder to explain. Other machine learning approaches allow you to determine which input characteristics most influence the outcome, but this relationship can be difficult or impossible to establish with deep learning.

Assume that a credit card company maintains customer transactions as records in a table. Each record in this table contains information about the transaction, including an ID that uniquely identifies the customer, as well as details about the transaction, including the date and time of the transaction, the ID of the vendor, the location of the transaction, and the currency and amount of the transaction. In addition to this information, which is added to the table every time a transaction is reported, every record has a field to indicate whether the transaction was reported as a fraud.

The credit card company plans to train a deep learning model on the historical data in this table and use this trained model to predict whether new incoming transactions are fraudulent. The goal is to identify potential fraud as quickly as possible (and take corrective action) rather than waiting days for the customer or vendor to report that a particular transaction is fraudulent.

Let's examine the customer transaction table. Figure 1.1 contains a snippet of what some records in this table would look like.

				Training data (X)					Label (Y)
customer ID	transaction date	transaction time	vendor ID	City	Country	currency	amount		fraud
1000123	13-Apr-18	14:45	X000456	Washing	US	USD	30.21		0
1000188	14-Mar-18	10:31	X000433	Dallas	US	USD	322.00		0
1000290	11-Feb-18	22:40	X000501	Tokyo	Japan	YEN	10000000.00		1
1000104	05-Feb-18	6:20	W00089	Paris	France	EUR	7.90		0

Figure 1.1   Dataset for credit card fraud example

The columns customer ID, transaction date, transaction time, vendor ID, City, Country, currency, and amount contain details about individual credit card transactions for the previous quarter. The fraud column is special because it contains the label: the value that we want the deep learning model to predict when it has been trained on the training data. Assume that the default value in the fraud column is 0 (meaning "not a fraud"), and that when one of our customers or vendors reports a fraudulent transaction, the value in the fraud column for that transaction in the table is set to 1.

As new transactions arrive, we want to be able to predict whether they are fraudulent so that we can quickly take corrective action. By training the deep learning model on the historical dataset, we will be defining a function that can predict whether new credit card transactions are fraudulent. In this example of supervised learning (http://mng.bz/pzBE), the model is trained by means of a dataset that incorporates examples with labels. The dataset that is used to train the model includes the value that the trained model will predict (in this case, whether a transaction is fraudulent). By contrast, in unsupervised learning the training dataset does not include labels.

Now that we have introduced the credit card fraud example, let's use it to take a brief tour of some of the concepts of deep learning. For a more in-depth description of these concepts, see François Chollet's *Deep Learning with Python,* 2nd ed. (http://mng.bz/OvM2), which includes excellent descriptions of these concepts:

- *Deep learning* is a machine learning approach in which multilayer artificial neural networks are trained by setting weights and offsets at each layer by optimizing a *loss function* (the delta between the actual outcome [the values in the fraud column] and the predicted outcome) through the use of gradient-based optimization and backpropagation.
- Neural networks in a deep learning model have a series of layers, starting with the input layer, followed by several hidden layers, and culminating with an output layer.
- In each of these layers, the output of the previous layer (or, in the case of the first layer, the training data, which for our example is the dataset columns from customer ID, date, time, vendor ID, City, Country, currency and amount) goes through a series of operations (multiplication by a matrix of weights, addition of an offset [bias], and application of a nonlinear activation function) to produce the input for the next layer. In figure 1.2, each circle (node) has its own set of weights. The inputs are multiplied by those weights, the bias is added, and an activation function is applied to the result to produce the output that is taken in by the next layer.

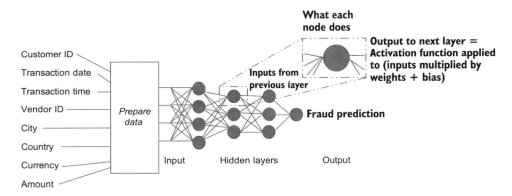

Figure 1.2   Multilayered neural network

- The final output layer generates the prediction of the model based on the input. In our example of predicting credit card fraud, the output indicates whether the model predicts a fraud (output of 1) or not a fraud (output of 0) for a given transaction.
- Deep learning works by iteratively updating the weights in the network to minimize the loss function (the function that defines the aggregate difference between the predictions of the model and the actual result values in the training dataset). As the weights are adjusted, the model's predictions in aggregate get closer to the actual result values in the fraud column of the input table. With each training iteration, the weights are adjusted based on the gradient of the loss function.

You can think of the gradient of the loss function as being roughly equivalent to the slope of a hill. If you make small, incremental steps in the direction opposite the slope of the hill, you will eventually get to the bottom of the hill. By making small changes to the weights in the direction opposite to the gradient for each iteration through the network, you reduce the loss function bit by bit. A process called *backpropagation* is used to get the gradient of the loss function, which can then be applied to update the weights for each node in the neural network in such a way that with repeated applications, the loss function is minimized and the accuracy of the model's predictions is maximized. The training process is summarized in figure 1.3.

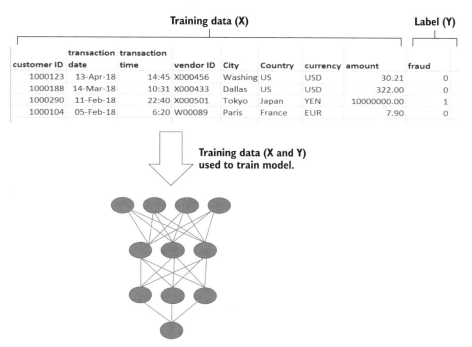

				Training data (X)				Label (Y)	
customer ID	transaction date	transaction time	vendor ID	City	Country	currency	amount	fraud	
1000123	13-Apr-18	14:45	X000456	Washing	US	USD	30.21	0	
1000188	14-Mar-18	10:31	X000433	Dallas	US	USD	322.00	0	
1000290	11-Feb-18	22:40	X000501	Tokyo	Japan	YEN	10000000.00	1	
1000104	05-Feb-18	6:20	W00089	Paris	France	EUR	7.90	0	

Training data (X and Y) used to train model.

Figure 1.3 Training data is used when weights are iteratively updated in the network to train the model.

- When the training is complete (the weights in the model have been repeatedly updated using the gradient provided by backpropagation to achieve the desired performance with the training data), the resulting model can be used to make predictions on new data that the model has never seen.

The output of the process is a trained deep learning model that incorporates the final weights and can be used to predict outputs from new input data, as shown in figure 1.4.

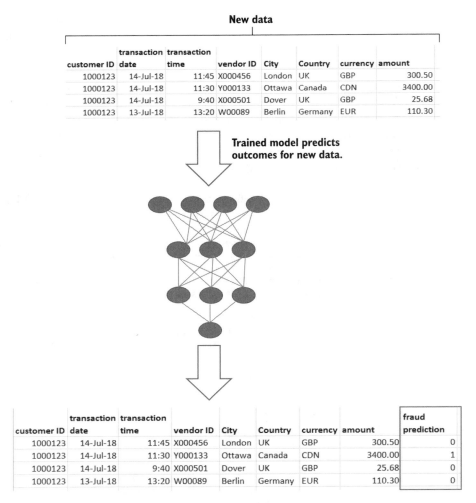

New data

customer ID	transaction date	transaction time	vendor ID	City	Country	currency	amount
1000123	14-Jul-18	11:45	X000456	London	UK	GBP	300.50
1000123	14-Jul-18	11:30	Y000133	Ottawa	Canada	CDN	3400.00
1000123	14-Jul-18	9:40	X000501	Dover	UK	GBP	25.68
1000123	13-Jul-18	13:20	W00089	Berlin	Germany	EUR	110.30

Trained model predicts outcomes for new data.

customer ID	transaction date	transaction time	vendor ID	City	Country	currency	amount	fraud prediction
1000123	14-Jul-18	11:45	X000456	London	UK	GBP	300.50	0
1000123	14-Jul-18	11:30	Y000133	Ottawa	Canada	CDN	3400.00	1
1000123	14-Jul-18	9:40	X000501	Dover	UK	GBP	25.68	0
1000123	13-Jul-18	13:20	W00089	Berlin	Germany	EUR	110.30	0

Figure 1.4   A trained model generates predictions on new data.

This book does not cover the mathematical basis of deep learning. The section on the mathematical building blocks of deep learning in *Deep Learning with Python*, 2nd ed., provides a clear, concise description of the math behind deep learning. You can also see the reference to the deeplearning.ai curriculum in chapter 9 for a good overview of the math behind deep learning.

1.2   Benefits and drawbacks of deep learning

The core point of deep learning is both simple and profound: a trained deep learning model can incorporate a function of incredible complexity that accurately characterizes patterns implicit in the data on which the model is trained. Given enough labeled data to train on (such as a large-enough dataset of credit card transactions with a column to indicate whether each transaction is a fraud), deep learning can define a model that predicts the label values for new data that the model never saw during the training process. The functions that deep learning defines in the form of trained models can include millions of parameters, well beyond what any human could create by hand.

In some use cases, such as image recognition, deep learning models have the benefit of being trainable on data that is closer to the raw input data than is possible with non-deep-learning machine learning approaches. Those approaches may require extensive *feature engineering* (hand-coded transformations of the input data and new columns in the input table) to achieve good performance.

The benefits of deep learning don't come free. Deep learning has several significant drawbacks that you need to be prepared to deal with. For deep learning to work, you need

- *Lots of labeled data*—You may need millions of examples, depending on the domain.
- *Hardware capable of doing massive matrix manipulations*—As you will see in chapter 2, a modern laptop may be sufficient to train a simple deep learning model. Bigger models will require specialized hardware (GPUs and TPUs) to train efficiently.
- *Tolerance for the model's imperfect transparency*—When you compare deep learning with classic, non-deep-learning machine learning, it can be more difficult to spell out why a deep learning model is making the predictions it is making. In particular, if a model is trained on a certain set of features (customer ID, transaction date, transaction time, and so on), it can be difficult to determine which features contribute most to the model's capability to predict an outcome.
- *Significant engineering to avert common pitfalls*—These pitfalls include overfitting (the model is accurate for the data it was trained on, but doesn't generalize to new data) and vanishing/exploding gradients (backpropagation blows up or grinds to a halt because the modifications to the weights become too large or too small at each step).
- *Ability to manipulate multiple hyperparameters*—Data scientists need to control a set of knobs called *hyperparameters*, including learning rate (the size of the steps taken each time the weights are updated), regularization (various tactics to avert overfitting), and the number of times the training process iterates through the input dataset to train the model. Adjusting these knobs to get a good result can be like trying to fly a helicopter. As a helicopter pilot needs to coordinate hands and feet in harmony to keep the machine on a steady path and avoid crashing, a data scientist training a deep learning model needs to coordinate the hyperparameters in harmony to get desired results out of the model and avoid pitfalls such as overfitting. See chapter 5 for details about the hyperparameters used to train the model for this book's extended example.

- *Tolerance for less-than-perfect accuracy*—Deep learning is, by its nature, not going to produce 100% accurate predictions. If absolute accuracy is required, it's better to use a more deterministic approach.

Here are some mitigations for these drawbacks:

- *Lots of labeled data*—Deep learning's thirst for massive amounts of labeled data can be tempered with *transfer learning*: reusing models or subsets of models that are trained to perform one task on a related task. A model trained on a large, general set of labeled image data can be used to jump-start a model that is being applied to a specific domain in which labeled image data is scarce. The extended example in this book does not apply transfer learning, but you can see *Transfer Learning for Natural Language Processing* by Paul Azunre (http://mng.bz/GdVV) for details on the key role that transfer learning plays in deep learning use cases such as natural language processing and computer vision.
- *Hardware capable of doing massive matrix manipulations*—Today, it's easy to get access to environments (including the cloud environments introduced in chapter 2) with sufficient hardware power to train challenging models at modest cost. The extended deep learning example in this book can be exercised faster in a cloud environment with hardware specifically designed for deep learning, but you can also exercise it on a reasonably provisioned modern laptop.
- *Tolerance for the model's imperfect transparency*—Several vendors (including Amazon, Google, and IBM) now offer solutions to help make deep learning models more transparent and explain the behavior of deep learning models.
- *Significant engineering to avert common pitfalls*—Algorithm improvements keep making their way into common deep learning frameworks to help insulate you from problems like exploding gradients.
- *Ability to manipulate multiple hyperparameters*—Automated approaches to optimizing hyperparameters have the potential to reduce the complexity of tuning hyperparameters and make the experience of training a deep learning model less like flying a helicopter and more like driving a car, in that a limited set of inputs (steering wheel, accelerator) has direct results (car changes direction, car changes speed).

Less-than-perfect accuracy remains a challenge. The impact of imperfect accuracy depends on the problem that you are trying to solve. If you are predicting whether a client is going to churn (take its business to a competitor), being right 85% or 90% of the time may be more than sufficient for the problem. If you are predicting a potentially fatal medical condition, however, the intrinsic limits of deep learning are harder to get around. How much inaccuracy you can tolerate will depend on the problem you are solving.

1.3   *Overview of the deep learning stack*

A variety of deep learning frameworks is available today. The two most popular are TensorFlow (https://www.tensorflow.org), which dominates in industrial applications of deep learning, and PyTorch (https://pytorch.org), which has a strong following in the research community.

In this book, we're going to use Keras (https://keras.io) as our deep learning library. Keras began life as a freestanding project that could be used as a frontend for a variety of deep learning frameworks. As explained in chapter 5, as of TensorFlow 2.0, Keras is integrated into TensorFlow. Keras is the recommended high-level API for TensorFlow. The code accompanying this book has been validated with TensorFlow 2.0, but you should not have any issues using later versions of TensorFlow.

Here is a brief introduction to the main components of the stack:

- *Python*—This easy-to-learn, flexible interpreted language is by far the most popular language for machine learning. Python's growth in popularity has closely tracked the machine learning renaissance in the past decade, and it now far outstrips its closest rival, R, as the lingua franca of machine learning. Python has a huge ecosystem and a massive set of libraries that cover not only everything you want to do with machine learning, but also the gamut of development. In addition, Python has a huge developer community, and you can easily find answers online to almost any Python question or problem. The code examples in this book are written entirely in Python, with the exception of the YAML config files described in chapter 3; an SQL example in chapter 2; and the deployments described in chapter 8, which include code in Markdown, HTML, and JavaScript.

- *Pandas*—This Python library gives you everything you need to conveniently deal with tabular, structured data within Python. You can easily import structured data (whether from CSV or Excel files or directly from a table in a relational database) into a Pandas dataframe and then manipulate it with table operations (such as dropping and adding columns, filtering by column values, and joining tables). You can think of Pandas as being Python's answer to SQL. Chapter 2 contains several examples of loading data into Pandas dataframes and using Pandas to perform common SQL-type operations.

- *scikit-learn*—scikit-learn is an extensive Python library for machine learning. The extended example in this book makes extensive use of this library, including the data transformation utilities described in chapters 3 and 4 and the facility described in chapter 8, to define trainable data pipelines that prepare data both for training the deep learning model and for getting predictions from the trained model.

- *Keras*—Keras is a straightforward library for deep learning that gives you ample flexibility and control while abstracting out some of the complexity of the low-level TensorFlow API. Keras has a large, active community that includes beginners and experienced machine learning practitioners, and it's easy to find solid examples of using Keras for deep learning applications.

1.4   Structured vs. unstructured data

The title of this book contains two terms that do not commonly appear together: *deep learning* and *structured data*. Structured data (in the context of this book) refers to data that is organized in tables with rows and columns—the kind of data that resides in relational databases. Deep learning is an advanced machine learning technique that has demonstrated success on a range of problems with data that is not commonly stored in tables, such as images, video, audio, and text.

Why apply deep learning to structured data? Why combine a data paradigm that is 40 years old with cutting-edge deep learning? Aren't there simpler approaches to solving problems that involve structured data? Aren't there better applications of the power of deep learning than attempting to train models with data that resides in tables?

To answer these valid questions, we're first going to define in a bit more detail what we mean by structured and unstructured data; in section 1.5, we'll address these and other objections to applying deep learning to structured tabular data.

In this book, *structured data* is data that has been organized to reside in a relational database with rows and columns. The columns can contain numeric values (such as currency amounts, temperatures, time durations, or other quantities expressed as integer or floating-point values) or non-numeric values (such as strings, embedded structured objects, or unstructured objects).

All relational databases support SQL (albeit with varying dialects) as the primary interface to the database. Common relational databases include the following:

- *Proprietary databases*—Oracle, SQL Server, Db2, Teradata
- *Open source databases*—Postgres, MySQL, MariaDB
- *Propriety database offerings based on open source*—AWS Redshift (based on Postgres)

Relational databases can include relationships between tables, such as foreign keys (in which the permissible values in the column of one table depend on the values in an identified column in another table). Tables can be joined to create new tables that contain combinations of the rows and columns from the tables participating in the join. Relational databases can also incorporate sets of code, such as sets of SQL statements called stored procedures, that can be invoked to access and manipulate data in the database. For the purposes of this book, we will be focusing on the row and typed column nature of tables rather than the additional intertable interactions and code interfaces provided by relational databases.

Relational databases are not the only possible repositories of structured tabular data. As shown in figure 1.5, data in Excel or CSV files is intrinsically structured in rows and columns, although unlike in relational tables, the types of the columns are not encoded as part of the structure but inferred from the column contents. The dataset for the main example in this book comes from a set of Excel files.

For the purposes of this book, we will not be looking at unstructured data—data that is not organized to reside in tabular form in a relational database. As shown in figure 1.6,

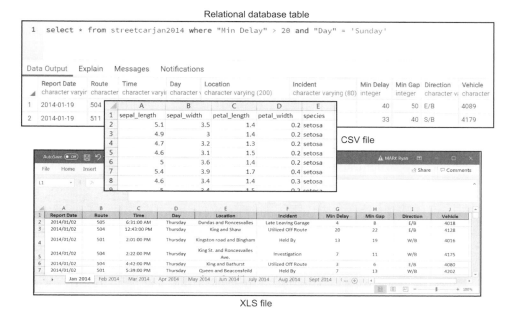

Figure 1.5   **Examples of tabular structured data**

unstructured data includes image, video, and audio files, as well as text and tagged formats such as XML, HTML, and JSON. By this definition, unstructured data doesn't necessarily have *zero* structure. The key/value pairs in JSON are a kind of structure, for

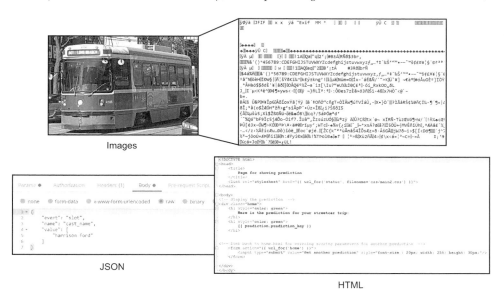

Figure 1.6   **Examples of unstructured data**

example, but in its native state JSON is not organized in a tabular form with rows and columns, so for the purposes of this book, it is unstructured. To complicate matters further, structured data can contain unstructured elements, such as columns in a table that contain freeform text or that refer to XML documents or BLOBs (binary large objects).

Many books cover applications of deep learning to unstructured data such as images and text. This book takes a different direction by focusing exclusively on deep learning applied to tabular structured data. Sections 1.5 and 1.6 provide some justification for this focus on structured data, first discussing some reasons why you might be skeptical about a focus on structured data, and then reviewing the benefits of exploring a structured data problem with deep learning.

1.5   *Objections to deep learning with structured data*

Many of the celebrated applications of deep learning have involved unstructured data such as images, audio, and text. Some deep learning experts question whether deep learning should be applied to structured data at all and insist that a non-deep-learning approach is best for structured data.

To motivate your exploration of deep learning with structured data, let's review some of the objections:

- *Structured datasets are too small to feed deep learning.* Whether this objection is valid depends on the domain. Certainly, there are many domains (including the problem explored in this book) in which the labeled structured dataset contains tens of thousands or even millions of examples, making them large enough to be in contention for training a deep learning model.
- *Keep it simple.* Deep learning is hard and complicated, so why not use an easier solution, such as non-deep-learning machine learning or traditional business intelligence applications? This objection was more valid three years ago than it is today. Deep learning has reached a tipping point in terms of simplicity and widespread use. Thanks to the popularity of deep learning, the tools available to exploit it are much easier to use. As you will see in the extended coding examples in this book, deep learning is now accessible to nonspecialists.
- *Handcrafted deep learning solutions are becoming less necessary.* Why go through the effort of creating an end-to-end deep learning solution, particularly if you are not a full-time data scientist, if handcrafted solutions will increasingly be replaced by solutions that require little or no coding? The fast.ai library (https://docs.fast.ai), for example, allows you to create powerful deep learning models with a few lines of code, and data science environments like Watson Studio offer GUI-based model builders (as shown in figure 1.7) that let you create a deep learning model without doing any coding at all.

  With these solutions, why make the effort to learn how to code a deep learning model directly? To understand how to use low-code or no-code solutions, you still need to understand how a deep learning model is put together, and the fastest way to learn that is to write the code to harness deep learning frameworks. If you deal primarily with tabular data in your job, it makes sense to be able to apply deep learning to that data. By coding a deep learning solution to a problem that involves structured tabular data that you understand thoroughly, you gain understanding of the concepts, strengths, and limitations of deep learning. Armed with that understanding, you will be able to exploit deep learning (whether hand-coded or not) to solve further problems. The extended example in this book takes you through an end-to-end example of applying deep learning to structured tabular data. In chapter 9, you will learn how to adapt the example in this book to your own structured data datasets.

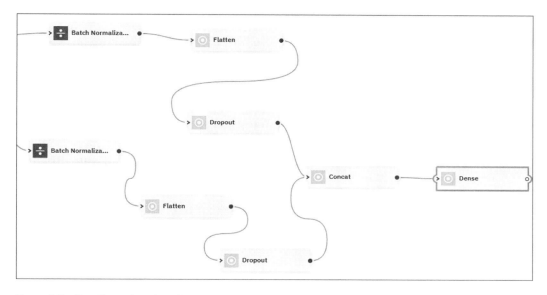

Figure 1.7   Creating a deep learning model by using a GUI (Watson Studio)

In this section, we looked at common objections to using deep learning to solve problems involving structured data and reviewed subjective responses. A subjective response is not sufficient, however; we also need to compare working code implementations of deep learning versus non-deep learning. In chapter 7, we make a head-to-head comparison of two solutions to the extended example in this book: the deep learning solution and a solution based on a non-deep-learning approach called XGBoost. We compare these two approaches in terms of performance, model training time, code complexity, and flexibility.

1.6   Why investigate deep learning with a structured data problem?

In section 1.5, we reviewed some of the objections to applying deep learning to structured data. Let's assume that you are satisfied with how these objections were handled. There's still the question of what benefit you will get by taking the time to go through an extended example of applying deep learning to structured data. Many books can take you through the process of applying deep learning to a wide variety of problems and datasets. What distinguishes this book? What is the benefit of going through an end-to-end problem using a structured dataset with deep learning?

Let's start with the big picture: there is a lot more unstructured data in the world than structured data (https://learn.g2.com/structured-vs-unstructured-data). If 80% of data is unstructured, why bother trying to apply deep learning to the small subset of all data that is structured? Although there may be four times as much unstructured data as structured data, the slice of the pie that is structured is extremely important. Banks, retailers, insurance companies, manufacturers, governments—the building blocks of modern life—run on relational databases. Every day as you go about your daily activities, you generate updates in dozens or even hundreds of tables in various relational databases. When you pay for something with your debit card, make a mobile phone call, or check your bank balance online, you are accessing or updating data in a relational database. On top of the importance of structured data to our daily lives, many jobs revolve around structured tabular data. Using deep learning on images and video is fun, but what if your job doesn't deal with this kind of data? What if your job is all about tables in relational databases or CSV and Excel files? If you master the techniques of applying deep learning to structured data, you will be able to apply these techniques to solve real problems with the kinds of datasets that you encounter in your job.

In this book, you'll learn from start to finish how to apply deep learning to a tabular structured dataset. You'll learn how to prepare a real-world dataset (with all the typical warts and problems that these datasets have) for training a deep learning model, how to categorize the dataset by the column types in the table, and how to create a simple deep learning model that is automatically defined by this categorization of the data. You will learn how this model combines layers that are adapted to each category of data so that you can take advantage of different types of data in the source tables (text, categorical, and continuous) to train the model. You will also learn how to deploy the deep learning model and make it available for other people to use. The techniques that you will learn in this book are applicable to a wide variety of structured datasets and will allow you to unlock the potential of deep learning to solve problems with these datasets.

1.7   An overview of the code accompanying this book

The heart of this book is an extended coding example that applies deep learning to solve a problem with a real-world structured dataset. Chapter 2 introduces the problem and describes all the code used in this example. In this section, we briefly summarize the most important programs used to solve the problem.

The code that accompanies this book is made up of a series of Jupyter Notebooks and Python programs that take you from the raw input dataset to a deployed, trained deep learning model. You can find all the code, along with associated data and configuration files, at http://mng.bz/v95x. Following are some of the key files in the repo:

- *chapter2.ipynb*—Code snippets associated with introductory code in chapter 2.
- *chapter5.ipynb*—Code snippets associated with using Pandas to do SQL-type operations, as described in chapter 2.
- *Data preparation notebook*—Code to ingest the raw dataset and perform common data cleansing and preparation steps. The output of this notebook is a Python pickle file that contains the Pandas dataframe with the cleansed training data.
- *Basic data exploration notebook*—Basic exploratory data analysis of the dataset for the main example in this book, as described in chapter 3.
- *Data preparation for geocoding*—Code for preparing the latitude and longitude values derived from location values in the main dataset, as described in chapter 4.
- *Time-series forecasting data exploration notebook*—Additional exploration of the dataset for the main example in this book, using time-series forecasting techniques, as described in chapter 3.
- *Deep learning model training notebook*—Code to refactor the cleansed data in a format that accounts for periods when there are no delays for a given streetcar and prepares this refactored form of the data for input to the Keras deep learning model, as described in chapters 5 and 6. The output of this notebook is a trained deep learning model.
- *XGBoost model training notebook*—Code for exercising a non-deep-learning model. This notebook is identical to the notebook for training the deep learning model up to the actual model training code. In chapter 7, we compare the results of this model with the deep learning model.
- *Web deployment*—Code for a simple web-based deployment of the trained deep learning model, as described in chapter 8.
- *Facebook Messenger deployment*—Code for a deployment of the trained deep learning model as a chatbot in Facebook Messenger, as described in chapter 8.

The raw dataset used by the main example in the book is not in the repo but is published at http://mng.bz/4B2B.

1.8 What you need to know

To get the most out of this book, you should be comfortable with coding in Python in the context of Jupyter Notebooks as well as raw Python files. You should also be familiar with non-deep-learning machine learning approaches. In particular, you should have a grasp of the following concepts: overfitting, underfitting, loss function, and objective function. You should be comfortable with basic operations in one of the common cloud environments, such as AWS, Google Cloud, or Azure. For the deployment section, you should have some basic familiarity with web programming. Finally, you should have a background in relational databases and be comfortable with SQL.

This book covers the essentials of deep learning but does not dig into the theoretical details. Instead, it takes you through an extended example of applying deep learning on a practical example. If you need a deeper examination of deep learning and its implementation in the Python environment, *Deep Learning with Python* is an excellent resource. I heartily recommend the whole book as a complement to this one. Here are three chapters that provide additional background on general deep learning topics:

- "The mathematical building blocks of neural networks"—Provides background on concepts that are fundamental to deep learning, including tensors (the core theoretical data container for deep learning) and backpropagation.
- "Getting started with neural networks"—Walks through a variety of simple deep learning problems covering classification (predicting which class an input data point belongs to) and regression (predicting a continuous value target for an input data point).
- "Advanced deep learning best practices"—Examines a variety of deep learning architectures and includes details on Keras callbacks (a topic introduced in chapter 6 of this book) and monitoring your deep learning model with TensorBoard.

In this book, I emphasize providing a practical exploration of the end-to-end process of deep learning with tabular, structured data, starting with the raw input data and going right to the deployed, trained deep learning model. Because this book covers such a broad scope, it won't always be possible to go into details about every related technical topic. Throughout this book, where appropriate, I will refer to *Deep Learning with Python*, other Manning publications, and technical articles for more details on related topics. In addition, chapter 9 recommends resources on the theoretical background of deep learning.

Summary

- Deep learning is a powerful technology that has come into its own in the past decade. So far, the celebrated applications of deep learning deal with nontabular data, such as images and text. In this book, I demonstrate that deep learning should also be considered for problems related to tabular, structured data.
- Deep learning applies a set of techniques (including gradient-based optimization and backpropagation) to input data to automatically define functions that can predict outcomes on new data.
- Deep learning has produced state-of-the-art results in a range of domains, but it has drawbacks compared with other machine learning techniques. These drawbacks include a lack of transparency about which features matter most to the model and a thirst for training data.

- Some people think that deep learning should not be applied to tabular, structured data. These people say that deep learning is too complex, structured datasets are too small to train deep learning models, and simpler alternatives are adequate for structured data problems.
- At the same time, structured data is essential to modern life. Why limit deep learning's scope to images and freeform text? Many important problems involve structured data, so it's worthwhile to learn how to harness deep learning to solve structured data problems.

Introduction to
the example problem
and Pandas dataframes

This chapter covers

- Development environment options for deep learning
- Introduction to Pandas dataframes
- Introduction to the major example used in this book to illustrate deep learning on structured data: predicting streetcar delays
- Format and scope of the example dataset
- More details on common objections to using deep learning with structured data
- A peek ahead at the process of training a deep learning model

In this chapter, you'll learn about the options that you can pick for a deep learning environment and how to bring tabular structured data into your Python program. You will get an overview of Pandas, the Pythonic facility for manipulating tabular structured data. You will also learn about the major example that is used throughout this book to demonstrate deep learning for structured data, including details about the dataset used in the major example and the overall structure of the code for this example. Then you will get more details on the objections to deep learning with structured data that were introduced in chapter 1. Finally, we will take a peek ahead and go through a round of training the deep learning model to whet your appetite for the rest of the extended example that is examined in chapters 3–8.

2.1 Development environment options for deep learning

Before you can start a deep learning project, you need to have access to an environment that provides the hardware and software stack that you need. This section describes the choices that you have for deep learning environments.

Before you look at environments specifically intended for deep learning, it is important to know that you can work through the extended code example in this book in a standard Windows or Linux environment. Using an environment with deep-learning-specific hardware will expedite the model training process, but doing so is not necessary. I ran the code examples in this book on my Windows 10 laptop with 8 GB of RAM and a single-core processor, as well as in the Paperspace Gradient environment (described in this section). Model training was about 30% faster in Gradient, but that meant a difference of only a minute or two in training time for each of the experiments described in chapter 7. For bigger deep learning projects, I strongly recommend one of the deep-learning-enabled environments described in this section, but a reasonably provisioned modern laptop is sufficient for the extended example in this book. If you decide to try to run the code examples on your local system, ensure that your Python version is at least 3.7.4. If you are doing a fresh install of Python or using a virtual Python environment, you will need to install Pandas, Jupyter, sci-kit learn, and TensorFlow 2.0. As you work your way through the examples, you may need to install additional libraries.

> **IMPORTANT** The majority of the code samples in the book can be run in the same Python environment. The one exception is the Facebook Messenger deployment described in chapter 8. This deployment needs to be done in a Python environment with TensorFlow 1.x, whereas the model training requires a Python environment with TensorFlow 2.0 or later. To get around this contention on TensorFlow levels, you should take advantage of Python virtual environments to run the code examples. I suggest that you bring your base Python environment up to the latest TensorFlow 1.x level and use it for everything except for running the model training notebook. Create a virtual environment for the model training notebook, and in that environment, install TensorFlow 2.0. Doing this will give you the benefits of TensorFlow 2.0 for the model training step while maintaining backward compatibility and stability for the rest of your Python environment. You can find details on setting up a Python virtual environment in this article: http://mng.bz/zrjr.

Several cloud vendors provide complete deep learning environments for around the cost of a cup of coffee per hour. Each cloud environment has its strengths and weaknesses, with some (Azure and IBM Cloud) emphasizing ease of creating your first project and others (Amazon Web Services [AWS]) providing the benefits of scale and incumbency. Here are some cloud vendors that provide deep learning environments:

- *AWS* can be accessed here: http://mng.bz/0Z4m. The SageMaker environment in AWS abstracts some of the complexity of managing machine learning models. AWS includes good tutorials on SageMaker, including one (http://mng.bz/9A0a) that takes you through the end-to-end process of training and deploying a model.
- *Google Cloud* (http://mng.bz/K524) also has easy-to-use tutorials, including one (http://mng.bz/jVgy) that shows you how to deploy a deep learning model on the Google Cloud platform.
- *Azure* (http://mng.bz/oREN) is the Microsoft cloud environment and includes several options for deep learning projects. The tutorial at http://mng.bz/8Gp2 provides a simple introduction.
- *Watson Studio Cloud* (http://mng.bz/nz8v) provides an environment focused on machine learning that you can exploit without having to delve into all the details of IBM Cloud. The article at http://mng.bz/Dz29 provides a quick overview, along with links to companion overview articles for AWS SageMaker, Google Cloud, and Azure.

All these cloud environments provide what you need for a deep learning project, including Python, most of the required libraries, and access to deep learning acceleration hardware, including graphic processing units (GPUs) and tensor processing units (TPUs).

The training of deep learning models depends on massive matrix manipulations, and these accelerators allow these operations to run faster. As noted previously, it's possible to train simple deep learning models in an environment that doesn't have GPUs or TPUs, but the training process will run more slowly. See section 2.11 for details on which parts of the extended example in this book will benefit from being run in an environment with deep-learning-specific hardware.

In addition to providing the hardware and software needed for deep learning, the cloud environments listed in this section cater to a wide spectrum of users beyond people who are interested in developing deep learning models. Here are two cloud environments that are specialized for machine learning:

- *Google Colaboratory* (Colab; http://mng.bz/QxNm) is a free Jupyter Notebooks environment provided by Google.
- *Paperspace* (https://towardsdatascience.com/paperspace-bc56efaf6c1f) is a cloud environment laser focused on machine learning. You can use the Paperspace Gradient environment (https://gradient.paperspace.com/) to create with one click a Jupyter Notebooks environment where you can start your deep learning project. Figure 2.1 shows a Gradient notebook in the Paperspace console.

You can use any of these cloud environments to exercise the code that accompanies this book. For the sake of simplicity and to maximize the time you spend learning about deep learning, if you are going to use a cloud environment instead of your local

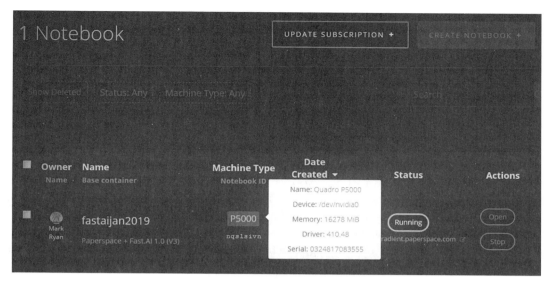

Figure 2.1   Paperspace Gradient: one-click deep learning cloud environment

system, I recommend that you take advantage of Paperspace Gradient. You will get a reliable environment that provides exactly what you need without having to worry about any of the additional cloud artifacts that other cloud environments offer. Gradient requires a credit card to set up. You can expect to pay about $1 per hour for a basic Gradient environment. Depending on how quickly you work through the code and how diligent you are about shutting down your Gradient notebook when you aren't using it, you can expect to pay a total $30–$50 to work through the code examples in this book.

If cost is a key consideration and you don't want to use your local system, Colab is a good alternative cloud environment. Your experience with Colab will not be as smooth as that with Paperspace Gradient, but you won't have to worry about cost. See appendix A for more details on what you need to know to get set up with Colab, along with a description of the pros and cons of Colab compared with Paperspace Gradient.

In addition to Colab and Paperspace Gradient, the mainline cloud providers (including AWS, Google Cloud Platform, and IBM Cloud) provide ML environments that you can use for deep learning development. All the providers offer some kind of limited free access to their ML environments. If you are already using one of these platforms, and you can tolerate paying after you have exhausted your free access, one of these mainline providers could be a good option for you.

2.2   Code for exploring Pandas

When you have cloned the GitHub repo (http://mng.bz/v95x) associated with this book, you'll find the code related to exploring Pandas in the notebooks subdirectory. The next listing shows the files that contain the code described in this chapter.

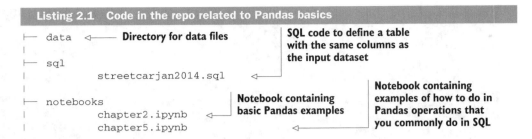

Listing 2.1   Code in the repo related to Pandas basics

2.3   *Pandas dataframes in Python*

If you are reading this book, you will be familiar with relational databases and the organization of data in tables with rows and columns. You can think of the Pandas library as Python's native (Pythonic) approach to representing and manipulating tabular structured data. The key structure in Pandas is the *dataframe*. You can think of a dataframe as being a Python approach to a relational table. Like a table, a dataframe

- Has rows and columns (and columns can have different data types).
- Can have indexes.
- Can be joined with other dataframes based on the values in certain columns.

Before I go into more detail about Pandas dataframes, suppose that you want to manipulate a simple tabular dataset, the Iris dataset (https://gist.github.com/curran/a08a1080b88344b0c8a7), in Python by

- Loading the CSV file into a Python structure
- Counting the number of rows in the dataset
- Counting how many rows in the dataset have setosa as the species

Figure 2.2 shows what a subset of the Iris dataset looks like as a CSV file.

	A	B	C	D	E
1	sepal_length	sepal_width	petal_length	petal_width	species
2	5.1	3.5	1.4	0.2	setosa
3	4.9	3	1.4	0.2	setosa
4	4.7	3.2	1.3	0.2	setosa
5	4.6	3.1	1.5	0.2	setosa
6	5	3.6	1.4	0.2	setosa
7	5.4	3.9	1.7	0.4	setosa
8	4.6	3.4	1.4	0.3	setosa
9	5	3.4	1.5	0.2	setosa

Figure 2.2   Iris dataset as a CSV file

To do this, you need to create a Pandas dataframe containing the contents of the dataset. You can find the code in the next listing in the chapter2.ipynb notebook.

> **Listing 2.2 Creating a Pandas dataframe from CSV referenced by URL**

Import the pandas library.
```
import pandas as pd
url="https://gist.githubusercontent.com/curran/a08a1080b88344b0c8a7/\
raw/d546eaee765268bf2f487608c537c05e22e4b221/iris.csv"     ←─── Raw GitHub URL
                                                                for Iris dataset

iris_dataframe=pd.read_csv(url)     ←─── Read the contents of the URL
iris_dataframe.head()               ←───   into a Pandas dataframe.
```
**Display the first few rows
from the new dataframe.**

Run this cell in the chapter2 notebook, and note the output. The head() call lists the first few (by default, five) rows from the dataframe in an easy-to-read format, as shown in figure 2.3.

	sepal_length	sepal_width	petal_length	petal_width	species
0	5.1	3.5	1.4	0.2	Setosa
1	4.9	3.0	1.4	0.2	Setosa
2	4.7	3.2	1.3	0.2	Setosa
3	4.6	3.1	1.5	0.2	Setosa
4	5.0	3.6	1.4	0.2	Setosa

Figure 2.3 Output of head() for the dataframe loaded with the Iris dataset

Compare with the first few rows of the raw dataset:

```
sepal_length,sepal_width,petal_length,petal_width,species
5.1,3.5,1.4,0.2,setosa
4.9,3.0,1.4,0.2,setosa
4.7,3.2,1.3,0.2,setosa
4.6,3.1,1.5,0.2,setosa
5.0,3.6,1.4,0.2,setosa
```

The raw CSV file and Pandas dataframe have the same column names and the same values, but what's up with the first column in the dataframe? By default, every row in a Pandas dataframe is named, and this name (contained in the first column of the dataframe by default) is a sequential number, starting at zero for the first row. You can also think of this first column as being the default index for the dataframe.

Now you want to get the number of rows in the dataframe. The following statement returns the total number of rows in the dataframe:

```
iris_dataframe.shape[0]
150
```

Finally, you want to count the number of rows in the dataframe with setosa as the species. In the following statement, `iris_dataframe[iris_dataframe["species"] == 'setosa']` defines a dataframe containing only the rows from the original dataframe in which `species = "setosa"`. Using the `shape` attribute the same way that you did to get the row count for the original dataframe, you can use this Python statement to get the number of rows in the dataframe with `species = "setosa"`:

```
iris_dataframe[iris_dataframe["species"] == 'setosa'].shape[0]
50
```

We will explore many more features of Pandas dataframes as we go through the main example in this book. Also, section 2.5 contains examples of using Pandas to perform common SQL operations. For now, this exploration has taught you how to bring tabular structured data into a Python program where you can prepare it to train a deep learning model.

2.4   *Ingesting CSV files into Pandas dataframes*

In section 2.3, you saw how to ingest a CSV file identified as a URL into a Pandas dataframe, but suppose that you have your own private copy of a dataset that you have modified. You want to load data from that modified file in your filesystem into a dataframe. In this section, you'll look at how to read a CSV file from the filesystem into a dataframe. In chapter 3, you'll learn how to ingest an XLS file with multiple tabs into a single dataframe.

Suppose that you want to load the Iris dataset into a dataframe, but you have made modifications to your own copy of the dataset (called iriscaps.csv) on your local filesystem, capitalizing the species names to meet the style guidelines for the application that uses this dataset. You need to load this modified dataset from a file on your filesystem instead of from the original Iris dataset. The code to bring a CSV file from the filesystem into a Pandas dataframe (shown in the following listing) resembles the code you have already seen for loading a dataframe from a URL.

Listing 2.3   Creating a Pandas dataframe from CSV referenced by filename

Import the pandas library.

```
import pandas as pd
file = "iriscaps.csv"#                    Define the filename.
iris_dataframe=pd.read_csv(os.path.join(path,file))     Read the contents of
iris_dataframe.head()                                    the file into a Pandas
                                                         dataframe.
```

Display the first few rows from the new dataframe.

How do you get the correct value for path, the directory where the data files reside? All the code samples in this book assume that all the data exists in a directory called data that is a sibling of the directory containing the notebook. In this repo, the top-level directories' notebooks and data contain the code files and data files, respectively.

Listing 2.4 is the code that gets the directory containing the notebook (rawpath). Then the code uses that directory to get the directory containing the data files by going first to the parent directory of the directory containing the notebook, and then to the data directory in the parent directory.

Listing 2.4   Getting the path for the data directory

```
rawpath = os.getcwd()           Get the directory that        Get the directory
print("raw path is",rawpath)    this notebook is in.          that the data files
path = os.path.abspath(os.path.join(rawpath, '..', 'data'))   are in.
print("path is", path)
```

Note that you use the same read_csv function, but the argument is the filesystem path of the file as opposed to a URL. Figure 2.4 shows the modified dataset with the species name capitalized.

	sepal_length	sepal_width	petal_length	petal_width	species
0	5.1	3.5	1.4	0.2	Setosa
1	4.9	3.0	1.4	0.2	Setosa
2	4.7	3.2	1.3	0.2	Setosa
3	4.6	3.1	1.5	0.2	Setosa
4	5.0	3.6	1.4	0.2	Setosa

Figure 2.4   Dataframe loaded from a file in which the species values have been capitalized

In this section, you've reviewed how to load a Pandas dataframe with the contents of a CSV file in the filesystem. In chapter 3, you'll see how to load a dataframe with the contents of an XLS file.

2.5   *Using Pandas to do what you would do with SQL*

Section 2.3 introduced the Pandas library as the Python solution for manipulating structured, tabular data. In this section, we will dig deeper into this part of the stack to show some examples of how you can use Pandas to accomplish tabular operations that you are used to doing with SQL. This section is not an exhaustive SQL-to-Pandas dictionary; see the articles at http://mng.bz/1XGM and http://sergilehkyi.com/translating-sql-to-pandas for more SQL-to-Pandas examples. Following are some examples that illustrate how to use Pandas to produce the same results as SQL.

To exercise the following examples

1 Create a table called streetcarjan2014 in a relational database (the example assumes Postgres) by loading a CSV file with the contents of the first tab of the 2014 XLS file in the streetcar delay dataset. Ensure that the type of "Min Delay" is numeric.

2 Use the chapter5.ipynb notebook to create a Pandas dataframe from the same CSV file. This notebook assumes that the CSV file is in a directory called data that is a sibling of the directory containing the notebook.

Now let's look at some pairs of equivalent SQL and Pandas statements. First, to get the first three rows of the table

- *SQL*—select * from streetcarjan2014 limit 3
- *Pandas*—streetcarjan2014.head(3)

Figure 2.5 shows the SQL query and results, and figure 2.6 shows the same for Pandas.

Query Editor	Query History									Scratch Pa

```
1   select * from streetcarjan2014 limit 3
```

Data Output   Explain   Messages   Notifications

	Report Date character varyir	Route character	Time character varyir	Day character v	Location character varying (200)	Incident character varying (80)	Min Delay integer	Min Gap integer	Direction character v	Vehicle character v
1	2014-01-02	505	6:31:00 AM	Thursday	Dundas and Roncesvalles	Late Leaving Garage	4	8	E/B	4018
2	2014-01-02	504	12:43:00 PM	Thursday	King and Shaw	Utilized Off Route	20	22	E/B	4128
3	2014-01-02	501	2:01:00 PM	Thursday	Kingston road and Bingham	Held By	13	19	W/B	4016

Figure 2.5 SQL first three records

```
streetcarjan2014.head(3)
```

	Report Date	Route	Time	Day	Location	Incident	Min Delay	Min Gap	Direction	Vehicle
0	2014-01-02	505	6:31:00 AM	Thursday	Dundas and Roncesvalles	Late Leaving Garage	4	8.0	E/B	4018.0
1	2014-01-02	504	12:43:00 PM	Thursday	King and Shaw	Utilized Off Route	20	22.0	E/B	4128.0
2	2014-01-02	501	2:01:00 PM	Thursday	Kingston road and Bingham	Held By	13	19.0	W/B	4016.0

Figure 2.6 Pandas first three records

To have a single condition on a select statement

- *SQL*—select "Route" from streetcarjan2014 where "Location " = 'King and Shaw'
- *Pandas*—streetcarjan2014[streetcarjan2014.Location == "King and Shaw"].Route

To list the unique entries in a column

- *SQL*—select `distinct "Incident" from streetcarjan2014`
- *Pandas*—`streetcarjan2014.Incident.unique()`

To have multiple conditions on a `select` statement

- *SQL*—select `* from streetcarjan2014 where "Min Delay" > 20 and "Day" = 'Sunday'`
- *Pandas*—`streetcarjan2014[(streetcarjan2014['Min Delay'] > 20) & (streetcarjan2014['Day'] == "Sunday")]`

Figure 2.7 shows the SQL query and results, and figure 2.8 shows the same for Pandas.

```
1  select * from streetcarjan2014 where "Min Delay" > 20 and "Day" = 'Sunday'
```

Data Output   Explain   Messages   Notifications

	Report Date character varyir	Route character	Time character varyi	Day character	Location character varying (200)	Incident character varying (80)	Min Delay integer	Min Gap integer	Direction character v:	Vehicle character
1	2014-01-19	504	8:33:00 AM	Sunday	King and Queen	Held By	40	50	E/B	4089
2	2014-01-19	511	7:17:00 PM	Sunday	Bathurst and Front	Investigation	33	40	S/B	4179

Figure 2.7   SQL `select` with multiple conditions

```
streetcarjan2014[(streetcarjan2014['Min Delay'] > 20) & (streetcarjan2014['Day'] == "Sunday")]
```

	Report Date	Route	Time	Day	Location	Incident	Min Delay	Min Gap	Direction	Vehicle
305	2014-01-19	504	8:33:00 AM	Sunday	King and Queen	Held By	40	50.0	E/B	4089.0
311	2014-01-19	511	7:17:00 PM	Sunday	Bathurst and Front	Investigation	33	40.0	S/B	4179.0

Figure 2.8   Pandas `select` with multiple conditions

To have `order by` on a `select` statement

- *SQL*—select `"Route", "Min Delay" from streetcarjan2014 where "Min Delay" > 20 order by "Min Delay"`
- *Pandas*—`streetcarjan2014[['Route','Min Delay']][(streetcarjan2014['Min Delay'] > 20)].sort_values('Min Delay')`

In this section, we have gone through a few examples of how to use Pandas to do common SQL operations. As you continue to use Pandas, you will find many other ways that Pandas can make it easy for you to use your SQL experience in the world of Python.

2.6   *The major example: Predicting streetcar delays*

Now that you have had a taste of how tabular structured data is brought into a Python program, let's examine the major example used throughout this book: predicting streetcar delays.

To have a successful deep learning project, you need data and a well-defined problem to solve. In this book, I am using a publicly available dataset (http://mng.bz/4B2B) published by the city of Toronto that describes every delay encountered in the city's streetcar system since January 2014. The problem to solve is how to predict delays in the Toronto streetcar system so that they can be prevented. In this chapter, you will learn about the format of this dataset. In subsequent chapters, you will learn how to correct the issues in the dataset that need to be fixed before it can be used to train a deep learning model.

Why does the problem of streetcar delays in Toronto matter? Before World War II, many cities in North America had streetcar systems. These systems, called *trams* in some parts of the world, consist of light rail vehicles, usually running individually, powered by electricity drawn from overhead cables or sometimes from rails in the street, and running on rails in common space with other road traffic. Although some of Toronto's streetcar network is on a dedicated right-of-way, the majority of the system runs on public streets mixed with other traffic.

In the postwar period, most North American cities replaced their streetcars with buses. Some cities kept a token streetcar service as a tourist attraction. Toronto, however, was unique among North American cities because it maintained its extensive streetcar network as a critical part of its overall public transit system. Today, streetcars service four of the five busiest surface routes in Toronto and carry up to 300,000 passengers every weekday.

The streetcar network has many advantages over buses and subways, the other modes of transit that make up Toronto's public transit system. Compared with buses, streetcars last longer, produce no emissions, carry at least twice as many passengers per driver, are cheaper to build and maintain, and provide more flexible service.

Streetcars have two big disadvantages: they are vulnerable to obstructions in general traffic, and they cannot easily get around these obstructions. When a streetcar gets blocked, it can cause compounded delays in the streetcar network and contribute to overall gridlock on the city's busiest streets.

Using the streetcar delay dataset provided by the city of Toronto, we will apply deep learning to predict and prevent streetcar delays. Figure 2.9 shows a heat map of streetcar delays superimposed on a map of Toronto. You can find the code to generate this map in the streetcar_data-geocode-get-boundaries notebook. The areas with the most streetcar delays (the darker blobs on the map) are the busiest streets in the core of the city.

Before I go into detail about the dataset for this problem, it makes sense to explain why I chose this particular problem. Why not chose a standard business problem like customer churn (predicting whether a customer is going to cancel a service) or

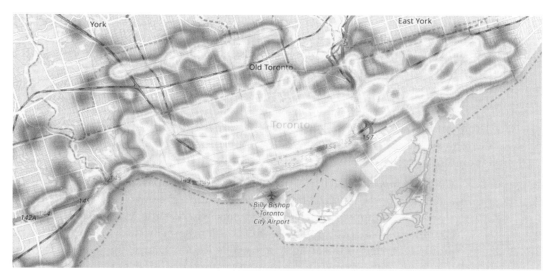

Figure 2.9   The Toronto streetcar network: heat map of delays

inventory control (predicting when a retail outlet is going to run out of stock of a particular item)? Why choose a problem that is specific to a particular activity (public transit) and a particular place (Toronto)? Here are some of the reasons for selecting this problem:

- It has a "Goldilocks" dataset (not too big and not too small). A really huge dataset presents additional data management problems that are not central to learning about deep learning. A big dataset can also mask inadequacies in the code and algorithm. The adage "He who has the most data wins" may apply to deep learning, but when you're learning, there is something to be said for not having masses of data as a crutch. On the other hand, if you have too little data, deep learning simply doesn't have enough signal to detect. The streetcar dataset (currently, more than 70,000 rows) is big enough to be applicable to deep learning, but not so big that it makes exploration difficult.

- The dataset is live. It gets updated every couple of months, so there is ample opportunity to test a model with data that it has never seen before.

- The dataset is real and raw. This dataset was collected over several years for several purposes, none of which was to train a deep learning model. As you will see in the next two chapters, this dataset has many errors and anomalies that need to be dealt with before the dataset can train a deep learning model. In practice, you will see similarly messy datasets across many business applications. By going through the process of cleaning up the real-world streetcar dataset, warts and all, you will be prepared to tackle other real-world datasets.

- Businesses have to deal with competitive and regulatory pressures that make it impossible for them to share their datasets openly, which makes it difficult to find real, nontrivial datasets from serious businesses. Public agencies, by contrast, often have a legal obligation to publish their datasets. I've taken advantage of Toronto's openness about the streetcar delay dataset to build the primary example for this book.

- The problem is accessible to a broad audience and is not tied to any particular industry or discipline.

Although the streetcar problem has the advantage of not being specific to any business, it can be directly related to common business problems to which deep learning is commonly applied, including

- *Customer support*—Each row in the dataset is comparable to a ticket in a customer support system. The Incident column is similar to the freeform text abstracts that appear in ticketing systems, whereas the Min Delay and Min Gap columns play a role similar to the problem-severity information that is commonly recorded in ticketing systems. The Report Date, Time, and Day columns map to the timestamp information in customer support ticketing systems.
- *Logistics*—Like logistics systems, the streetcar network has a spatial nature (implicit in the Route, Location, and Direction columns in the dataset) and a temporal nature (implicit in the Report Date, Time, and Day columns).

2.7 Why is a real-world dataset critical for learning about deep learning?

When you are learning about deep learning, why is it so important to work with a dataset that is real and messy? When you think about applying deep learning to a real-world dataset, you can compare it to being asked to create a Blu-ray disc from a box full of media collected over the past four decades. This box contains an assortment of formats, including analog video in 3:4 aspect ratio, analog photos, mono audio recording, and digital video. One thing is clear: none of the media in the box was created with Blu-ray in mind because most of it was recorded before Blu-ray existed. You will have to preprocess each of the media sources to prepare it for the Blu-ray package, such as correcting color, cleaning up VHS judder, and fixing the aspect ratio in the analog video. For the mono audio, you will need to remove tape hiss and extrapolate the mono audio track to stereo. Figure 2.10 summarizes this process of assembling various elements to generate a Blu-ray disc.

Similarly, you can bet that the problems in your organization that are candidates for deep learning have datasets that were *not* collected with deep learning in mind. You will need to clean up, transform, and extrapolate to get a dataset that is ready to train a deep learning model.

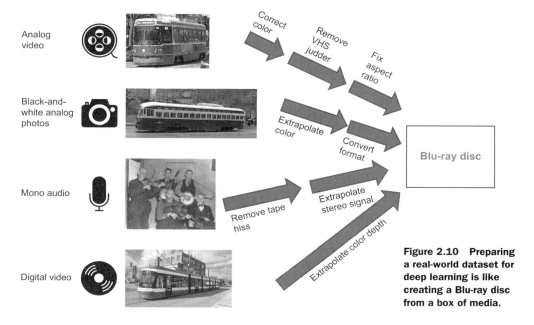

Figure 2.10 Preparing a real-world dataset for deep learning is like creating a Blu-ray disc from a box of media.

2.8 *Format and scope of the input dataset*

Now that we have reviewed the streetcar delay problem and the importance of working with a real-world dataset, let's dig into the structure of the streetcar delay dataset (http://mng.bz/4B2B). This dataset has the following file structure:

- An XLS file for each year
- In each XLS file, a tab for each month

Figure 2.11 shows the file structure of the streetcar delay dataset.

2014

	Report Date	Route	Time	Day	Location	Incident	Min Delay	Min Gap	Direction	Vehicle
2	2014-01-02	505	6:31:00 AM	Thursday	Dundas and Roncesvalles	Late Leaving Garage	4	8	E/B	4018
3	2014-01-02	504	12:42:00 PM	Thursday	King and Shaw	Utilized Off Route	20	22	E/B	4128

	Report Date	Route	Time	Day	Location	Incident	Min Delay	Min Gap	Direction	Vehicle
2	2014-02-01	504	11:45:00 AM	Saturday		General Delay	0	0	E/B	
3	2014-02-01	501	5:43:00 PM	Saturday	Broadview and queen	Mechanical	9	15	E/B	4208
4	2014-02-03	511	5:51:00 AM	Monday	queen and Roncesvales	Late Leaving Garage	5	10	E/B	4095
5	2014-02-03	401	6:01:00 AM	Monday	queen and roncesvales	Late Leaving Garage	10	20	W/B	4241
6	2014-02-03	512	6:08:00 AM	Monday	queen and Roincesvalles	Late Leaving Garage	4	8	E/B	4100

	Report Date	Route	Time	Day	Location	Incident	Min Delay	Min Gap	Direction	Vehicle
2	2014-12-01	510	1:28:00 AM	Monday	Spadina and Oxford	Emergency Services	77	87	B/W	4124
3	2014-12-01	306	3:59:00 AM	Monday	Gerrard and Kingsmount Park Rd.	Investigation	41	71	W/B	4044
4	2014-12-01	512	5:02:00 AM	Monday	Exhibition Loop	Late Leaving Garage	8	16	W/B	4171
5	2014-12-01	504	5:36:00 AM	Monday	Queen and Roncesvalles	Late Leaving Garage	6	12	E/B	4233
6	2014-12-01	506	5:52:00 AM	Monday	Coxwell and Gerrard	Mechanical	4	8	E/B	4077

2019

	Report Date	Route	Time	Day	Location	Incident	Min Delay	Min Gap	Direction	Vehicle
2	01-Jan-19	301	1:08:00 AM	Tuesday	Queen/Braodview	Held By	6	13	E/B	4193
3	01-Jan-19	514	1:20:00 AM	Tuesday	Bathurst/College	Investigation	8	16	N/B	1030

	Report Date	Route	Time	Day	Location	Incident	Min Delay	Min Gap	Direction	Vehicle
2	01-Feb-19	504	12:14:00 AM	Friday	King and jarvis	Diversion	34	33	W/B	4405
3	01-Feb-19	504	5:17:00 AM	Friday	Broadview/Millbrook	Held By	10	29	W/B	4447
4	01-Feb-19	506	6:11:00 AM	Friday	Leslie and Gerrard	Held By	12	18	E/B	4068
5	01-Feb-19	509	6:42:00 AM	Friday	Exibition Loop	Mechanical	6	12	B/W	
6	01-Feb-19	506	7:06:00 AM	Friday	Dundas and Howard Park	Mechanical	6	12	W/B	4073

Figure 2.11 File structure of the streetcar delay dataset

	Report Date	Route	Time	Day	Location	Incident	Min Delay	Min Gap	Direction	Vehicle
2	2014-01-02	505	6:31:00 AM	Thursday	Dundas and Roncesvalles	Late Leaving Garage	4	8	E/B	4018
3	2014-01-02	504	12:43:00 PM	Thursday	King and Shaw	Utilized Off Route	20	22	E/B	4128
4	2014-01-02	501	2:01:00 PM	Thursday	Kingston road and Bingham	Held By	13	19	W/B	4016
5	2014-01-02	504	2:22:00 PM	Thursday	King St. and Roncesvalles Ave.	Investigation	7	11	W/B	4175

Figure 2.12   Columns in the streetcar delay dataset

Figure 2.12 shows the columns in the streetcar delay dataset:

- *Report Date*—The date (YYYY/MM/DD) when the delay-causing incident occurred
- *Route*—The number of the streetcar route
- *Time*—The time (hh:mm:ss AM/PM) when the delay-causing incident occurred
- *Day*—The name of the day
- *Location*—The location of the delay-causing incident
- *Incident*—The description of the delay-causing incident
- *Min Delay*—The delay, in minutes, in the schedule of the following streetcar
- *Min Gap*—The total scheduled time, in minutes, from the streetcar ahead of the following streetcar
- *Direction*—The direction of the route (E/B, W/B, N/B, S/B, B/W, and variants), where B/W indicates both ways
- Vehicle—The ID number of the vehicle involved in the incident

It's worth taking a bit more time to review the characteristics of some of these columns:

- *Report Date*—This column embeds a lot of information that could be valuable for the deep learning model. In chapter 5, we will revisit this column to add derived columns to the dataset for subcomponents of this column: year, month, and day of month.
- *Day*—Does this column duplicate information that is already encoded in the Report Date column? For the purposes of this problem, is it relevant that an incident happened on a Monday that also happened to be the last day of the month? We will explore these questions in chapter 9.
- *Location*—This column is the most interesting one in the dataset. It encodes the geographical aspect of the dataset in a challenging, open-ended format. In chapter 4, we will revisit this column to answer some important questions, including why this data isn't encoded as longitude and latitude and how the unique topography of the streetcar network manifests itself in the values in the Location column. In chapter 9, we will look at the most effective way to encode this information for the deep learning model.

The dataset currently has more than 70,000 records, and 1,000 to 2,000 new records are added every month. Figure 2.13 shows the number of records per year since the beginning of the dataset in January 2014. The raw record count is the number of records in the input dataset. The cleaned record count is the number of records after

Year	Raw record count	Cleaned record count
2014	11,027	9,340
2015	12,221	10,877
2016	14,021	11,908
2017	13,762	9,890
2018	15,612	12,011
2019	11,882	7,474

Figure 2.13   Streetcar dataset record count by year

records with invalid values (such as specifying delays on routes that aren't valid streetcar routes) are dropped, as described in chapter 3.

2.9   *The destination: An end-to-end solution*

Throughout the rest of this book, we will work through the problem of predicting streetcar delays. We will clean up the input dataset, build a deep learning model, train it, and then deploy it to help users get predictions on whether their streetcar trips are going to be delayed.

Figure 2.14 shows one of the results you will get after following through the extended example in this book. You will be able to get predictions on whether a particular streetcar trip will be delayed from the deep learning model that you trained with data derived from the raw dataset introduced in this chapter.

Figure 2.15 summarizes the end-to-end journey that you will take through this book with the extended example of streetcar delays, from the raw dataset introduced in this chapter to the model deployments that allow users to get predictions on whether their streetcar trips will be delayed. Note that the two deployment methods shown in figure 2.15 (Facebook Messenger and web deployment, respectively) are two means to

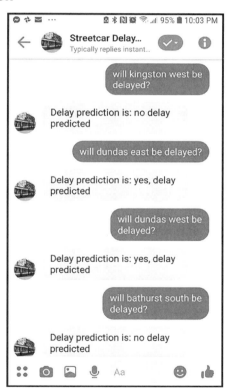

Figure 2.14   One result of the extended example: Facebook Messenger deployment

the same end: making the trained deep learning model accessible to users who want to get predictions on whether their streetcar trips are going to be delayed.

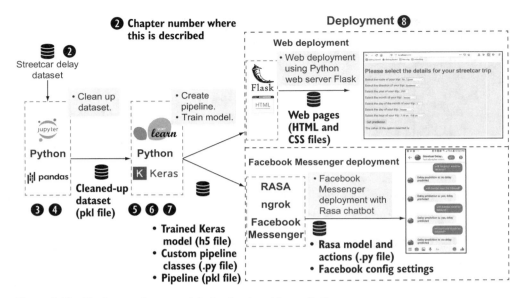

Figure 2.15   The journey from raw data to streetcar trip predictions

The numbers in figure 2.15 highlight what's covered in each chapter:

- Chapter 2 introduces the raw dataset that we will be using in the extended example.
- Chapters 3 and 4 describe the steps you take to clean up the raw dataset and prepare it to train a deep learning model.
- Chapter 5 describes how to create a simple deep learning model using the Keras library.
- Chapter 6 describes how to train the Keras deep learning model using the dataset you prepared in chapters 3 and 4.
- Chapter 7 describes how to conduct a series of experiments to determine the impact of changing aspects of the deep learning model and of replacing the deep learning model with a non-deep-learning approach.
- Chapter 8 shows how to deploy the deep learning model you trained in chapter 6. You will use the pipeline facility from the scikit-learn library to process the trip data that users provide so that the trained deep learning model can make predictions. Chapter 8 leads you through two deployment options. First, we go through deploying the trained model via a web page served by Flask (https://flask.palletsprojects.com/en/1.1.x), a basic web application framework for Python. This deployment method is straightforward, but the user experience is limited. The second deployment approach provides a richer user experience by using the Rasa chatbot framework to interpret the user's trip prediction requests and display the trained model's predictions in Facebook Messenger.

2.10   *More details on the code that makes up the solutions*

The end-to-end journey described in section 2.9 is implemented through a series of Python programs and the files that are inputs and outputs to each program. As described in chapter 1, these files are available in the repo for this book: http://mng .bz/v95x. The next listing shows the key directories in the repo and summarizes the files in each directory.

Listing 2.5   Directory structure of the repo

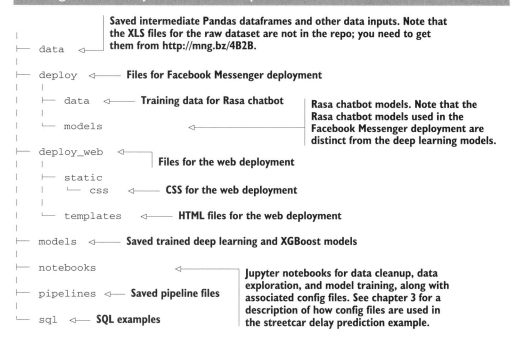

Figures 2.16 and 2.17 describe the same end-to-end journey as figure 2.15 from the perspective of the Python programs and the files that flow between them. Figure 2.16 shows the progression from the raw dataset to a trained deep learning model:

- We begin with the raw dataset made up of XLS files as described in this chapter. When you have run the data preparation notebook, you can save the data from the XLS files as a pickled dataframe that you can use to conveniently rerun the data preparation notebook. Chapter 3 explains the pickle facility that lets you serialize Python objects in files so that objects can be saved between Python sessions.
- The dataset is cleaned up (duplicate values are mapped to a common value, for example, and records with invalid values are removed) by the data preparation notebook streetcar_data_preparation.ipynb to generate a cleansed pickled dataframe. This part of the process is described in chapters 3 and 4.

- The cleansed pickled dataframe is input to the model training notebook streetcar _model_training.ipynb that refactors the dataset and uses it to generate pickled pipeline files and a trained deep learning model file. This part of the process is described in chapters 5 and 6.

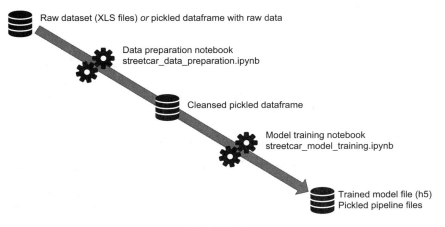

Figure 2.16   File progression from raw dataset to trained model

Figure 2.17 picks up the story from the trained model file and pickled pipeline files generated by the model training notebook. The pipelines are used in the deployments to take the trip information entered by users (such the streetcar route and direction) and transform this information into a format that the trained deep learning model can take

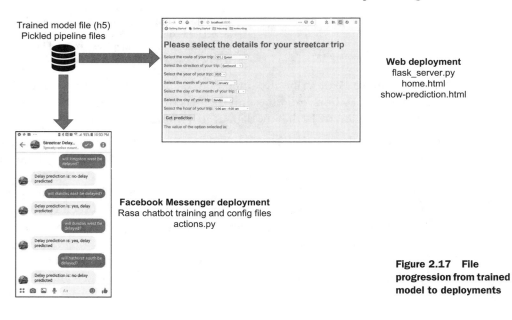

Figure 2.17   File progression from trained model to deployments

in to make a prediction. As you will see in chapter 8, these pipelines appear twice in the process. First, they transform the data that is used to train the deep learning model; then they transform user input so that the trained model can generate a prediction for it. Chapter 8 describes two kinds of deployment: web deployment, where the user enters the trip information in a web page, and Facebook Messenger deployment, where the user enters the trip information in a Messenger session.

In this section, you have seen two perspectives on the journey from the input dataset to a deployed deep learning model that you can use to predict whether a streetcar trip is going to be delayed. This journey covers a broad range of technical components, but don't worry if some of these components aren't familiar to you. We'll examine them one by one as we go through the chapters. By the time you complete chapter 8, you will have an end-to-end deep learning with structured data solution for predicting streetcar delays.

2.11 *Development environments: Vanilla vs. deep-learning-enabled*

In section 2.1, we reviewed your options for the environment to use in this book. In this section, we'll review which subsets of the code would benefit from a deep-learning-enabled environment and which are fine with a *vanilla* system—one that does not have access to any deep-learning-specific hardware such as GPUs and TPUs. This vanilla system could be your local system (after you have installed Jupyter Notebooks, Python, and the required Python libraries) or a non-GPU/non-TPU cloud environment.

Figure 2.18 shows the end-to-end solution highlighting which areas would benefit from a deep-learning-enabled environment and which can be worked in a vanilla environment:

- The data preparation code (described in chapters 2–4) can be used in either a vanilla environment or a deep learning environment. The operations that you will be performing in these sections do not require any deep-learning-specific hardware. I have run the data preparation code in both Paperspace Gradient and on my local Windows machine, which has no deep-learning-specific hardware.
- The model training code described in chapters 5–7 will run more slowly if you don't have access to deep-learning-specific hardware, such as the GPUs available in Paperspace, Azure, or Colab, or the TPUs available in Google Cloud Services and Colab.
- The deployment code described in chapter 8 can be used in either a vanilla environment or a deep learning environment. I have done the deployment on both Azure (using a standard, non-GPU-enabled VM) and on my local Windows machine. The trained model does not require deep-learning-specific hardware when it is deployed.

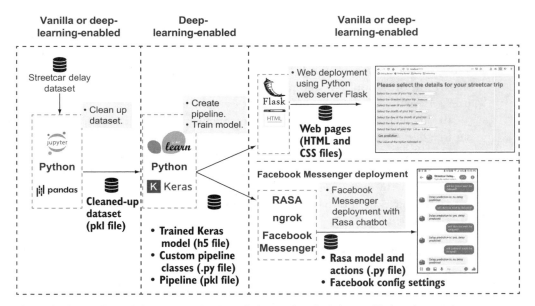

Figure 2.18   Portions of the process that benefit from a deep-learning-enabled environment

2.12 *A deeper look at the objections to deep learning*

In chapter 1, we briefly reviewed some of the pros and cons of deep learning. It's worthwhile to do a more detailed comparison of deep learning with non-deep-learning machine learning. For the sake of simplicity, in this chapter we will simply refer to the latter as *classic machine learning*.

We need to contrast classic machine learning with deep learning when we're dealing with problems with structured tabular data. The conventional wisdom is to use classic machine learning, rather than deep learning, on structured data. The whole point of this book is to examine how deep learning can be applied to structured data, so we need to provide some motivation for this approach and examine the reasoning behind the dictum "If it's structured data, don't use deep learning."

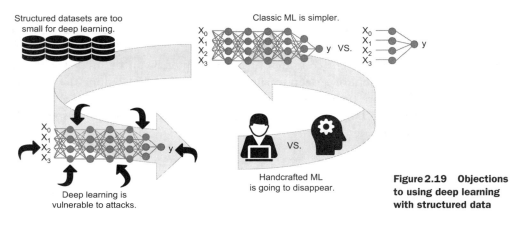

Figure 2.19   Objections to using deep learning with structured data

Let's dig a bit deeper into the objections to deep learning introduced in Chapter 1 and illustrated in figure 2.19:

- *Structured datasets are too small to feed deep learning.* There is a very valid point behind this objection, even if the whole objection does not hold up to scrutiny. Certainly, many structured datasets are too small for deep learning, and perhaps that's the source of the perception that structured datasets are too small for deep learning. It is not uncommon, however, for relational tables to have tens of millions and even billions of rows. The top commercial relational database vendors support tables with more than a billion rows. Easy-to-find, open source structured datasets do tend to be small, so when you're looking for a problem to investigate, it's easier to find a structured dataset that is small and appropriate for classic machine learning than it is to find a large, open source structured dataset. So the problem with dataset size is more a question of convenience than an intrinsic size problem with structured datasets. Luckily, the streetcar dataset used in this book is both openly available *and* big enough to make it an interesting subject for deep learning.

- *Keep it simple.* The most common argument for choosing classic machine learning over deep learning for structured datasets is simplicity. The rationale is that classic machine learning algorithms are simpler, easier to use, and more transparent than deep learning. In chapter 7, you will see a direct comparison of the deep learning solution to the streetcar delay prediction problem and a solution based on XGBoost, a non-deep-learning approach. Both implementations use the same data preparation steps and the same pipelines, which constitute most of the code that makes up the solution. The heart of the solution is the definition, training, and evaluation of the model where the two solutions diverge. In that section of the solution, the deep learning approach has about 60 lines of code compared with fewer than 20 for XGBoost. Although the XGBoost solution has fewer lines of code at the heart of its solution, this section of the code represents less than 10% of the total lines of code in either approach. Also, the additional complexity in the heart of the deep learning approach allows it to be much more flexible because it can handle datasets with columns containing freeform text.

- *Deep learning is vulnerable to adversarial attacks.* There are well-publicized examples of deep learning systems being fooled into incorrect scoring of data examples that were purposely altered to exploit vulnerabilities in the system. An image of a panda, for example, can be doctored in a way that is imperceptible to humans but tricks a deep learning model into misidentifying the image. You can see this image at http://mng.bz/BE2g. To us, the doctored image still looks like a panda, but the deep learning system scores the image as that of a gibbon.

  I argued in chapter 1 that the crown jewels of commerce and government reside in structured data. If it's possible for a malicious actor to mislead a deep learning system, why would we trust a deep learning system with the analysis of such valuable data? Is this vulnerability unique to deep learning? The article at http://mng.bz/dwyX argues that classic machine learning suffers from the same vulnerability to spoofing as deep learning. If that's the case, why has so much attention been given to deep learning being fooled? The hype around deep learning invites counter narratives, and the examples of deep learning being fooled make better sound bites. It's more interesting to hear about a deep learning model mistaking a giraffe for a polar bear than it is to hear about a linear regression model predicting an outcome incorrectly due to a doctored value in one column of an input table. Finally, the vulnerability of both deep learning and classic machine learning to adversarial attacks depends on the attackers getting inside information about the nature of the models. If there is proper governance of model security, the crown jewels of data should not be threatened by adversarial attacks.

- *The days of handcrafted deep learning solutions are coming to an end.* The world of machine learning is moving fast enough, and its potential impact is large enough, that it would be unwise to predict how nonspecialists will harness machine learning in the early 2030s. Think about the interest in multimedia in the mid-1990s. Back then, even people who were not directly involved in creating multimedia platforms had to concern themselves with the arcana of sound card device drivers and IRQ conflicts if they wanted to take advantage of multimedia. Today, we take the audio and video capabilities of computers for granted, and only a select few need to worry about the details of multimedia. The term *multimedia* itself is now quaint due to lack of use; the technology has become so ubiquitous that we don't need a term for it anymore. Will machine learning and deep learning share the same fate? It's possible that automated solutions like Google's Auto ML (https://cloud.google.com/automl) will mature to the point that only a relatively small set of deep ML specialists will need to do hand-coding of machine learning solutions. Even if that does happen, the fundamental concepts behind deep learning, as well as the practical steps that need to be taken to harness deep learning on a real-world dataset, will still be important to understand. These concepts are to machine learning what the periodic table is to chemistry. Unless we specialize in chemistry or a related discipline, most of us won't have to directly apply the foundational concepts expressed in the periodic table. It's still critical to learn about the periodic table, however, and understand what it tells us about the nature of matter. In a similar way, the fundamental concepts of deep learning will still be useful to understand, even if the implementation of machine learning systems is largely automated in the near future. You will be able to make better judgments about the applicability of deep learning because you understand at some level how it works.

We've examined in more detail some of the objections to deep learning. One objection in particular—deep learning is too difficult for nonspecialists to use—was more true five years ago than it is today. What changed in recent years to make deep learning a contender in more problem areas and to make it accessible to nonspecialists? We'll answer this question in the next section. First, we can ask which approach is better for dealing with structured data: deep learning or classic machine learning. In chapters 5 and 6, you will see the code for the deep learning model to predict streetcar delays. You will also see the results of a series of experiments to measure the performance of the trained deep learning model. In addition, chapter 7 describes an alternative solution to the streetcar delay prediction problem that uses a classic machine learning algorithm, XGBoost. In that chapter, you will be able to directly compare the code for the deep learning solution with the code for the XGBoost solution. You will also see a head-to-head comparison of the performance of the two solutions so that you can draw your own conclusions about which approach is better suited to solving this problem.

2.13　*How deep learning has become more accessible*

In section 2.12, we reviewed some of the objections to deep learning. What has changed to make this comparison even worth making, and why is deep learning now a viable approach alongside classic machine learning? Figure 2.20 summarizes some of the changes in the past decade that have opened up the power of deep learning to a wider audience.

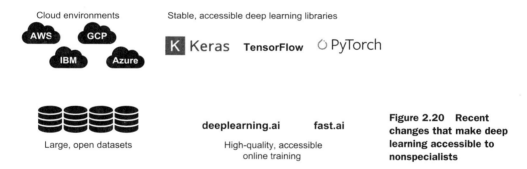

Figure 2.20　Recent changes that make deep learning accessible to nonspecialists

Following are some more details on the changes listed in figure 2.20:

- *Cloud environments*—As outlined in section 2.1, all the major cloud vendors provide deep learning environments that include the software stack and the specialized hardware needed for efficient training of deep learning models. The choice available in these environments, from the deep-learning-focused Gradient environment of Paperspace to the all-encompassing breadth of AWS, the hardware options and value for money have been improving year by year. Deep learning is no longer the preserve of the lucky few who work for tech giants or well-endowed academic institutions that can afford dedicated, on-premises hardware for deep learning.
- *Stable, usable deep learning libraries*—Since the initial release of Keras in early 2015, it's been possible to take advantage of the power of deep learning

through an intuitive and easy-to-learn interface. The release of PyTorch (https://pytorch.org) in late 2016 and TensorFlow 2.0 in mid-2019 gave developers even more usable choices for deep learning.

- *Large, open datasets*—In the past decade, there has been an explosion of large datasets that lend themselves to deep learning. The advent of social media and smartphones in the 2000s, government initiatives to provide open datasets, and Google's Dataset Search (https://toolbox.google.com/datasetsearch) combined to make large, interesting datasets accessible. To complement this tsunami of data, sites such as Kaggle (https://www.kaggle.com) provide a community of machine learning investigators who want to exploit these datasets.

- *High-quality, accessible educational material on deep learning*—This material includes excellent online courses for self-study. Since 2017, courses such as deeplearning.ai and fast.ai have made it possible for nonspecialists to learn about deep learning and, particularly in the case of fast.ai, exercise what they have learned in real coding examples. These courses mean that you don't need to get a graduate degree in artificial intelligence to learn about deep learning.

2.14   *A first taste of training a deep learning model*

Over the course of the next six chapters, we will work through the code in the extended example, starting with cleaning up data in chapter 3 and ending with deploying the trained model in chapter 8. If you think of the extended example as being an action movie, the big car chase takes place in chapter 6 when we train the deep learning model. To give you a taste of the climax, in this section we will go through a simplified scenario of training a deep learning model.

If you cloned the repo described in section 2.10, you see the following files, which we will use in this section:

- In the notebooks directory, the notebook streetcar_model_training.ipynb contains the code for defining and training the deep learning model. The config file streetcar_model_training_config.yml lets you set the parameters for the model training process.

- In the data directory, you will find a ready-made, cleaned-up dataset file called 2014_2019_df_cleaned_remove_bad_values_may16_2020.pkl. You can use this file as input to the model training notebook, so you don't have to run the dataset cleanup code for this scenario. If the trained deep learning model is a gourmet meal, you can think of this cleaned-up dataset file as being a dish of ingredients that have been cleaned and chopped up, ready to cook. When you go through chapters 3 and 4, you will be rinsing and slicing the ingredients yourself, but for the purposes of this section, the prep work has been done for you, and you will simply be popping everything into the oven.

Here are the steps to follow to do a simple training run of the deep learning model:

1 Update the streetcar_model_training_config.yml file to set the parameters as shown in the next listing.

Listing 2.6 Items that need to be updated in the config file for a simple training run

Modifier to generate unique names for output pipeline and trained model files

Filename for input file to the model training process

```
modifier: 'initial_walkthrough_2020'
pickled_dataframe: '2014_2019_df_cleaned_remove_bad_values_may16_2020.pkl'
current_experiment: 9
get_test_train_acc: False
```

Switch to control whether the extended calculation of test and training accuracy is run. This section of code can take a lot of time to run, so for this preliminary training run, we set this switch to False.

Preset experiment that specifies the characteristic of the training run, including how many runs are done through the training set, whether the training accounts for imbalances in the training set, and whether the training stops early if the model is no longer improving.

2 Open the model training notebook in the environment you chose for the example, and run all cells in the notebook.
3 When the notebook has finished running, check the models subdirectory for a file called scmodelinitial_walkthrough_2020_9.h5. This file is the trained model that has all the weights that were learned in the training process.

You have successfully trained a deep learning model. If you wanted to, you could follow the instructions in chapter 8 to create a simple website that would invoke this model to make predictions on whether a given streetcar trip would be delayed. But although this model is a functionally complete trained deep learning model, its performance isn't the best. If you examine the end of the notebook, you will see a colored box called a confusion matrix that summarizes how good of a model you got in this training run. The confusion matrix looks something like figure 2.21.

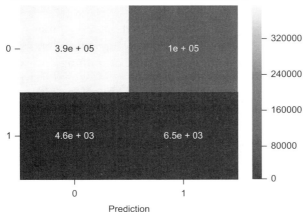

Confusion matrix for streetcar delay prediction (weighted)

Figure 2.21 Example confusion matrix

The top-left and bottom-right quadrants show the number of correct predictions that the model made on the test set (that is, a subset of the dataset that was not used in the training process), and the top-right and bottom-left quadrants show the number of predictions that the model got wrong. Chapter 6 provides a detailed description of the confusion matrix and how to interpret it, along with details on the parameters that make up a training experiment. For now, simply note that the bottom row of the confusion matrix shows that about 40% of the time, the model predicted no delay when a delay occurred. As you will see in chapter 6, this outcome is the worst one for our users, so having it occur so frequently is not good. What can you do to get a better deep learning model? What is the difference between the raw input dataset described in section 2.8 and the cleaned-up dataset that was fed into this training run? Now that you have had a taste of training a deep learning model, see chapters 3–7 to answer these questions, and then see chapter 8 to make your trained deep learning model available to the outside world.

Summary

- Two of the fundamental decisions in a deep learning project are what environment to use and what problem to tackle.
- You can choose your local system to run a deep learning project, or you can choose a full-featured cloud environment like Azure or AWS. In between are environments specifically designed for deep learning, including Paperspace and Google Colab.
- Pandas is the standard Python library for working with tabular datasets. If you are familiar with SQL, you will find that Pandas can conveniently do what you are used to doing with SQL.
- One of the biggest objections to applying deep learning to structured data is that deep learning is too complex. Thanks to the accessibility of environments that target deep learning development, better deep learning frameworks, and deep learning education aimed at nonspecialists, this objection is not as relevant as it was five years ago.
- The code for the major example in this book is designed so that you can run subsets of it without having to run all the preceding steps. You can do deep learning model training runs directly to get a taste of training, for example.

Preparing the data, part 1: Exploring and cleansing the data

This chapter covers

- Using config files in Python
- Ingesting XLS files into Pandas dataframes and saving dataframes with pickle
- Exploring the input dataset
- Categorizing data into continuous, categorical, and text categories
- Correcting gaps and errors in the dataset
- Calculating data volume for a successful deep learning project

In this chapter, you'll learn how to bring tabular structured data from an XLS file into your Python program and how to use the pickle facility in Python to save your data structure between Python sessions. You'll learn how to categorize the structured data in the three categories needed by the deep learning model: continuous, categorical, and text. You will learn how to detect and deal with gaps and errors in the dataset that must be corrected before it can be used to train a deep learning model. Finally, you will get some pointers on how to assess whether a given dataset is large enough to be applicable to deep learning.

3.1 Code for exploring and cleansing the data

After you have cloned the GitHub repo associated with this book (http://mng.bz/ v95x), the code related to exploring and cleansing the data will be in the notebooks sub-directory. The next listing shows the files that contain the code described in this chapter.

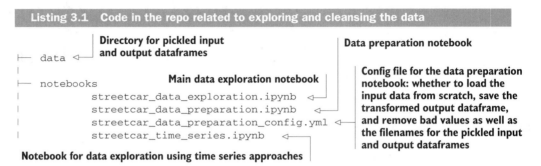

Listing 3.1   Code in the repo related to exploring and cleansing the data

3.2 Using config files with Python

The main code to clean up the dataset is contained in the notebook streetcar_ data_preparation.ipynb. This notebook has a companion config file, streetcar_ data_preparation_config.yml, that is used to set the main parameters. Before exploring the data preparation code, let's examine how this config file and the other config files are used in the streetcar delay prediction example.

Config files are files that are external to your Python program where you can set parameter values. Your Python program reads the config file and uses the values from it for the parameters in the Python program. With config files, you separate setting the parameter values from the Python code, so you can update the parameter values and rerun your code without having to make updates to the code itself. This technique reduces the risk of introducing errors into your code when you update parameter values and keeps your code neater. For the streetcar delay prediction example, we have config files for all the major Python programs, as shown in figure 3.1.

Python program	Description	Config file	Directory in the repo
streetcar_data_preparation.ipynb	Data preparation	streetcar_data_preparation_config.yml	notebooks
streetcar_model_training.ipynb	Model training	streetcar_model_training_config.yml	notebooks
flask_server.py	Web deployment	deploy_web_config.yml	deploy_web
actions.py	Facebook Manager deployment custom actions	deploy_config.yml	deploy

Figure 3.1   Summary of the config files used in the streetcar delay prediction example

You can define config files for your Python program as JSON (https://www.json.org/json-en.html) or YAML (https://yaml.org). For the streetcar delay prediction example in this book, we use YAML. Listing 3.2 shows the config file used by the streetcar_data_preparation notebook, streetcar_data_preparation_config.yml.

Listing 3.2   Config file for data preparation streetcar_data_preparation_config.yml

Parameter used to control whether the raw XLS files are read directly. If this parameter is True, the raw dataset is read from the original XLS files. If this parameter is False, the dataset is read from a pickled dataframe.

You can organize your config files with categories. This config file has one category for general parameters and another for filenames.

Parameter used to control whether the output dataframe is saved to a pickle file

Parameter used to control whether bad values are included in the output dataframe

```
general:
    load_from_scratch: False
    save_transformed_dataframe: False
    remove_bad_values: True
file_names:
    pickled_input_dataframe: 2014_2019_upto_june.pkl
    pickled_output_dataframe: 2014_2019_df_cleaned_remove_bad_oct18.pkl
```

Filename of the pickled data frame to read if load_from_scratch is set to False

Filename of the pickled data frame to write if save_transformed_dataframe is True

The next listing is the code in the streetcar_data_preparation notebook that reads the config file and sets the parameters based on the values in the config file.

Listing 3.3   Code in the data preparation notebook that ingests the config file

Define the path for the fully qualified config file. Note that the name of the config file is one parameter that needs to be hardcoded in the Python code, although this should not be a problem because the name of the config file should not change. Also note that we use os.path.join to combine the directory and filename into a single path. We use this function because it makes the pathname platform independent.

Get the path for the notebook.

```
current_path = os.getcwd()
path_to_yaml = os.path.join(current_path,
    'streetcar_data_preparation_config.yml')
try:
    with open (path_to_yaml, 'r') as c_file:
        config = yaml.safe_load(c_file)
except Exception as e:
    print('Error reading the config file')
```

Define the Python dictionary config containing the key/value pairs from the config file.

```
load_from_scratch = config['general']['load_from_scratch']
save_transformed_dataframe = config['general']['save_transformed_dataframe']
remove_bad_values = config['general']['remove_bad_values']
pickled_input_dataframe = config['file_names']['pickled_input_dataframe']
pickled_output_dataframe = config['file_names']['pickled_output_dataframe']
```

Copy the values from the config dictionary into the variables used throughout the rest of the program.

In this section, you have seen why we use config files with the major Python programs in the streetcar delay prediction example along with a description of the details of the config file for the data preparation code. Config files are particularly handy for this example because we are using pickle files to save the interim results. By setting the values for the filenames of these pickle files in config files, we can rerun the code on different interim result sets without having to modify the code itself.

3.3   Ingesting XLS files into a Pandas dataframe

In chapter 2, we examined the format of the input dataset for the streetcar delay problem. In this section, we will go over how to ingest this dataset into a Pandas dataframe in Python. The input dataset is made up of multiple XLS files. To start, let's go through the process of ingesting a single XLS file into a Pandas dataframe as shown in the notebook for this chapter.

First, you need to install the library to read Excel files:

```
!pip install xlrd
```

Then you need to get the metadata (tab names) for the XLS file and iterate through the list of tab names to load all the tabs into one dataframe, as shown in the next listing.

Listing 3.4   Code to iterate through the tabs in the XLS file

```
def get_path():                          ⟵──┤ Function that returns the
    rawpath = os.getcwd()                     │ path of the data directory
    path = os.path.abspath(os.path.join(rawpath, '..', 'data'))
    return(path)

import pandas as pd
path = get_path()
file = "ttc-streetcar-delay-data-2014.xlsx"   ⟵──┐
xlsf = pd.ExcelFile(os.path.join(path,file))   ⟵──┤
df = pd.read_excel(os.path.join(path,file),sheet_name=xlsf.sheet_names[0])
for sheet_name in xlsf.sheet_names[1:]:
    print("sheet_name",sheet_name)
    data = pd.read_excel(os.path.join(path,file),sheet_name=sheet_name)  ⟵──┐
    df = df.append(data)                 ⟵──┐
```

Import the pandas library.

Define the base path and the filename.

Load metadata about the Excel file; then load the first sheet of the XLS file into a dataframe.

Load the current sheet into a dataframe.

Iterate through the remaining sheets in the XLS file, appending their contents to the dataframe.

Append this dataframe to the aggregated dataframe.

The output shows the tab names starting with the second tab name (because the first name is loaded before the `for` loop):

```
sheet_name Feb 2014
sheet_name Mar 2014
sheet_name Apr 2014
sheet_name May 2014
sheet_name Jun 2014
sheet_name July 2014
```

```
sheet_name Aug 2014
sheet_name Sept 2014
sheet_name Oct 2014
sheet_name Nov 2014
sheet_name Dec 2014
```

After the dataframe is created from the input XLS files, you will notice some unexpected columns in the head() output for the dataframe (figure 3.2).

	Day	Delay	Direction	Gap	Incident	Incident ID	Location	Min Delay	Min Gap	Report Date	Route	Time	Vehicle
0	Thursday	NaN	E/B	NaN	Late Leaving Garage	NaN	Dundas and Roncesvalles	4.0	8.0	2014-01-02	505	06:31:00	4018.0
1	Thursday	NaN	E/B	NaN	Utilized Off Route	NaN	King and Shaw	20.0	22.0	2014-01-02	504	12:43:00	4128.0
2	Thursday	NaN	W/B	NaN	Held By	NaN	Kingston road and Bingham	13.0	19.0	2014-01-02	501	14:01:00	4016.0
3	Thursday	NaN	W/B	NaN	Investigation	NaN	King St. and Roncesvalles Ave.	7.0	11.0	2014-01-02	504	14:22:00	4175.0
4	Thursday	NaN	E/B	NaN	Utilized Off Route	NaN	King and Bathurst	3.0	6.0	2014-01-02	504	16:42:00	4080.0

Figure 3.2   Loaded dataframe with extraneous columns

In addition to the expected Min Delay and Min Gap columns, there are unexpected Delay and Gap columns, as well as an unexpected Incident ID column. It turns out that the source dataset has some anomalies introduced in the April and June tabs of the 2019 XLS file, as shown in figure 3.3. The April tab of the 2019 XLS file has columns called Delay and Gap (rather than Min Delay and Min Gap, like all the other tabs in the original dataset), along with an Incident ID column. The June tab of the 2019 XLS file has a different issue: instead of the Min Delay and Min Gap columns, it has columns called Delay and Gap.

Report Date	Route	Time	Day	Location	Incident ID	Incident	Delay	Gap	Direction	Vehicle
01-Apr-19	512	4:26:00 AM	Monday	Roncesvalles Yard.		1 Mechanical	10	20	E/B	4460

Report Date	Route	Time	Day	Location	Incident	Delay	Gap	Direction	Vehicle
01-Jun-19	501	12:27:00 AM	Saturday	Queen and Bay	Held By	16	21	W/B	4474

Figure 3.3   Anomalies in the April 2019 and June 2019 tabs of the 2019 XLS file

Because these anomalous columns appear in two tabs in the 2019 XLS file, if you read in the complete dataset including the XLS file for 2019, then the overall dataframe gets these columns as well. The data preparation notebook includes the code in the following listing, which corrects the problem by copying over the needed data and then deleting the extraneous columns.

Listing 3.5   Code to correct the anomalous columns

```
def fix_anomalous_columns(df):
    df['Min Delay'].fillna(df['Delay'], inplace=True)
    df['Min Gap'].fillna(df['Gap'], inplace=True)
```

> **If there is NaN in the Min Delay or Min Gap columns, copy over the value from Delay or Gap.**

```
del df['Delay']
del df['Gap']
del df['Incident ID']
return(df)
```

Now that the useful values have been copied from Delay and Gap, remove the Delay and Gap columns.

Return the updated dataframe.

Remove the Incident ID column; it's extraneous.

After this cleanup, the output of `head()` confirms that the anomalous columns have been eliminated and that the dataframe has the expected columns (see figure 3.4).

	Report Date	Route	Time	Day	Location	Incident	Min Delay	Min Gap	Direction	Vehicle
0	2014-01-02	505	06:31:00	Thursday	Dundas and Roncesvalles	Late Leaving Garage	4.0	8.0	E/B	4018.0
1	2014-01-02	504	12:43:00	Thursday	King and Shaw	Utilized Off Route	20.0	22.0	E/B	4128.0
2	2014-01-02	501	14:01:00	Thursday	Kingston road and Bingham	Held By	13.0	19.0	W/B	4016.0
3	2014-01-02	504	14:22:00	Thursday	King St. and Roncesvalles Ave.	Investigation	7.0	11.0	W/B	4175.0
4	2014-01-02	504	16:42:00	Thursday	King and Bathurst	Utilized Off Route	3.0	6.0	E/B	4080.0

Figure 3.4   The beginning of the dataframe containing all tabs of the input XLS file

We check the output of `tail()` to confirm that the end of the dataframe is also as expected (see figure 3.5).

	Report Date	Route	Time	Day	Location	Incident	Min Delay	Min Gap	Direction	Vehicle
869	2014-12-31	509	22:30:00	Wednesday	Union Loop to Exhibition Loop	General Delay	10.0	20.0	B/W	NaN
870	2014-12-31	504	22:54:00	Wednesday	King and Dunn	Emergency Services	11.0	16.0	E/B	4128.0
871	2014-12-31	505	23:00:00	Wednesday	Dundas West Station to Broadview Station	General Delay	10.0	12.0	B/W	NaN
872	2014-12-31	511	23:01:00	Wednesday	CNE	Mechanical	8.0	16.0	N/B	4160.0
873	2014-12-31	504	23:18:00	Wednesday	King and Bathurst	Mechanical	7.0	14.0	E/B	4128.0

Figure 3.5   The end of the dataframe containing all tabs of the input XLS file

There's an important lesson to be learned from these anomalies in the source streetcar dataset. With a live, real-world dataset, we need to be prepared to be nimble to account for changes in the dataset. While I was writing this book, the anomalies described in this section were introduced into the dataset, so I needed to be prepared to update the data preparation code to address these anomalies. When you are dealing with a dataset that you don't control, you need to be able to take unintended changes in the dataset in stride.

Now that you know how to load a single XLS file, let's work through how to ingest the entire input dataset by bringing data from multiple XLS files into a single Pandas dataframe.

The code examples in this section come from the streetcar_data_preparation notebook. This notebook assumes that you have copied all the XLS files from the raw input dataset (http://mng.bz/ry6y) to a directory called data, which is a sibling of the directory that contains the notebook.

The code in the streetcar data preparation notebook uses two functions to ingest multiple XLS files into a single dataframe. The `reloader` function primes the process by loading the first tab of the first file into a dataframe and then calls the `load_xls` function to load the remaining tabs of the first file, along with all the tabs of all the other XLS files. The code in the next listing assumes that the XLS files in the data directory are exactly the XLS files that make up the dataset.

Listing 3.6   Code to ingest the XLS file

Load all the tabs of all the XLS files in a list of XLS files, minus the tab that has the seeded dataframe.

```
def load_xls(path, files_xls, firstfile, firstsheet, df):
    '''
    load all the tabs of all the XLS files in a list of XLS files, minus
tab that has seeded dataframe

    Parameters:
    path: directory containing the XLS files
    files_xls: list of XLS files
    firstfile: file whose first tab has been preloaded
    firstsheet: first tab of the file that has been preloaded
    df: Pandas dataframe that has been preloaded with the first tab
of the first XLS file and is loaded with all the data
when the function returns

    Returns:
    df: updated dataframe

    '''
    for f in files_xls:
        print("filename",f)
        xlsf = pd.ExcelFile(path+f)
        for sheet_name in xlsf.sheet_names:
            print("sheet_name",sheet_name)
            if (f != firstfile) or (sheet_name != firstsheet):
                print("sheet_name in loop",sheet_name)
                data = pd.read_excel(path+f,sheetname=sheet_name)
                df = df.append(data)
    return (df)
```

Iterate through all the XLS files in the directory.

Iterate through all the sheets in the current XLS file.

Append the dataframe for the current sheet to the overall dataframe.

The code in the following listing shows the `reloader` function that calls the `load_xls` function to ingest all XLS files and saves the result in a pickled dataframe.

Listing 3.7   Code to ingest multiple XLS files and save the result in a pickled dataframe

Given a path and a filename, load all the XLS files in the path into a dataframe.

```
def reloader(path,picklename):
    files_xls = get_xls_list(path)
    print("list of xls",files_xls)
    dfnew = pd.read_excel(path+files_xls[0])
```

Get the list of all XLS files in the path.

Seed the initial tab on the initial XLS file.

```
xlsf = pd.ExcelFile(path+files_xls[0])                       ◁──┐  Get the list of sheets
dflatest = load_xls(path,files_xls,files_xls[0], \              │  in the first file.
 ┌─▷ ⇨ xlsf.sheet_names[0], dfnew)
 │   dflatest.to_pickle(os.path.join(path,picklename))  ◁──┐  Save the dataframe
 │   return(dflatest)  ◁─────────────────┐                 │  to a pickle file.
Load the remaining tabs              Return the dataframe loaded
from all the other XLS files.        with all tabs of all XLS files.
```

How do you get the correct value for path, the directory where you have copied the XLS files that make up the dataset? The code assumes that all the data exists in a directory called data, which is a sibling of the directory that contains the notebook. The next listing is the code snippet introduced in chapter 2 that gets the correct path for the directory containing the XLS files; it gets the current directory (where the notebook resides) and the path for the directory called data that is a sibling of this directory.

> **Listing 3.8   Code to get the path of the data directory**

```
rawpath = os.getcwd()                ◁──┐  Get the directory that
print("raw path is",rawpath)            │  this notebook is in.
path = os.path.abspath(os.path.join(rawpath, '..', 'data'))  ◁──
print("path is", path)
```

Get the fully qualified path of the directory data that is a sibling of the directory that this notebook is in.

3.4   *Using pickle to save your Pandas dataframe from one session to another*

A Pandas dataframe exists for the life of your notebook session. This consideration is an important one, particularly when you are using a cloud environment such as Paperspace. When you have shut down the notebook (either explicitly or by closing your cloud session), you lose the dataframes you created during your session. The next time you want to do more work, you have to reload the data from scratch. What can you do if you want your Pandas dataframe to persist between sessions, to save you from having to reload the data from its source every time, or if you want to share a dataframe between two notebooks?

For modest-sized datasets, the answer to the problem of keeping a dataframe beyond the life of a session is pickle. This extremely useful standard Python library allows you to save your Python objects (including Pandas dataframes) as files in your filesystem that you can later read back into Python. Before I go into the details of how to use pickle, it behooves me to acknowledge that not everybody is a fan of pickle. Ben Frederickson, for example, argues that pickle is less efficient than serialization alternatives like JSON and can expose you to security issues if you unpickle files whose origin is not known (https://www.benfrederickson.com/dont-pickle-your-data). In addition, pickle isn't the right choice for every use case. It isn't recommended if you need to share serialized objects between programming languages (pickle is for Python only), for example, or between levels of Python. You can run into issues if you pickle an object in one level of Python and then try to bring it into another piece of code that is running at a different Python level. For the purposes of the example described in this book, I am sticking with pickle because it simplifies the serialization process and because the provenance of all the pickle files is known.

Suppose that you want to work with the publicly available Iris dataset rather than copy it to your filesystem, but you are working in an environment in which your internet connection is not reliable. For the sake of this example, assume that you are using a locally installed machine learning framework, such as Jupyter Notebooks installed in your local system, so you can work on notebooks when you are offline. You want to be able to load the dataframe while you are connected to the internet and then save the dataframe to your filesystem so you can reload the dataframe and keep working when you are offline.

First, you load the Iris dataset into a dataframe, just as you did in chapter 2 (listing 3.9), as shown next.

Listing 3.9   Code to ingest a CSV file using a URL reference

```
url="https://gist.githubusercontent.com/curran/a08a1080b88344b0c8a7/\
    raw/d546eaee765268bf2f487608c537c05e22e4b221/iris.csv"      ◁──  Raw GitHub URL
iris_dataframe=pd.read_csv(url)     ◁──                              for Iris dataset
                                    Read the contents of the URL
                                    into a Pandas dataframe.
```

Next, you call the `to_pickle()` method to save the dataframe to a file in your filesystem, as shown in the following listing. By convention, pickle files have the extension `pkl`.

Listing 3.10   Code to save a dataframe as a pickle file

```
file = "iris_dataframe.pkl"                          ◁──  Define a filename
iris_dataframe.to_pickle(os.path.join(path,file))         for the pickle file.
Write the dataframe to the named pickle file.
```

Now when you are on a flight with no internet connection and want to keep working with this dataset, all you have to do is call the `read_pickle` method with the pickle file you saved as the argument, as the next listing shows.

Listing 3.11   Code to read a pickle file into a dataframe

```
file = "iris_dataframe.pkl"
iris_dataframe_from_pickle = pd.read_pickle(os.path.join(path,file))   ◁──
iris_dataframe_from_pickle.head()
                                      Call the read_pickle function to read
                                      the pickle file into a dataframe.
```

The output of `head()` shows that you have the data loaded into a dataframe again without having to go back to the original source dataset (figure 3.6).

Figure 3.7 summarizes the flow from the original source dataset (CSV file) to a Pandas dataframe, then to a pickle file, and finally back to the Pandas dataframe.

	sepal_length	sepal_width	petal_length	petal_width	species
0	5.1	3.5	1.4	0.2	setosa
1	4.9	3.0	1.4	0.2	setosa
2	4.7	3.2	1.3	0.2	setosa
3	4.6	3.1	1.5	0.2	setosa
4	5.0	3.6	1.4	0.2	setosa

Figure 3.6   Results of unpickling a dataframe that was saved in a pickle file

Figure 3.7   Life cycle of a dataset

Pickling is extremely useful if you have a large dataset that takes some time to load into a dataframe from its external source. For large datasets, unpickling a saved dataframe can be much faster than reloading the dataframe from its external source.

3.5   *Exploring the data*

Now that we've learned how to ingest the complete input dataset into a Pandas dataframe and how to make this dataset persistent between sessions, we need to explore the data to understand its characteristics. By using the facilities that are available in Python to visualize the data, we can explore the data to find patterns and anomalies that help us make good choices for the downstream processes. You can find the code for this section in the streetcar_data_exploration notebook and in the streetcar _time_series notebook.

First let's use `describe()` on the raw dataframe (see figure 3.8).

	Route	Min Delay	Min Gap	Vehicle
count	69603.000000	69549.000000	69528.000000	65142.000000
mean	501.186070	12.697523	18.147480	4388.337923
std	43.712495	29.781860	33.623384	1539.555810
min	1.000000	0.000000	0.000000	0.000000
25%	501.000000	5.000000	9.000000	4075.000000
50%	505.000000	6.000000	12.000000	4161.000000
75%	509.000000	12.000000	20.000000	4246.000000
max	999.000000	1400.000000	4216.000000	163242.000000

Figure 3.8   Output of `describe()`

Here are a few items to note:

- Route and Vehicle are being interpreted as continuous; we need to correct the types of these two columns.
- The maximum delay is 23 hours, and the maximum gap is 72 hours. Both values look incorrect. We need to check the records to confirm whether they are incorrect.
- The average delay is 12 minutes; the average gap is 18 minutes.

Taking a random sample of the dataset by using `sample()`, we get the output shown in figure 3.9.

	Report Date	Route	Time	Day	Location	Incident	Min Delay	Min Gap	Direction	Vehicle
307	2016-09-09	504	16:55:00	Friday	King and Roncesvalles	Held By	51.0	56.0	W/B	4166.0
488	2014-06-13	501	16:02:00	Friday	Gerrard and Greenwood	Utilized Off Route	11.0	17.0	W/B	4246.0
1654	2017-12-31	506	01:45:00	Sunday	Gerrard and Broadview	Investigation	10.0	20.0	E/B	4135.0
84	2015-09-02	501	22:43:00	Wednesday	Queen and Ohara	Mechanical	6.0	12.0	W/B	4230.0
1030	2015-01-26	504	10:21:00	Monday	King and Sherbourne	Mechanical	12.0	16.0	W/B	4074.0
367	2015-03-10	510	17:07:00	Tuesday	Spadina and Queen	Utilized Off Route	3.0	6.0	N/B	4173.0
877	2014-05-29	501	10:45:00	Thursday	Queen at Coxwell	Emergency Services	0.0	0.0	E/B	4226.0
168	2017-11-06	506	07:33:00	Monday	High Park Loop	Utilized Off Route	16.0	21.0	E/B	4032.0
833	2015-10-29	504	06:49:00	Thursday	Roncesvalles& Queen	Mechanical	4.0	8.0	W/B	NaN
345	2018-01-05	504	13:46:00	Friday	Dufferin and King	Mechanical	2.0	5.0	W/B	4133.0

Figure 3.9   Output of `sample()` on the raw input dataframe

What does this output tell us?

- Some incidents have zero-length delays and gaps, which isn't what we'd expect from a dataset that is supposed to record delays. We need to review these records to determine whether the zero-length delays and gaps are intentional or errors.
- Location values do not have consistent junction words: `at`, `and`, and `&` all appear in this random sample
- Incident may be a categorical column. We should count the number of unique values to determine whether it makes sense to treat Incident as a categorical column.

If we look at the number of unique values for Incident, we see that it is a small enough number for Incident to be a categorical column:

```
print("incident count",df['Incident'].nunique())
incident count 9
```

This confirms that Incident should be treated as a categorical column rather than a freeform text column.

Let's explore the relative size of Min Delay and Min Gap in the next listing by counting how many times one value is larger than the other for a given incident.

Listing 3.12   Code to count how many times Min Delay is bigger or smaller than Min Gap

```
df[df['Min Gap'] > df['Min Delay']].shape       Get the number of records in which
(65176, 10)                                     Min Gap is greater than Min Delay.
          Number of these records

df[df['Min Gap'] < df['Min Delay']].shape       Get the number of records in which
(1969, 10)                                      Min Gap is less than Min Delay.
          Number of these records
```

The result tells us that Min Gap is usually longer than Min Delay for a given incident, but about 3% of the time, Min Delay is longer. This isn't what we'd expect. We need to review these records where Min Delay is longer than Min Gap to determine whether they are errors.

Next, let's look at a view that clusters the number of incidents by month (see figure 3.10). You can find the code to generate the charts in this section in the streetcar_time _series notebook. Each dot in this view represents the total incidents in a month for a given year. Tight vertical clusters of dots mean that the number of incidents doesn't vary much from year to year.

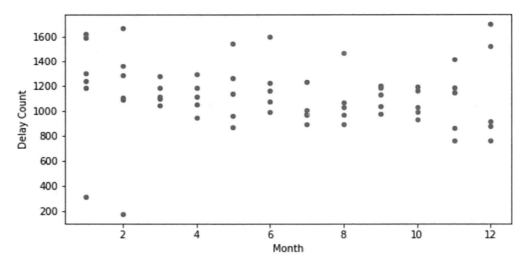

Figure 3.10   Delay incidents by month

The next listing shows the code that generates this chart.

Listing 3.13   Code to generate the delay incidents by month chart

```
dfmonthav.plot.scatter(x = 'Month', y = 'Delay Count')      Plot with the month
plt.show()                                                  of the year on the x
          Render the plot.                                  axis and count of
                                                            delays on the y axis
```

What does this view tell us?

- The number of incidents in March, April, September, and October (and arguably July) doesn't vary as much from year to year as in other months.
- January, February, and December have the ranges with the highest top ends.

Can we draw any conclusions from these observations? Perhaps there are more incidents during the months with more extreme temperatures. Perhaps the number of incidents is more variable during months with unpredictable weather. Both of these conclusions are reasonable, but neither is certain. We need to let the data drive the conclusions. It is possible that weather is a contributing factor to the number of delays, but we need to be careful not to assign causality without supporting data. In chapter 9, we discuss adding weather as an additional data source to the streetcar prediction model. The delays by month chart indicates this might be a useful exercise.

Now let's look at a rolling average of delay duration. The data point for each month on this chart is the average of the delay duration for the six preceding months (see figure 3.11).

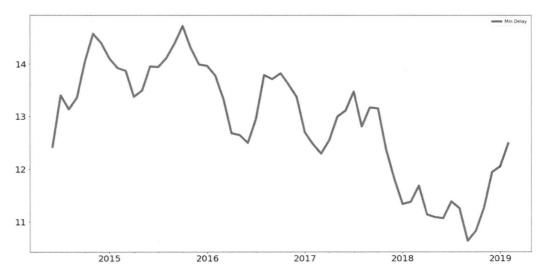

Figure 3.11 Rolling average delay duration

The following listing is the code that generates this chart.

Listing 3.14 Code to generate the rolling average delay duration chart

```
mean_delay = dfmonthav[['Min Delay']]
mean_delay.rolling(6).mean().plot(figsize=(20,10), linewidth=5, fontsize=20)
plt.show()
```

Render the plot.

Plot the six-month rolling average of delay duration with data points by month.

Figure 3.11 tells us that there has been an overall trend of delay incidents getting shorter, with an uptick in 2019.

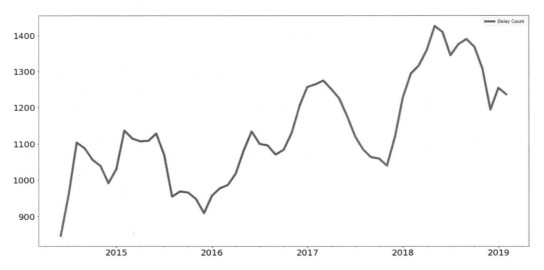

Figure 3.12   Rolling average delay count

Python offers many options for exploring a dataset. This section showed a useful subset of these options along with possible actions to take as a result of the exploration.

The next listing is the code for the chart in figure 3.12.

> **Listing 3.15   Code to generate the rolling average delay count chart**

```
count_delay = dfmonthav[['Delay Count']]
count_delay.rolling(6).mean().plot(figsize=(20,10), \
linewidth=5, fontsize=20)
plt.show()
```

Render the plot.

Plot the six-month rolling average of delay counts with data points by month.

Figure 3.12 suggests that the trend toward delay count is increasing, opposite the trend toward delay duration.

3.6   *Categorizing data into continuous, categorical, and text categories*

Now that you have explored the data, it's time to tackle the problem of how to categorize the columns in the dataset. The approach described in this book is based on grouping the input columns into three categories:

- *Continuous*—These values are numeric and are values to which arithmetic can be applied. Examples of continuous values include temperatures, currency values, time spans (such as elapsed hours), and counts of objects and activities.

- *Categorical*—These values can be single strings, such as the days of the week, or collections of one or more strings that constitute an identifier, such as the names of the U.S. states. The number of distinct values in categorical columns can range from two to several thousand.
- *Text*—These values are sets of strings.

This categorization is critical for two reasons:

- Like other machine learning algorithms, deep learning algorithms work on numerical values. The final data stream that is fed into the deep learning model needs to consist entirely of numerical values, so all non-numerical values need to be transformed into numerical values. The categorization tells us whether such a transformation is needed for a column and, if so, what kind of transformation is needed.
- As you will see in chapter 5, the layers of the deep learning models are built up automatically based on the categories of the input columns. Each type of column (continuous, categorical, and text) generates layers with different characteristics. By categorizing the input columns, you make it possible for the code in the streetcar_model_training notebook to build a deep learning model automatically, which means that if you add columns to or drop columns from your dataset, the model will be updated automatically when you rerun the notebook.

Figure 3.13 shows how the columns can be categorized for the input streetcar delay dataset:

	Report Date	Route	Time	Day	Location	Incident	Min Delay	Min Gap	Direction	Vehicle
		Categorical		**Categorical**		**Text**	**Continuous**		**Categorical**	
0	2014-01-02	505	06:31:00	Thursday	Dundas and Roncesvalles	Late Leaving Garage	4.0	8.0	E/B	4018.0
1	2014-01-02	504	12:43:00	Thursday	King and Shaw	Utilized Off Route	20.0	22.0	E/B	4128.0
2	2014-01-02	501	14:01:00	Thursday	Kingston road and Bingham	Held By	13.0	19.0	W/B	4016.0
3	2014-01-02	504	14:22:00	Thursday	King St. and Roncesvalles Ave.	Investigation	7.0	11.0	W/B	4175.0
4	2014-01-02	504	16:42:00	Thursday	King and Bathurst	Utilized Off Route	3.0	6.0	E/B	4080.0

Figure 3.13   Categorizing columns in the input dataset for the main example in this book

Here is a description of the categorization of each column:

- Min Delay and Min Gap are measurements of elapsed time and thus are continuous columns.
- Incident is a categorical column that describes what caused the interruption of service. There are nine valid values.
- Route is a categorical column. There are 12 valid values.
- Day is a categorical column with seven valid values.

- Location is a categorical column, even though it is a freeform field when the data is entered. This column is an example that requires preprocessing to map a large number of potential values to a smaller set of unique values. In chapter 4, we'll discuss the pros and cons of mapping these location strings to strictly defined longitude and latitude values.
- Direction is a categorical column with five valid values: the four compass points and a value to indicate multiple directions.
- Vehicle is a categorical column, even though the values in it look like floating-point values when they are initially brought into a dataframe. The values in this column are actually four-character identifiers for 300 or so active streetcar vehicles. In chapter 4, we will deal with the mismatch between the type that Python assigns to this column and the actual type of the data.

What about the temporal columns Report Date and Time? In chapter 5, we'll describe an approach to parsing the values in these columns into new categorical columns that identify the most interesting temporal aspects of the incidents: year, month, day of month, and hour.

Note that in some cases, a column could legitimately fit into more than one category. A column containing timestamps, for example, could be treated as continuous or categorical, depending on the requirements of your business problem. The good news is that the approach described in this book is flexible enough that you can change your mind about the category for a column and retrain the model with minimal disruption.

3.7   *Cleaning up problems in the dataset: missing data, errors, and guesses*

The streetcar delay problem is a good illustration of applying deep learning to tabular structured data because the input dataset is messy, with lots of missing, invalid, and extraneous values. Real-world problems that we want to solve with deep learning involve these kinds of messy datasets, so cleaning up messy data is one thing we need to learn how to do if we want to harness deep learning to solve practical problems with tabular, structured data.

We need to clean up these problems in the dataset for a variety of reasons:

- The missing values need to be dealt with because the deep learning model cannot be trained on datasets that have missing values.
- The invalid values need to be dealt with because, as you will see in chapter 7, training the deep learning model with the invalid values still in place reduces the performance of the trained model.
- The extraneous values—multiple distinct tokens for the same real-world characteristic (such as E/B, e/b, and eb for *eastbound*)—need to be dealt with because carrying them through the rest of the process increases the complexity of the model without providing any additional signal to be picked up in the training process.

Following are the characteristics we want the dataset to have when the cleanup process is complete:

- *All values are numeric.* Machine learning algorithms depend on all the data being numeric. Missing values need to be replaced, and non-numeric values (in categorical or text columns) need to be replaced by numeric identifiers.
- *Records with invalid values are identified and eliminated.* The reason for eliminating invalid values (such as locations that are outside the geographic area of the streetcar network or vehicle IDs that are not valid streetcar IDs) is to prevent the model from being trained with data that isn't a reflection of the real-world problem.
- *Extraneous categories are identified and eliminated.* We know that the Direction column should have only five valid values (the compass points plus an identifier to indicate both directions). All records need to use the same consistent categories.

First, let's take a look at the missing values in each column. Deep learning models work only with numbers as input. All the values that are used to train deep learning models must be numbers. The reason is that the data that is used to train the deep learning model needs to repeatedly undergo the process described in chapter 1: multiplication by weights, addition of bias values, and application of an activation function. These operations cannot work with missing values, character values, or anything else that is not a number, so dealing with missing values is a fundamental part of cleaning up the input dataset.

How can you tell which columns are missing values and how many rows in each column are missing values? Here's a simple command whose output is the number of missing values in each column:

```
df.isnull().sum(axis = 0)
Report Date      0
Route            0
Time             0
Day              0
Location       270
Incident         0
Min Delay       58
Min Gap         77
Direction      232
Vehicle          0
```

The output tells us that Location, Min Delay, Min Gap, and Direction all have missing values that need to be dealt with. The `fill_missing` function iterates through all the columns in a dataframe and replaces empty values with a placeholder value depending on the column category, as the next listing shows.

Listing 3.16   Code to replace missing values with placeholder values

```
def fill_missing(dataset):
    print("before mv")
    for col in collist:
        dataset[col].fillna(value="missing", inplace=True)
    for col in continuouscols:
        dataset[col].fillna(value=0.0,inplace=True)
    for col in textcols:
        dataset[col].fillna(value="missing", inplace=True)
    return (dataset)
```

Fill missing values according
to the column category.

We are going to fill missing values in continuous columns with
zeros. Note that for some columns, the mean of the values in
the column would be a valid substitute for missing values.

If we call this function with the dataframe where we loaded the input dataset as the
argument

```
df = fill_missing(df)
```

and then rerun the command to count empty values, we can see that all the missing
values have been dealt with:

```
df.isnull().sum(axis = 0)
Report Date    0
Route          0
Time           0
Day            0
Location       0
Incident       0
Min Delay      0
Min Gap        0
Direction      0
Vehicle        0
```

Now that we have fixed the missing values, let's explore in depth the remaining
cleanup action for one of the columns of the input dataset: Direction.

The Direction column indicates which direction of traffic was affected by the incident in a given record. According to the readme file that accompanies the dataset,
there are seven valid values for Direction:

- B, b, or BW for incidents that affect traffic going in both directions. When we
  clean up the values in this column, we will use a single value to indicate both
  directions.
- NB, SB, EB, and WB for incidents that affect traffic going in a single direction
  (northbound, southbound, eastbound, or westbound).

Now let's look at the actual number of unique values in the Direction column in the
dataframe where we've loaded the input data:

```
print("unique directions before cleanup:",df['Direction'].nunique())
unique directions before cleanup: 95
```

What's going on? How can there be 95 distinct values in a column that has only seven legitimate values? Let's take a look at the output of `value_counts` for the Direction column to get an idea of where all these unique values are coming from:

```
df['Direction'].value_counts()
W/B                     32466
E/B                     32343
N/B                      6006
B/W                      5747
S/B                      5679
missing                   232
EB                        213
eb                        173
WB                        149
wb                        120
SB                         20
nb                         18
NB                         18
sb                         14
EW                         13
eastbound                   8
bw                          7
5                           7
w/b                         7
w                           6
BW                          4
8                           4
ew                          4
E                           4
w/B                         4
s                           4
2                           4
W                           3
b/w                         3
10                          3
                      . . .
e/w                         1
```

As you can see, the 95 values in the Direction column come from a combination of redundant tokens and errors. To correct these problems, we need to

- Get a consistent case for the values in this column to avoid problems like EB and eb being treated as distinct values.
- Remove / from values in this column to avoid problems like wb and w/b being treated as distinct values.
- Make the following substitutions to eliminate redundant tokens for compass points:
  - e for eb and eastbound
  - w for wb and westbound
  - n for nb and northbound

- – s for sb and southbound
- – b for bw
- ▪ Replace all remaining tokens (including the missing token that we inserted for missing values) with a single token, bad direction, to signify a value that could not be mapped to any of the valid directions.

We apply the direction_cleanup function in the next listing to the Direction column to make these changes.

Listing 3.17   Code to clean up the Direction column

```
def check_direction (x):          ⟵——— Function to replace invalid direction
    if x in valid_directions:          values with a common string
        return(x)
    else:
        return("bad direction")
```

Function to clean up direction values

Remove / from all values.

```
def direction_cleanup(df):      ⟵
    print("Direction count pre cleanup",df['Direction'].nunique())
    df['Direction'] = df['Direction'].str.lower()
    df['Direction'] = df['Direction'].str.replace('/','')      ⟵
    df['Direction'] =
        df['Direction'].replace({'eastbound':'e','westbound':'w', \
        'southbound':'s','northbound':'n'})
    df['Direction'] = df['Direction'].replace('b','',regex=True)
    df['Direction'] = df['Direction'].apply(lambda x:check_direction(x))   ⟵
    print("Direction count post cleanup",df['Direction'].nunique())
    return(df)
```

Lowercase all values.

Remove extraneous b from strings like eb and nb.

Replace eastbound, westbound, and so on with single letter direction tokens.

Call check_direction to replace any remaining invalid values with a common string.

The output shows the effect of these changes:

```
Unique directions before cleanup: 95
Unique directions after cleanup: 6
```

Here are the counts by the remaining unique values in the Direction column:

```
w                32757
e                32747
n                 6045
b                 5763
s                 5719
bad direction      334
```

Note that now we have only six valid values instead of the seven specified in the readme. We have combined the three "both way" tokens—B, b, and BW—into b and added a new token, bad direction, for erroneous direction values. This cleanup is essential for the refactoring of the input dataset that is described in chapter 5 to get a dataset with a record for every route/direction/time-slot combination. This refactoring depends on there being at most five direction values for any route, and thanks to the cleanup of the Direction column, we know that this condition is true.

The Direction column is only one of the columns that need to be cleaned up. Compared with other columns, Direction is relatively straightforward to clean up because it has a small number of valid values. Also, the operations to convert the input values to the set of valid values are relatively straightforward. We will go through a more complicated cleanup process for other columns in chapter 4.

3.8 Finding out how much data deep learning needs

If you do a naïve search to find out how much data you need to train a deep learning model, you will not get satisfying results. The answers are all variations on "It depends." Some famous deep learning models are trained on millions of examples. Generally speaking, nonlinear methods like deep learning require more data than linear methods such as linear regression to achieve adequate results. Like other machine learning methods, deep learning requires a training dataset that covers the combinations of inputs that could be encountered when the model is deployed. In the case of the streetcar delay prediction problem, we need to ensure that the training set includes records for all the streetcar routes for which a user might want predictions. If a new streetcar route were added to the system, for example, we would need to retrain the model with a dataset that includes delay information for that route.

The real question for us isn't the broad question "How much data does a deep learning model need to be trained adequately?" The question is "Does the streetcar dataset have enough data so that we can apply deep learning to it?" Ultimately, the answer depends on how well our model performs, and there is a lesson in this observation that the amount of data needed depends on the performance of the trained model. If you have a dataset with tens of thousands of entries, like the streetcar dataset, it is neither so small that deep learning is out of the question, nor so big as to guarantee that data volume won't be a problem. The only way to know for sure whether deep learning is applicable to your problem is to try it out and look at the performance. As described in chapter 6, for the streetcar delay prediction model, we measure test accuracy (that is, how well the model predicts delays for trips that it did not see during the training process) and other measurements that are connected to a good user experience with the model. The good news is that after you have completed this book, you will have all the tools you need to assess the performance of deep learning on tabular structured datasets.

We will take a closer look at model accuracy in chapter 6, but it's worth briefly reflecting on the question of accuracy now. How good does the accuracy of the streetcar prediction model need to be? For this problem, anything better than 70% will help, because it will make it possible for passengers to avoid long delays most of the time.

Summary

- A fundamental step in a deep learning project is ingesting the raw dataset so that it is available for you to manipulate in your code. When you have ingested the data, you can explore it and begin to clean it up.

- You can use config files in conjunction with your Python programs to keep your parameters organized and to make it easy to update parameters without having to touch the Python code.

- You can ingest a CSV file directly into a Pandas dataframe with a single function call. With a simple Python function, you can also ingest all the tabs in an XLS file or even in multiple XLS files into a dataframe.

- Python's pickle facility is an easy way to save objects in a Python program so you can use them across Python sessions. If you have a Python program that performs a series of transformations on a dataset, you can pickle the transformed dataframe, read the pickled dataframe in another Python program, and continue working on the dataset without having to redo the transformations.

- When you have ingested the dataset into a dataframe, Python offers many convenient functions for exploring the dataset to determine the type and range of values in each column as well as trends in the values in columns. This exploration can help you detect anomalies in the dataset and avoid making unsubstantiated assumptions about the data.

- When you clean up a dataset to prepare it for training a deep learning model, the problems that you need to fix include missing values, invalid values, and values indicated by multiple distinct tokens (such as e, e/b, and EB all indicating eastbound).

- The answer to the question "How much data do you need to train a deep learning model?" is "Enough data to train the model to meet your performance criteria." In most cases involving structured data, you need at least tens of thousands of records.

Preparing
the data, part 2:
Transforming the data

This chapter covers

- Dealing with more incorrect values
- Mapping complex, multiword values to single tokens
- Fixing type mismatches
- Dealing with rows that still contain bad values after cleanup
- Creating new columns derived from existing columns
- Preparing categorical and text columns to train a deep learning model
- Reviewing the end-to-end solution introduced in chapter 2

In chapter 3, we corrected a set of errors and anomalies in the input dataset. There's still more cleanup and preparation to be done in the dataset, and that's what we'll do in this chapter. We'll deal with remaining issues (including multiword tokens and type mismatches) and go over your choices about how to deal with the bad values that are still present after all the cleanup. Then we'll go over creating derived columns and how to prepare non-numeric data to train a deep learning model. Finally, we'll take a closer look at the end-to-end solution introduced in chapter 2 to see how the data preparation steps we have completed so far fit into our overall journey to a deployed, trained deep learning model for predicting streetcar delays.

You will see a consistent theme throughout this chapter: making updates to the dataset so that it more closely matches the real-world situation of streetcar delays. By eliminating errors and ambiguities to make the dataset better match the real world, we increase our chances of getting an accurate deep learning model.

4.1 Code for preparing and transforming the data

When you have cloned the GitHub repo (http://mng.bz/v95x) associated with this book, the code related to exploring and cleansing the data is in the notebooks subdirectory. The next listing shows the files described in this chapter.

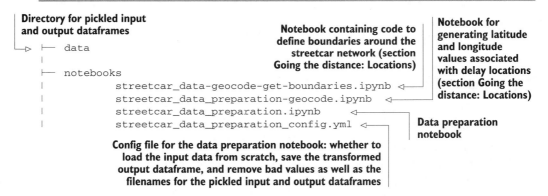

Listing 4.1 Code in the repo related to preparing the data

Directory for pickled input and output dataframes

Notebook containing code to define boundaries around the streetcar network (section Going the distance: Locations)

Notebook for generating latitude and longitude values associated with delay locations (section Going the distance: Locations)

```
data

notebooks
        streetcar_data-geocode-get-boundaries.ipynb
        streetcar_data_preparation-geocode.ipynb
        streetcar_data_preparation.ipynb
        streetcar_data_preparation_config.yml
```

Config file for the data preparation notebook: whether to load the input data from scratch, save the transformed output dataframe, and remove bad values as well as the filenames for the pickled input and output dataframes

Data preparation notebook

4.2 Dealing with incorrect values: Routes

In chapter 3, we cleaned up the Direction column. As you will recall, the valid values for this column corresponded to the compass points plus an extra token to indicate two directions. The valid values for the Direction column are universal (north, east, south, west) and not specific to the streetcar delay problem. What about columns that have values that are unique to the streetcar use case: Route and Vehicle? How do we clean up these columns, and what lessons can we learn from this cleanup that are applicable to other datasets?

If you look at the beginning of the data preparation notebook, you will notice a cell with the valid streetcar routes (figure 4.1).

Streetcar routes

From https://www.ttc.ca/Routes/Streetcars.jsp

	501	Queen		▸ Eastbound	▸ Westbound
	502	Downtowner		▸ Eastbound	▸ Westbound
	503	Kingston Rd		▸ Eastbound	▸ Westbound
	504	King		▸ Eastbound	▸ Westbound
	505	Dundas		▸ Eastbound	▸ Westbound
	506	Carlton		▸ Eastbound	▸ Westbound
♿	509	Harbourfront	🚲	▸ Eastbound	▸ Westbound
♿	510	Spadina	🚲	▸ Northbound	▸ Southbound
	511	Bathurst		▸ Northbound	▸ Southbound
	512	St Clair		▸ Eastbound	▸ Westbound

All Night Streetcar Routes ⌷PRESTO⌷ ⌷POP⌷☛

	301	Queen		▸ Eastbound	▸ Westbound
	304	King		▸ Eastbound	▸ Westbound
	306	Carlton		▸ Eastbound	▸ Westbound
♿	310	Spadina	🚲	▸ Northbound	▸ Southbound

Figure 4.1   Valid streetcar routes

The following listing shows the code in the data preparation notebook that cleans up the values in the Route column.

Listing 4.2   Code to clean up values in the Route column

Define a list containing all the valid route values.

```
valid_routes = ['501','502','503','504','505','506','509', \
'510','511','512','301','304','306','310']
```

```
print("route count",df['Route'].nunique())
route count 106
```

Print out a count of all the unique values in the Route column.

```
def check_route (x):
    if x in valid_routes:
        return(x)
    else:
        return("bad route")
```

Function to replace route values that aren't in the list of valid values with a placeholder value

```
df['Route'] = df['Route'].apply(lambda x:check_route(x))
```

Apply the check_route function to the Route column.

```
print("route count post cleanup",df['Route'].nunique())
df['Route'].value_counts()
route count post cleanup 15
```

Print out the revised count of all unique values in the Route Column.

When the data in the input dataset was entered, the values in the Route column were not limited to valid routes, so the column contains many values that aren't valid streetcar routes. If we don't fix this situation, we will be training our deep learning model with data that doesn't reflect the real-world situation. The refactoring of the dataset to make each record a route/direction/time-slot combination (chapter 5) will not be possible unless we clean up the values in the Route column.

It is worthwhile to review the cleanup process for the Route and Vehicle columns because the same dilemma can occur in many real-world datasets: you have a column that has a strictly defined list of valid values, but bad values still occur in the dataset because of the way that the data is entered or because of lax error checking in the data entry process.

How bad is the problem with the Route column? When we list the values in the Route column, we see that there are 14 valid streetcar routes, but the Route column contains more than 100 distinct values.

We define a simple function, `check_route`, that checks the values in the Route column and replaces any values that aren't in the list of valid route values with a `bad value` token. We apply this function to the entire Route column, using lambda so that the function is applied to every value in the column. See http://mng.bz/V8gO for more details on the power of applying functions to Pandas dataframes by using lambda.

We check the number of unique values in the Route column again after applying the `check_route` function to confirm that the Route column no longer contains any unexpected values. As we expect, the Route column now has 15 distinct values: the 14 valid route values, plus `bad route` to indicate that the original dataset had a value that is not a valid route.

4.3   *Why only one substitute for all bad values?*

You may ask whether we have any options for bad route values other than substituting a single value for all the bad values. What if we are losing some kind of signal in the invalid route values when we substitute a single placeholder for all of them? Perhaps it would make sense to replace bad values with placeholders that reflect why the value is bad, such as the following:

- `Bus_route`—For values in the Route column that are not valid streetcar routes but are valid bus routes.

- `Obsolete_route`—For values in the Route column that are former streetcar routes.
- `Non_ttc_route`—For values in the Route column that are valid route designations for bus routes from outside Toronto that are not run by the Toronto Transit Commission (TTC). The municipalities that surround Toronto (including Mississauga to the west, Vaughn to the northwest, Markham to the northeast, and Durham to the east) have their own distinct transit operators, and it is theoretically possible that a bus route of one of these non-TTC operators could be delayed by a streetcar delay. There are no instances of non-TTC routes in the Route column in the current dataset, but that doesn't mean that such a non-TTC route could not appear in the dataset in the future. As we will see in chapter 9, we can expect that a model will get retrained on new data repeatedly after it is put in production, so the data preparation code should be resilient to allow potential future changes in the input dataset. Allowing for non-TTC route values in the Route column is an example of anticipating potential changes in the dataset.
- `Incorrect_route`—For values in the Route column that have never been valid routes for any transit operation in the greater Toronto area, including routes.

As it happens, for the streetcar delay problem, these distinctions are not relevant. We are interested only in delays for streetcar routes. But if the problem were framed differently, to include predicting delays for transit operations beyond streetcars, it could make sense to use finer-grained substitutions for bad values in the Route column, such as those in the preceding list. It is certainly worth asking whether all nonvalid values for a column are equivalent in terms of the goal of the project. In the case of the streetcar delay problem, the answer is yes, but the same answer doesn't necessarily apply to all structured data problems.

4.4 Dealing with incorrect values: Vehicles

In the same way that there is a fixed list of valid streetcar routes, there is also a fixed list of valid vehicles. You can see how this list of valid vehicles is compiled and view the sources for this information in the data preparation notebook (figure 4.2).

Streetcar vehicle IDs CLRV/ALRV

From https://en.wikipedia.org/wiki/Toronto_streetcar_system_rolling_stock#CLRVs_and_ALRVs

Class	Builder	Description	Fleet numbers	Fleet size	Year acquired	Year retired	Notes[35][36]
L1	SIG	CLRV	4000–4005	6	1977	2015–date	Prototypes for the CLRV, built in Switzerland.
L2	Hawker	CLRV	4010–4199	190	1977–1981	2009–date	air conditioning added to car #4041 in 2006.
--	Hawker	ALRV	4900	1	1982	1997	ALRV prototype. Tested in Toronto but never owned by TTC.
L3	Hawker	ALRV	4200–4251	52	1987–1988	2015–date	Longer, articulated version of the CLRV

Figure 4.2 Valid streetcar IDs

Bus identification

The following links define the valid non-streetcar vehicles that can be delayed by streetcar incidents

- Buses 1xxx: https://cptdb.ca/wiki/index.php/Toronto_Transit_Commission_1000-1149
- Buses 2xxx: https://cptdb.ca/wiki/index.php/Toronto_Transit_Commission_2000-2110, 2150-2155, 2240-2485, 2600-2619, 2700-2765, 2767-2858
- Buses 70xx: https://cptdb.ca/wiki/index.php/Toronto_Transit_Commission_7000-7134
- Buses 74xx: https://cptdb.ca/wiki/index.php/Toronto_Transit_Commission_7400-7499, 7500-7619, 7620-7881
- Buses 8xxx: https://cptdb.ca/wiki/index.php/Toronto_Transit_Commission_8000-8099
- Buses 9xxx: https://cptdb.ca/wiki/index.php/Toronto_Transit_Commission_9000-9026

Figure 4.3   Valid bus IDs

Buses can also be victims of streetcar delays. The list of valid bus IDs is more complex (figure 4.3).

As we did for the Route column, we define a function in the next listing that replaces invalid Vehicle values with a single token to indicate a bad value, reducing the number of values in the Vehicle column by more than half.

Listing 4.3   Code to clean up values in the Vehicle column

```
print("vehicle count pre cleanup",df['Vehicle'].nunique())
df['Vehicle'] = df['Vehicle'].apply(lambda x:check_vehicle(x))
print("vehicle count post cleanup",df['Vehicle'].nunique())

vehicle count pre cleanup 2438   ◁──────   Count of unique values in the
vehicle count post cleanup 1017  ◁────┐    Vehicle column precleanup
                                      │
         Count of unique values in the
         Vehicle column postcleanup   │
```

As it turns out, we will not end up using the Vehicle column in the model training described in chapters 5 and 6. First, in the deployment scenarios in chapter 8, the user will be somebody who wants to take a trip on a streetcar and needs to know whether it will be delayed. In this use case, the user will not know which specific vehicle they will be riding in. Because the user will not be able to provide the vehicle ID at the time they want to get a prediction, we cannot train the model with the data in the Vehicle column. But we could use the Vehicle column in a future variation of the model that is aimed at a different set of users (such as administrators of the transit authority that runs the streetcars) who would know the vehicle ID for a given trip, so it is worthwhile to clean up the values in the Vehicle column for potential future use.

4.5   *Dealing with inconsistent values: Location*

The Route and Vehicle columns are typical categorical columns because they have a fixed set of valid values that is easily defined. The Location column presents a different set of problems because it doesn't have a neatly defined set of valid values. It is worth spending some time going through the issues related to the Location column and how to fix them, because this column demonstrates the kind of messiness you will come across in real-world datasets. The values in this column are specific to the streetcar dataset, but the approaches that we will take to clean up these values (getting a consistent case, getting a consistent order for values, and replacing inconsistent tokens that refer to the same real-world entity with a single token) apply to many datasets.

Following are some of the idiosyncrasies of the values in the Location column:

- The values in the Location column can be street junctions ("Queen and Connaught") or landmarks ("CNE Loop," "Main Station," "Leslie Yard").
- There are thousands of valid street junction values. Because routes go beyond their namesake streets, a route can have valid junction values that don't include the route name. "Broadview and Dundas" is a valid location value for an incident on the King route, for example.
- The landmark values can be commonly known (such as "St. Clair West station"), or they can be specific to the inner workings of the streetcar network (such as "Leslie Yard").
- The order of the street names isn't consistent ("Queen and Broadview," "Broadview and Queen").
- Many locations have multiple tokens to represent them ("Roncy Yard," "Roncesvalles Yard," and "Ronc. Carhouse" represent the same location).
- The total count of values in the Location column is much larger than any of the other columns we have looked at so far:

```
print("Location count pre cleanup:",df['Location'].nunique())
Location count pre cleanup: 15691
```

Here are the steps we are going to take to clean up the Location column:

- Convert all values to lowercase.
- Use consistent tokens. When multiple distinct values are used to indicate the same location ("Roncy Yard," "Roncesvalles Yard," and "Ronc. Carhouse"), replace these distinct strings with a single string ("Roncesvalles yard") so that only one string is used to indicate any given location.
- Make the order of streets in junction values consistent (replace "Queen and Broadview" with "Broadview and Queen"). We do this by ensuring that street names in junctions are always ordered with the street name that comes first alphabetically coming first in the junction string.

We will track our progress by calculating the total percentage drop in the number of distinct values in the Location column after taking each step. After we make all the values in the Location column lowercase, the number of unique values drops by 15%:

```
df['Location'] = df['Location'].str.lower()
print("Unique Location values after lcasing:",df['Location'].nunique())
Unique Location values after lcasing: 13263
```

Next, we make a set of substitutions to remove duplicate values such as "stn" and "station." You may ask how we determine what values are duplicates. How do we know, for example, that "carhouse," "garage," and "barn" are all identical to "yard" and that we should substitute "yard" for those three values? This question is a good one because it leads to an important point about machine learning projects. To determine which terms in the Location column are equivalent, we need to have domain knowledge about Toronto (especially its geography) and about the streetcar network in particular. Any machine learning project is going to require a combination of technical expertise in machine learning and domain knowledge about the subject area to which machine learning is being applied. To really tackle the credit card fraud detection problem outlined in chapter 1, for example, we would need to have access to somebody who has deep understanding of the details of credit card fraud. For the major example in this book, I chose the streetcar delay problem because I know Toronto well and happen to have knowledge of the streetcar network that allows me to determine, for example, that "carhouse," "garage," and "barn" mean the same thing as "yard." The need for domain knowledge in a machine learning project should never be underestimated, and as you consider projects to tackle, you should ensure that you have somebody on the team who has adequate knowledge of the domain of the project.

What is the effect of the changes we have applied to the Location column? So far, these changes bring the total reduction of unique values to 30%:

```
Unique Location values after substitutions: 10867
```

Finally, for all the location values that are street junctions, make the order of the street names consistent, such as by eliminating the difference between "broadview and queen" and "queen and broadview." With this transformation, the total reduction in unique values is 36%:

```
df['Location'] = df['Location'].apply(lambda x:order_location(x))
print("Location values post cleanup:",df['Location'].nunique())
Location values post cleanup: 10074
```

By cleaning up the location values (making all values lowercase, removing duplicate values, and ensuring a consistent order for junction pairs), we have reduced the number of distinct location values from more than 15,000 to 10,074—a drop of 36%. In addition to making the training data reflect the real world more accurately, reducing the number of unique values in this column can save us real money, as we will see in section 4.6.

4.6   *Going the distance: Locations*

Is the cleanup described in section 4.5 all we can do to clean up the Location values? One more possible transformation can give us high-fidelity values in the Location column: replace freeform text Location values with longitude and latitude. The geocode preparation notebook contains an approach to this transformation that uses Google's geocoding API (http://mng.bz/X06Y).

Why would we want to replace the freeform text locations with longitude and latitude? Advantages of using longitude and latitude instead of freeform locations include

- Locations are as exact as the geocode API can make them.
- Output values are numeric and can be used to train a deep learning model directly.

Disadvantages include

- Thirty-five percent of the locations are not street junctions/addresses, but locations that are specific to the streetcar network, such as "birchmount yard." Some of these locations will not resolve to longitude and latitude values.
- The topology of the streetcar network and the pattern of effect of delays are not directly related to a real-world map. Consider two potential locations for delays: "king and church" = latitude 43.648949 / longitude -79.377754 and "queen and church" = latitude 43.652908 / longitude -79.379458. From the point of view of latitude and longitude, these two locations are close together, but in terms of the streetcar network, they are distant because they are on separate lines.

This section (and the code in the geocode preparation notebook) assume that you are using Google's geocoding API. This approach has several advantages, including copious documentation and a wide user base, but it's not free. To get the latitude and longitude values for a dataset with 60,000 locations in a single batch run (that is, not spreading the run over multiple days to keep it within the free clip level for geocoding API calls), you can expect to spend around $50. Several alternatives to the Google geocoding API could save you money. Locationiq (https://locationiq.com), for example, provides a free tier that allows you to process a larger dataset of locations in fewer iterations than you would need to stay within the free limit for Google's geocoding API.

Because calls to the Google geocoding API are not free, and because an account is limited to the number of calls to this API that it can make in a 24-hour period, it's important to prepare the location data so that we make the minimum number of geocoding API calls to get the latitude and longitude values.

To make the minimal number of geocoding API calls, we start by defining a new dataframe, df_unique, with a single column that contains exactly the list of unique Location values:

```
loc_unique = df['Location'].unique().tolist()
df_unique = pd.DataFrame(loc_unique,
➥  columns=['Location'])
df_unique.head()
```

	Location
0	broadview and gerrard
1	galley and roncesvalles
2	king and sherborne
3	main st. and upper gerrard
4	gerrard and sumach

Figure 4.4 Dataframe that contains only distinct location values

Figure 4.4 shows a snippet of rows from this new dataframe.

We define a function that calls the Google geocode API, takes a location as an argument, and returns a JSON structure. If the structure returned is not empty, parse the structure, and return a list with the latitude and longitude values. If the structure is empty, return a placeholder value, as shown in the following listing.

Listing 4.4 Code to get the latitude and longitude values for a street junction

```
def get_geocode_result(junction):

    geo_string = junction+", "+city_name                Check to see
    geocode_result = gmaps.geocode(geo_string)          whether the
    if len(geocode_result) > 0:              ⟵          result is empty.
        locs = geocode_result[0]["geometry"]["location"]
        return [locs["lat"], locs["lng"]]
    else:
        return [0.0,0.0]
```

If we call this function with a location that the geocoding can interpret, we get back a list with the corresponding latitude and longitude values:

```
get_geocode_result("queen and bathurst")[0]
43.6471969
```

If we call this function with a location that the geocoding cannot interpret, we get the placeholder value back:

```
locs = get_geocode_result("roncesvalles to longbranch")
print("locs ",locs)
locs  [0.0, 0.0]
```

We call the `get_geocode_results` function to create a new column in this dataframe that contains the longitude and latitude values. Dumping both values into one column requires doing some additional processing to get what we want: individual columns for longitude and latitude. But making the call this way reduces the number of geocoding API calls we need to make, saving money and helping us keep within the daily limit for geocoding API calls:

```
df_unique['lat_long'] = df_unique.Location.apply(lambda s:
➥  get_geocode_result(s))
```

Next, we create individual columns for longitude and latitude:

```
df_unique["latitude"] = df_unique["lat_long"].str[0]
df_unique["longitude"] = df_unique["lat_long"].str[1]
```

Finally, we join the `df_unique` dataframe with the original dataframe to get the longitude and latitude columns added to the original dataframe:

```
df_out = pd.merge(df, df_unique, on="Location", how='left')
```

As you can see, it takes several steps (including the initial setup of the Google geocoding API) to get latitude and longitude values added to the dataset. Understanding how to manipulate latitude and longitude values in the context of a Python program is a useful skill for many common business problems that have a spatial dimension, and latitude and longitude values make it possible to create visualizations (such as the one in figure 4.5) to identify hotspots for delays. As it turns out, the deep learning model described in chapters 5 and 6 does not use location data—either the freeform text or latitude and longitude. The freeform text locations cannot be used in the refactored dataset, and the process for converting freeform text locations into latitude and longitude is complicated and difficult to integrate into a pipeline. Chapter 9 includes a section on augmenting the model to incorporate location data to identify the subsection of a streetcar route on which a delay occurs.

Figure 4.5 Heat map showing hotspots for streetcar delays

4.7 *Fixing type mismatches*

To get the types that get assigned to the dataframe, you can use the `dtypes` attribute of the dataframe. The value of this attribute for the dataframe that is initially ingested for the streetcar delay dataset looks like this:

```
Day                object
Delay              float64
Direction          object
Gap                float64
Incident           object
Incident ID        float64
Location           object
Min Delay          float64
```

```
Min Gap                    float64
Report Date      datetime64[ns]
Route                       int64
Time                       object
Vehicle                   float64
```

Python does a good job of predicting the types of data as that data is ingested, but it is not perfect. Fortunately, it's easy to ensure that you don't get type surprises. This code ensures that continuous columns have a predictable type:

```
for col in continuouscols:
        df[col] = df[col].astype(float)
```

Similarly, values that look numeric, such as vehicle IDs, can be misinterpreted by Python, which assigns `float64` type to the Vehicle column (figure 4.6).

	Report Date	Route	Time	Day	Location	Incident	Min Delay	Min Gap	Direction	Vehicle
0	2015-01-01	504	01:25:00	Thursday	Broadview and Gerrard	Mechanical	9.0	18.0	S/B	4092.0
1	2015-01-01	504	01:44:00	Thursday	Roncesvalles and Galley	Held By	14.0	23.0	S/B	4030.0
2	2015-01-01	504	02:04:00	Thursday	King and Sherborne	Mechanical	9.0	18.0	E/B	4147.0
3	2015-01-01	306	02:12:00	Thursday	Main St. and Upper Gerrard	Investigation	29.0	39.0	S/B	4049.0
4	2015-01-01	306	05:05:00	Thursday	Gerrard and Sumach	Mechanical	30.0	60.0	W/B	4114.0

Figure 4.6   **Python misinterprets the type of the Vehicle column.**

To correct these types, we use the `astype` function to cast the columns to string type and then clip the end of the Vehicle column to remove the vestigial decimal point and zero:

```
df['Route'] = df['Route'].astype(str)
df['Vehicle'] = df['Vehicle'].astype(str)
df['Vehicle'] = df['Vehicle'].str[:-2]
```

4.8   *Dealing with rows that still contain bad data*

After all the cleanup, how many bad values are left in the dataset?

```
print("Bad route count pre:",df[df.Route == 'bad route'].shape[0])
print("Bad direction count pre:",df[df.Direction ==
     'bad direction'].shape[0])
print("Bad vehicle count pre:",df[df.Vehicle == 'bad vehicle'].shape[0])
Bad route count pre: 2544
Bad direction count pre: 407
Bad vehicle count pre: 14709
```

Compare this result with the total number of rows in the dataset:

```
df.shape output (78525, 13)
```

What happens to the size of the dataset if we remove all the rows that contain one or more of the remaining bad values?

```
if remove_bad_values:
    df = df[df.Vehicle != 'bad vehicle']
    df = df[df.Direction != 'bad direction']
    df = df[df.Route != 'bad route']

df.shape output post removal of bad records  (61500, 11)
```

Removing the bad values removes about 20% of the data. The question is this: What is the result of removing the bad values on the model performance? Chapter 7 describes an experiment that compares the results of training the model with and without the bad values. Figure 4.7 shows the result of this experiment.

Experiment	Epochs	Terminal validation accuracy	False negatives exercising model on test set	Recall on test set: true positive/(true positive + false negative)
No bad values	50	0.78	3,500	0.68
Bad values	50	0.79	6,400	0.53

Figure 4.7   Comparison of model performance with and without bad values in the training dataset

Although validation accuracy of the trained model with bad values not removed is around the same as validation accuracy for the model trained with bad values removed, recall and false negative count are much worse when we don't remove bad values. We can conclude that removing bad values is good for the performance of the trained model.

4.9   *Creating derived columns*

In some situations, you will want to create new columns derived from the columns in the original dataset. A column with date values (such as Report Date in the streetcar dataset) includes information (such as year, month, and day) that could be pulled into separate derived columns that could help the performance of the model.

Figure 4.8 shows the dataframe before derived columns based on Report Date are added.

Report Date	Route	Time	Day	Location	Incident	Min Delay	Min Gap	Direction	Vehicle	Report Date Time
2015-01-01	504	01:25:00	Thursday	Broadview and Gerrard	Mechanical	9.0	18.0	S/B	4092	2015-01-01 01:25:00
2015-01-01	504	01:44:00	Thursday	Roncesvalles and Galley	Held By	14.0	23.0	S/B	4030	2015-01-01 01:44:00
2015-01-01	504	02:04:00	Thursday	King and Sherborne	Mechanical	9.0	18.0	E/B	4147	2015-01-01 02:04:00
2015-01-01	306	02:12:00	Thursday	Main St. and Upper Gerrard	Investigation	29.0	39.0	S/B	4049	2015-01-01 02:12:00
2015-01-01	306	05:05:00	Thursday	Gerrard and Sumach	Mechanical	30.0	60.0	W/B	4114	2015-01-01 05:05:00

Figure 4.8   Dataframe before derived columns based on Report Date are added

Here is the code to create explicit columns for year, month, and day of month from the existing Report Date column:

```
merged_data['year'] = pd.DatetimeIndex(merged_data['Report Date']).year
merged_data['month'] = pd.DatetimeIndex(merged_data['Report Date']).month
merged_data['daym'] = pd.DatetimeIndex(merged_data['Report Date']).day
```

Figure 4.9 shows what the dataframe looks like after the derived columns are added.

Report Date	Route	Time	Day	Location	Incident	Min Delay	Min Gap	Direction	Vehicle	Report Date Time	year	month	daym
2015-01-01	504	01:25:00	Thursday	Broadview and Gerrard	Mechanical	9.0	18.0	S/B	4092	2015-01-01 01:25:00	2015	1	1
2015-01-01	504	01:44:00	Thursday	Roncesvalles and Galley	Held By	14.0	23.0	S/B	4030	2015-01-01 01:44:00	2015	1	1
2015-01-01	504	02:04:00	Thursday	King and Sherborne	Mechanical	9.0	18.0	E/B	4147	2015-01-01 02:04:00	2015	1	1
2015-01-01	306	02:12:00	Thursday	Main St. and Upper Gerrard	Investigation	29.0	39.0	S/B	4049	2015-01-01 02:12:00	2015	1	1
2015-01-01	306	05:05:00	Thursday	Gerrard and Sumach	Mechanical	30.0	60.0	W/B	4114	2015-01-01 05:05:00	2015	1	1

Figure 4.9   Dataframe with derived columns based on Report Date

In chapter 5, we will generate derived columns as part of the process of refactoring the dataset. By pulling year, month, and day of month out of the Report Date column and into their own columns, we simplify the process of deployment by making it straightforward to get date/time trip information from the user.

4.10   *Preparing non-numeric data to train a deep learning model*

Machine learning algorithms can be trained only on numeric data, so any non-numeric data needs to be transformed into numeric data. Figure 4.10 shows the dataframe with the categorical values in their original states.

Report Date	Route	Time	Day	Location	Incident	Min Delay	Min Gap	Direction	Vehicle	Report Date Time	year	month	daym	hour
2018-11-12	501	16:45:00	Monday	Queen and Connaught	Mechanical	5.0	10.0	W/B	4180	2018-11-12 16:45:00	2018	11	12	16
2017-10-27	512	19:03:00	Friday	St Clair West Station	Investigation	3.0	6.0	W/B	4400	2017-10-27 19:03:00	2017	10	27	19
2014-05-25	501	06:42:00	Sunday	Queen t Coxwell	Investigation	13.0	23.0	E/B	4249	2014-05-25 06:42:00	2014	5	25	6
2015-02-10	506	01:05:00	Tuesday	Main Station	Emergency Services	10.0	10.0	W/B	4124	2015-02-10 01:05:00	2015	2	10	1
2017-05-15	502	10:43:00	Monday	Bingham Loop	Mechanical	8.0	16.0	W/B	7729	2017-05-15 10:43:00	2017	5	15	10

Figure 4.10   Dataframe before categorical and text column values are replaced by numeric IDs

You can take either of two general approaches to replace categorical values with numerical values: *label encoding*, in which each unique categorical value in the column is replaced by a numeric identifier, or *one-hot encoding*, in which a new column gets generated for each unique categorical value. Rows get a 1 in the new column representing their original categorical value and a 0 in the other new columns.

Label encoding can cause problems for some machine learning algorithms that assign significance to the relative values of the numeric identifiers when they have no significance. If numeric identifiers replace the values for provinces of Canada, for example, starting with 0 for Newfoundland and Labrador and ending with 9 for British Columbia, it is not significant that the identifier for Alberta (8) is less than the identifier for British Columbia.

One-hot encoding has its problems as well. If a column has more than a few values, one-hot encoding can generate an explosion of new columns that can gobble up memory and make manipulation of the dataset difficult. For the streetcar delay dataset, we are sticking with label encoding to control the number of columns in the dataset.

The code snippet in the next listing, from the encode_categorical class defined in custom_classes, uses the LabelEncoder function from the sci-kit learn library to replace the values in categorical columns with numeric identifiers.

Listing 4.5 Code to replace categorical column values with numeric identifiers

```
def fit(self, X, y=None,  **fit_params):
    for col in self.col_list:
        print("col is ",col)
        self.le[col] = LabelEncoder()          ◁—— Create an instance
        self.le[col].fit(X[col].tolist())           of LabelEncoder.
    return self

def transform(self, X, y=None, **tranform_params):
    for col in self.col_list:
        print("transform col is ",col)
        X[col] = self.le[col].transform(X[col])   ◁—┐ Use the instance of
        print("after transform col is ",col)          │ LabelEncoder to replace
        self.max_dict[col] = X[col].max() +1          │ values in a categorical
    return X                                           │ column with numeric
                                                       │ identifiers.
```

For a complete description of this class, see the description of pipelines in chapter 8.

Figure 4.11 shows what the basic dataframe looks like after the categorical columns Day, Direction, Route, hour, month, Location, daym, and year are encoded.

One column still contains non-numerical data: Incident. This column contains multiword phrases that describe the kind of delay that occurred. If you recall the data exploration that we did in chapter 3, we determined that Incident can be treated as a categorical column. To illustrate how text columns are prepared, let's treat it as a text column for now, and apply the Python Tokenizer API to do the following:

- Change all values to lowercase.
- Remove punctuation.
- Replace all words with numeric IDs.

Report Date	Route	Time	Day	Location	Incident	Min Delay	Min Gap	Direction	Vehicle	Report Date Time	year	month	daym	hour
2018-11-12	50	16:45:00	1	9555	Mechanical	5.0	10.0	54	4180	2018-11-12 16:45:00	4	10	11	16
2017-10-27	61	19:03:00	0	12794	Investigation	3.0	6.0	54	4400	2017-10-27 19:03:00	3	9	26	19
2014-05-25	50	06:42:00	3	10244	Investigation	13.0	23.0	35	4249	2014-05-25 06:42:00	0	4	24	6
2015-02-10	55	01:05:00	5	7599	Emergency Services	10.0	10.0	54	4124	2015-02-10 01:05:00	1	1	9	1
2017-05-15	51	10:43:00	1	988	Mechanical	8.0	16.0	54	7729	2017-05-15 10:43:00	3	4	14	10

Figure 4.11   Dataframe with categorical column values replaced by numeric IDs

The following listing contains the code that accomplishes this transformation.

Listing 4.6   Code to prepare text columns to be part of a model training dataset

```
from keras.preprocessing.text import Tokenizer

for col in textcols:
    if verboseout:
        print("processing text col",col)
    tok_raw = Tokenizer(num_words=maxwords,lower=True)   ◁─┐   Tokenizer lowercases
    tok_raw.fit_on_texts(train[col])                           and removes
    train[col] = tok_raw.texts_to_sequences(train[col])        punctuation by default.
    test[col] = tok_raw.texts_to_sequences(test[col])
```

Figure 4.12 shows the result of applying this transformation to the Incident column.

Report Date Time	Report Date	Route	Time	Day	Location	Incident	Min Delay	Min Gap	Direction	Vehicle	Report Date Time	year	month	daym	hour	time_of_day	target
2015-11-18 05:43:00	2015-11-18	53	05:43:00	6	8627	[1]	5.0	11.0	35	4027	2015-11-18 05:43:00	1	10	17	5	morning_rush	0
2018-10-24 07:49:00	2018-10-24	53	07:49:00	6	5523	[8, 9]	10.0	16.0	54	n	2018-10-24 07:49:00	4	9	23	7	morning_rush	1
2018-06-23 16:32:00	2018-06-23	53	16:32:00	2	11541	[1]	6.0	12.0	54	4428	2018-06-23 16:32:00	4	5	22	16	aft_rush	1
2017-05-23 16:40:00	2017-05-23	61	16:40:00	5	12663	[2]	27.0	32.0	39	4131	2017-05-23 16:40:00	3	4	22	16	aft_rush	1
2015-08-28 19:55:00	2015-08-28	55	19:55:00	0	7599	[13, 14]	8.0	16.0	54	4171	2015-08-28 19:55:00	1	7	27	19	evening	1

Figure 4.12   Dataframe after values in categorical and text columns are replaced by numeric IDs

Figure 4.13 compares the before and after values in the Incident column. Each entry in the Incident column is now a list (or array, if you prefer a less Pythonic term) of numeric IDs. Note that the After view has a list entry for each word in the original column, and IDs are assigned consistently (the same word gets assigned a consistent ID regardless of where it appears in the column). Also note the following:

- In the end, we treated Incident as a categorical column, which means that multitoken values like "Emergency Services" were encoded to a single numeric value. In this section, we treated Incident as a text column to illustrate how this portion of the code works, so each token in "Emergency Services" is encoded separately.
- We have illustrated only a single text column, but the code works with datasets that have multiple text columns.

Before	After
Incident	Incident
Mechanical	[1]
Investigation	[2]
Investigation	[2]
Emergency Services	[13, 14]
Mechanical	[1]

Figure 4.13   Incident column before and after text values are encoded

4.11   *Overview of the end-to-end solution*

Before we examine deep learning and the stack that we'll use to tackle the streetcar delay problem, let's look at the entire solution for the problem by revisiting the end-to-end picture introduced in chapter 2. Figure 4.14 shows all the major elements that make up the solution, from the input dataset to the trained model deployed and accessed via a simple website or Facebook Messenger. The components are grouped in three sections: cleaning up the dataset, building and training the model, and deploying the model.

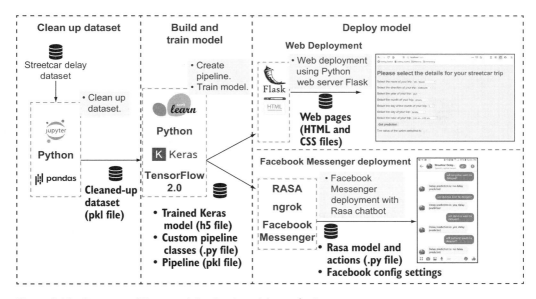

Figure 4.14   Summary of the complete streetcar delay project

Figure 4.15 zooms in on the components that we used to go from the input dataset to a cleaned-up dataset in chapters 2, 3 and 4, including Python and the Pandas library for dealing with tabular data.

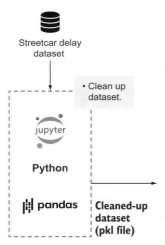

Figure 4.15   From input dataset to cleaned-up dataset

Figure 4.16 zooms in on the components that we will use in chapters 5 and 6 to build and train the deep learning model, including the deep learning library Keras and the pipeline facilities in the scikit-learn library.

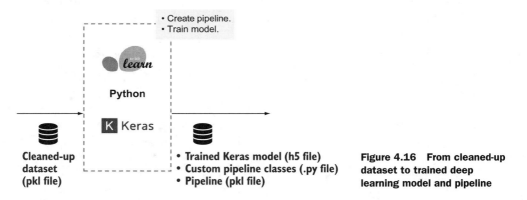

Figure 4.16   From cleaned-up dataset to trained deep learning model and pipeline

Figure 4.17 zooms in on the components that we will use in chapter 8 to deploy the trained deep learning model. For the web deployment, these components include the Flask web deployment library (to render HTML web pages on which the user can specify the details of their streetcar trip and see the trained deep learning model's prediction of whether the trip will be delayed). For the Facebook Messenger deployment, these components include the Rasa chatbot framework, ngrok for connecting Rasa and Facebook, and Facebook application configurations.

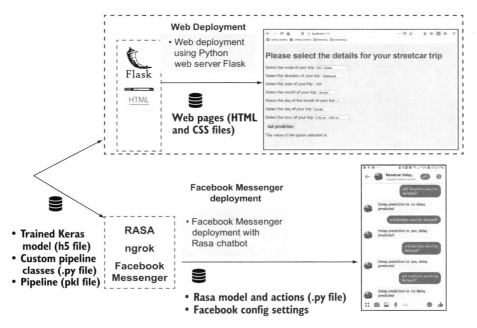

Figure 4.17 From trained model and pipeline to deployed deep learning model

Figures 4.18 and 4.19 show the goal: a trained deep learning model that has been deployed and can be used to get predictions on whether a given streetcar trip is going to be delayed, either on a web page (figure 4.18) or in Facebook Messenger (figure 4.19).

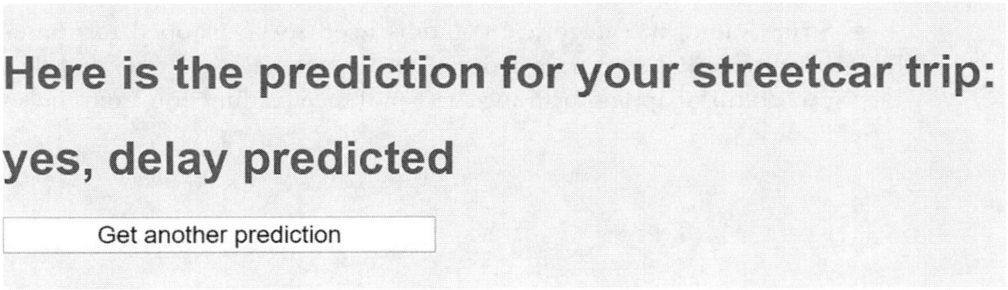

Here is the prediction for your streetcar trip: yes, delay predicted

Get another prediction

Figure 4.18 Streetcar delay predictions available on a web page

In this section, we've gone through a brief over-view of the end-to-end streetcar delay prediction project. Over the next four chapters, we will go over all the steps needed to get from the cleaned-up dataset in this chapter to a simple web page that uses the trained model to predict whether a given streetcar trip is going to be delayed.

Summary

- Cleaning up the data isn't the only prepa-ration we need to perform on the dataset. We also need to ensure that non-numeric values (such as strings in categorical col-umns) get converted to numeric values.

- If the dataset contains invalid values (such as route values that aren't actual streetcar routes or direction values that cannot be mapped to one of the compass points), these values can be replaced by a valid placeholder (such as the most common value in a categorical column), or the records that contain them can be removed from the dataset.

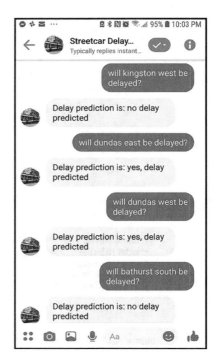

Figure 4.19   Streetcar delay predictions available in Facebook Messenger

- When a CSV or XLS file is ingested into a Pandas dataframe, the type of the col-umns is not always assigned correctly. If Python assigns an incorrect type to a column, you can convert the column to the required type.

- String values in categorical columns need to be mapped to numeric values because you cannot train a deep learning model with non-numeric data. You can do this mapping by using the `LabelEncoder` function from the scikit-learn library.

5

Preparing and building the model

This chapter covers

- Revisiting the dataset and determining which features to use to train the model
- Refactoring the dataset to include timeslots when there is no delay
- Transforming the dataset into the format expected by the Keras model
- Building a Keras model automatically based on the structure of the data
- Examining the structure of the model
- Setting parameters, including activation and optimization functions and learning rate

This chapter begins with a quick reexamination of the dataset to consider which columns can legitimately be used to train the model. Then we'll go over the transformations required to get the data from the format in which we have been manipulating it (Pandas dataframes) to the format expected by the deep learning model.

Next, we will go over the code for the model itself and see how the model is built up layer by layer based on the category of the input columns. We wrap up by reviewing methods you can use to examine the structure of the model and the parameters you can use to adjust how the model is trained.

All the preceding chapters in this book have been building up to this point. After examining the problem, preparing the data, we are finally ready to dig into the deep learning model itself. One thing to keep in mind as you go through this chapter: if you have not worked directly with deep learning models before, you may find the code for the model to be somewhat anticlimactic after all the detailed work required to prepare the data. This feeling may be familiar to you from using Python libraries for classic machine learning algorithms. The code to apply logistic regression or linear regression to a dataset that has been prepared for training isn't exciting, particularly if you have had to create nontrivial code to tame a real-world dataset. You can see the code described in this chapter in the streetcar_ model_training notebook.

5.1   Data leakage and features that are fair game for training the model

Before we get into the details of the code that constitutes the model, we need to review which columns (either columns from the original dataset or columns derived from the original columns) are legitimate to use to train the model. If we need to use the model to predict streetcar delays, we need to ensure that we avoid data leakage. *Data leakage* occurs when you train a model using data (including the outcome that you're trying to predict) from outside the training dataset. If you succumb to data leakage when you train a model by depending on data that isn't available at the point when you want to make a prediction, you risk the following problems:

- Undermining your ability to make predictions
- Getting a performance measurement for your model that is too optimistic

To understand the problem of data leakage, consider a simple model that predicts the sale price of houses in a given property market. For this model, you have a set of information about houses that have sold recently in this market. You can use this information to train a model that you will later use to predict the sales price of houses that are being put on the market, as shown in figure 5.1.

Figure 5.2 shows the features that are available for you to choose from in the sold-houses dataset.

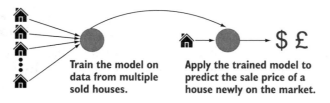

Train the model on data from multiple sold houses.

Apply the trained model to predict the sale price of a house newly on the market.

Figure 5.1   Training and applying a model to predict house prices

Feature	Example value	Available at prediction time?	Source of data leakage?
Number of bedrooms	3	yes	no
Number of bathrooms	2	yes	no
Floor space	1,700 sq ft	yes	no
Frontage	40 ft	yes	no
Time on market	3 weeks	no	yes
Asking price	$400,000	maybe	maybe
Selling price	$350,000	no	yes

Figure 5.2 Features available in the dataset of sold houses

Our goal is to make a prediction about the selling price for a house when it initially goes on the market, potentially weeks before it sells. When the house is ready to go on the market, the following features will be available:

- Number of bedrooms
- Number of bathrooms
- Floor space
- Frontage

We know that selling price (the feature that we want to predict) won't be available. What about these features?

- Time on market
- Asking price

Time on market won't be available when we want to make a prediction because the house has not been on the market yet, so we should not use this feature to train the model. Asking price is a bit more ambiguous; it may or may not be available at the point when we want to make the prediction. This example shows that we need a deeper understanding of the real-world business situation before we can determine whether a given feature will lead to data leakage.

5.2 *Domain expertise and minimal scoring tests to prevent data leakage*

What can you do to prevent the data leakage problems described in section 5.1? If you already have domain expertise in the business problem that your deep learning model is trying to solve, it will be easier for you to avoid data leakage. One of the rationales for this book is to enable you to exercise deep learning on problems in your everyday work so that you can take advantage of the domain expertise that you possess from doing your job.

Returning to the house-prices example (section 5.1), what would happen if you trained your model using features that have been identified as sources of data leakage, such as time on market? First, during the training, you probably would see model performance (measured by accuracy, for example) that looks good. This great performance, however, is misleading. It's the equivalent of a teacher being happy about her students' performance on a test when every student had a peek at the answers during the test. The students didn't legitimately do well because they were exposed to information that should not have been available to them at the time of the test. The second result of data leakage is that when you finish training the model and try to apply it, you will find that some of the features that you need to feed the model to get a prediction are missing.

In addition to applying domain knowledge (such as the time on market not being known when a house first goes on the market), what can you do to prevent data leakage? A minimal scoring test on an early iteration of the model can help. In the house-prices example, we could take a provisional version of the trained model and apply data from one or two houses that are newly on the market. The prediction may be poor because the training iterations are not complete, but this exercise will expose features the model requires that aren't available at prediction time, allowing us to remove them from the training process.

5.3   *Preventing data leakage in the streetcar delay prediction problem*

In the streetcar delay example, we want to predict whether a given streetcar trip is going to be delayed. In this context, including the Incident column as a feature to train the model would constitute data leakage, because before the trip is taken, we don't know whether a given trip will have a delay and, if so, the nature of the delay. We don't know what, if any, value the Incident column will have for a given streetcar trip before the trip is taken.

As shown in figure 5.3, the Min Delay and Min Gap columns also cause data leakage. Our label (the value we are trying to predict) is derived from Min Delay and is correlated with Min Gap, so both of these columns are potential sources of data leakage. We won't know these values when we want to predict whether a given streetcar trip is going to be delayed.

Looking at the problem another way, which columns contain information that will be legitimately available to us when we want to make delay predictions for a particular trip or a set of trips? The information that the user provides at prediction time is

Columns that can cause data leakage if they
are used as features to train the model

	Report Date	Route	Time	Day	Location	Incident	Min Delay	Min Gap	Direction	Vehicle
0	2014-01-02	505	06:31:00	Thursday	Dundas and Roncesvalles	Late Leaving Garage	4.0	8.0	E/B	4018.0
1	2014-01-02	504	12:43:00	Thursday	King and Shaw	Utilized Off Route	20.0	22.0	E/B	4128.0
2	2014-01-02	501	14:01:00	Thursday	Kingston road and Bingham	Held By	13.0	19.0	W/B	4016.0
3	2014-01-02	504	14:22:00	Thursday	King St. and Roncesvalles Ave.	Investigation	7.0	11.0	W/B	4175.0
4	2014-01-02	504	16:42:00	Thursday	King and Bathurst	Utilized Off Route	3.0	6.0	E/B	4080.0

Figure 5.3   Columns in the original dataset that can cause data leakage

described in chapter 8. The information provided by the user depends on the type of deployment:

- *Web* (figure 5.4)—In the web deployment of the model, the user selects seven scoring parameters (route, direction, and date/time details) that will be fed into the trained model to get a prediction.

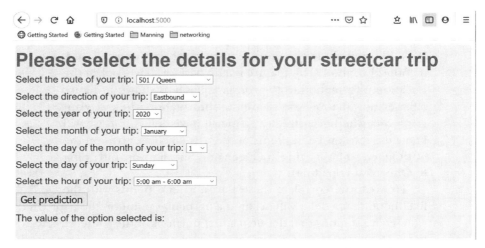

Figure 5.4   Information provided by the user in the web deployment of the model

- *Facebook Messenger* (figure 5.5)—In the Facebook Messenger deployment of the model, the date/time details default to the current time when the prediction is made if the user doesn't provide them explicitly. In this deployment, the user needs to provide only two scoring parameters: the route and the direction of their intended streetcar trip.

Let's check these parameters to ensure that we're not risking data leakage:

- *Route*—When we want to predict whether a streetcar trip will be delayed, we'll know what route (such as Route 501 Queen or Route 503 Kingston Road) the trip will take.
- *Direction*—We'll know the direction (northbound, southbound, eastbound or westbound) of the trip at the time we want to predict whether it will be delayed.

We will also know the following date/time information (because the user sets the values explicitly in

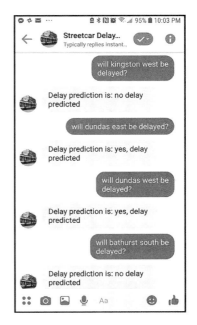

Figure 5.5   Information provided by the user in the Facebook Messenger deployment of the model

the web deployment or because we assume the current date/time in the Facebook Messenger deployment):

- Hour
- Day (day of the week, such as Monday)
- Day of month
- Month
- Year

We'd like to include one more feature in the data entry for predictions: Location. This feature is a bit trickier. If we look at the Location information in the source dataset as shown in figure 5.6, we know that we won't have this information when we want to predict whether a streetcar trip will have delays. But we will know the start and end points of the trip (such as a trip on the 501 Queen route starting at Queen and Sherbourne and going to Queen and Spadina).

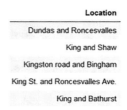

Location
Dundas and Roncesvalles
King and Shaw
Kingston road and Bingham
King St. and Roncesvalles Ave.
King and Bathurst

Figure 5.6   Values in the Location column

How can we correlate these start and end points with the likelihood that a delay will occur at a particular point on the trip? Unlike subway lines, which have stations that define distinct portions of the route, streetcar routes are fairly fluid. Many stops occur along a route, and these stops are not static, like those at subway stations; streetcar stops get moved. One approach that we will investigate in chapter 9 is dividing each route into sections and predicting whether a delay will occur in any of the sections that make up the entire trip along the streetcar route. For now, we are going to examine a version of the model that doesn't include location data so that we can go through the model from end to end the first time without too much additional complexity.

If we limit ourselves to training the streetcar delay model to the columns we have identified (route, direction, and the date/time columns), we can prevent data leakage and be confident that the model we are training will be capable of making predictions about new streetcar trips.

5.4   Code for exploring Keras and building the model

When you have cloned the GitHub repo (http://mng.bz/v95x) associated with this book, you'll find the code related to exploring Keras and building the streetcar delay prediction model in the notebooks subdirectory. The next listing shows the files that contain the code described in this chapter.

Listing 5.1   Code in the repo related to exploring Keras and building the model

```
├── data          ←┐  Directory for the pickled
│                   │  dataframe that is the output
├── notebooks     ←┘  of the data preparation steps       Notebook containing code to
│                                                          refactor the input dataset and
         streetcar_model_training.ipynb  ←─────────────── build the model
```

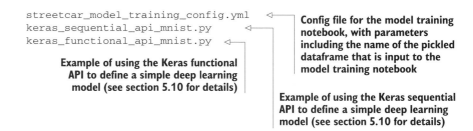

```
|              streetcar_model_training_config.yml
|              keras_sequential_api_mnist.py
|              keras_functional_api_mnist.py
```

Config file for the model training notebook, with parameters including the name of the pickled dataframe that is input to the model training notebook

Example of using the Keras functional API to define a simple deep learning model (see section 5.10 for details)

Example of using the Keras sequential API to define a simple deep learning model (see section 5.10 for details)

5.5   Deriving the dataframe to use to train the model

In chapters 1–4, we went through many steps to clean and transform the data, including

- Replacing redundant values with a single consistent value, such as replacing eastbound, e/b, and eb with e in the Direction column
- Removing records with invalid values, such as records with Route values that aren't valid streetcar routes
- Replacing categorical values with numeric identifiers

Figure 5.7 shows the outcomes of these transformations.

Report Date	Route	Time	Day	Location	Incident	Min Delay	Min Gap	Direction	Vehicle	Report Date Time	year	month	daym	hour
2018-11-12	50	16:45:00	1	9555	[1]	5.0	10.0	54	4180	2018-11-12 16:45:00	4	10	11	16
2017-10-27	61	19:03:00	0	12794	[2]	3.0	6.0	54	4400	2017-10-27 19:03:00	3	9	26	19
2014-05-25	50	06:42:00	3	10244	[2]	13.0	23.0	35	4249	2014-05-25 06:42:00	0	4	24	6
2015-02-10	55	01:05:00	5	7599	[13, 14]	10.0	10.0	54	4124	2015-02-10 01:05:00	1	1	9	1
2017-05-15	51	10:43:00	1	988	[1]	8.0	16.0	54	7729	2017-05-15 10:43:00	3	4	14	10

Figure 5.7   The input dataset after the transformations up to the end of chapter 4

Will this dataset be sufficient to train a model to meet our goal of predicting whether a given streetcar trip will be delayed? The answer is no. As it stands now, this dataset has only records for delays. What's missing is information about all the situations when there were no delays. What we need is a refactored dataset that also has records of all the times when there were no delays on a particular route in a particular direction.

Figure 5.8 summarizes the difference between the original dataset and the refactored dataset. In the original dataset, every record describes a delay, including the time, route, direction, and incident that caused the delay. In the refactored dataset, there is a record for every combination of time slot (every hour since January 1, 2014), route, and direction, whether or not there was a delay on that route in that direction during that time slot.

Figure 5.8   Comparing the original dataset with the refactored dataset

Figure 5.9 shows explicitly what the refactored dataset looks like. If there is a delay in a given time slot (an hour in a particular day) on a given route in a given direction, count is nonzero; otherwise, count is zero. The snippet of the refactored dataset in figure 5.9 shows that there were no delays on Route 301 in the eastbound direction between midnight and 5 a.m. on January 1, 2014.

	Report Date	count	Route	Direction	hour	year	month	daym	day	Min Delay	target
0	2014-01-01	0	301	e	0	2014	1	1	2	0.0	0
1	2014-01-01	0	301	e	1	2014	1	1	2	0.0	0
2	2014-01-01	0	301	e	2	2014	1	1	2	0.0	0
3	2014-01-01	0	301	e	3	2014	1	1	2	0.0	0
4	2014-01-01	0	301	e	4	2014	1	1	2	0.0	0

Figure 5.9   Refactored dataset with a row for each route/direction/time-slot combination

Figure 5.10 summarizes the steps to get the refactored dataset that has an entry for every time-slot/route/direction combination.

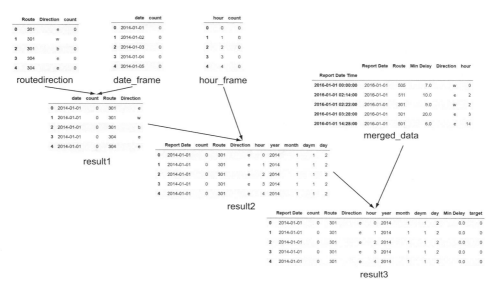

Figure 5.10   Refactoring the dataframe

Following are the steps:

1 Create a `routedirection_frame` dataframe containing a row for each route/ direction combination (figure 5.11).

2 Create a `date_frame` dataframe, containing a row for each date in the period from which training data will be selected (figure 5.12).

3 Create an `hour_frame` dataframe, containing a row for each hour of the day (figure 5.13).

	Route	Direction	count
0	301	e	0
1	301	w	0
2	301	b	0
3	304	e	0
4	304	e	0

Figure 5.11   routedirection _frame dataframe

	date	count
0	2014-01-01	0
1	2014-01-02	0
2	2014-01-03	0
3	2014-01-04	0
4	2014-01-05	0

Figure 5.12   date_frame dataframe

	hour	count
0	0	0
1	1	0
2	2	0
3	3	0
4	4	0

Figure 5.13   hour _frame dataframe

4 Combine these three dataframes to get the `result2` dataframe (figure 5.14).

	Report Date	count	Route	Direction	hour	year	month	daym	day
0	2014-01-01	0	301	e	0	2014	1	1	2
1	2014-01-01	0	301	e	1	2014	1	1	2
2	2014-01-01	0	301	e	2	2014	1	1	2
3	2014-01-01	0	301	e	3	2014	1	1	2
4	2014-01-01	0	301	e	4	2014	1	1	2

Figure 5.14   result2 dataframe

5 Add derived columns for the components of the date to the `result2` dataframe:

```
result2['year'] = pd.DatetimeIndex(result2['Report Date']).year
    result2['month'] = pd.DatetimeIndex(result2['Report Date']).month
    result2['daym'] = pd.DatetimeIndex(result2['Report Date']).day
    result2['day'] = pd.DatetimeIndex(result2['Report Date']).weekday
```

6 Drop extraneous columns from the input dataset (`merged_data` dataframe) and combine it with the `result2` dataframe to get the completed refactored dataframe (figure 5.15).

	Report Date	count	Route	Direction	hour	year	month	daym	day	Min Delay	target
0	2014-01-01	0	301	e	0	2014	1	1	2	0.0	0
1	2014-01-01	0	301	e	1	2014	1	1	2	0.0	0
2	2014-01-01	0	301	e	2	2014	1	1	2	0.0	0
3	2014-01-01	0	301	e	3	2014	1	1	2	0.0	0
4	2014-01-01	0	301	e	4	2014	1	1	2	0.0	0

Figure 5.15   Completed refactored dataframe

To compare the size of the dataset before and after refactoring, a dataset with 56,000 rows results in a refactored dataset with 2.5 million rows to cover a five-year period. The start and end of the time period covered by this refactored dataset is controlled by these variables, defined in the overall parameters block:

```
start_date =  date(config['general']['start_year'], \
config['general']['start_month'], config['general']['start_day'])
end_date = date(config['general']['end_year'], \
config['general']['end_month'], config['general']['end_day'])
```

The start date corresponds with the beginning of the delay dataset in January 2014. You can change the end date by updating the parameters in the config file streetcar_model_training_config.yml, but note that you want to keep `end_date` no later than the latest delay data from the original source (http://mng.bz/4B2B).

5.6 Transforming the dataframe into the format expected by the Keras model

The Keras model expects tensors as input. You can think of a tensor as being a generalization of a matrix. A matrix is a 2D tensor, and a vector is a 1D tensor. Figure 5.16 summarizes common terms for tensors by dimension.

Dimension	Common term	Example
0	scalar	1
1	vector	[1, 2, 3]
2	matrix	$\begin{bmatrix} 1 & 2 & 3 \\ 4 & 5 & 6 \\ 7 & 8 & 9 \end{bmatrix}$
3	3D matrix	$\begin{bmatrix} 1 & 2 & 3 \\ 4 & 5 & 6 \\ 7 & 8 & 9 \end{bmatrix}$ $\begin{bmatrix} 1 & 2 & 3 \\ 4 & 5 & 6 \\ 7 & 8 & 9 \end{bmatrix}$ $\begin{bmatrix} 1 & 2 & 3 \\ 4 & 5 & 6 \\ 7 & 8 & 9 \end{bmatrix}$

Figure 5.16 Tensor summary

When we have made all the data transformations that we need to make in Pandas dataframes, the final step before feeding this data into the model to train is putting the data in the tensor format required by the Keras model. By leaving this transformation as the final step before training the model, we get to enjoy the convenience and familiarity of Pandas dataframes until we need to put the data in the format expected by the Keras model. The code to perform this transformation is in the `transform` method of the `prep_for_keras_input` class, shown in the next listing. This class is part of the pipelines described in chapter 8 that perform transformations on data for training and scoring.

Listing 5.2 Code to put the data in the tensor format required by the model

```
def __init__(self):
        self.dictlist = []       <-- List that will contain numpy
        return None                  arrays for each column


def transform(self, X, y=None, **tranform_params):
```

```
    for col in self.collist:
        print("cat col is",col)
        self.dictlist.append(np.array(X[col]))
    for col in self.textcols:
        print("text col is",col)
        self.dictlist.append(pad_sequences(X[col], \
        ➥ maxlen=max_dict[col]))
    for col in self.continuouscols:
        print("cont col is",col)
        self.dictlist.append(np.array(X[col]))
    return self.dictlist
```

Append the numpy array for the current categorical column to the overall list.

Append the numpy array for the current text column to the overall list.

Append the numpy array for the current continuous column to the overall list.

This code is flexible. Like the rest of the code in this example, as long as the columns from the input dataset are categorized correctly, this code will work with a wide variety of tabular structured data. It isn't specific to the streetcar dataset.

5.7   *A brief history of Keras and TensorFlow*

We have reviewed the final set of transformations that the dataset needs to go through in preparation to train a deep learning model. This section provides background on Keras, the high-level deep learning framework used to create the model for the primary example in this book. We will begin in this section by briefly reviewing the history of Keras and its relationship with TensorFlow, the low-level deep learning framework. In section 5.8, we will review the steps required to migrate from TensorFlow 1.x to TensorFlow 2, the backend deep learning framework used for the code examples in this book. In section 5.9, we will briefly contrast the Keras/TensorFlow framework with the other major deep learning framework, PyTorch. In section 5.10, we will review two code examples that show how the layers of a deep learning model are built in Keras. With this background on Keras, we will be ready to examine how the Keras framework is used to implement the streetcar delay prediction deep learning model in section 5.11.

Keras began its life as a frontend for a variety of backend deep learning frameworks, including TensorFlow (https://www.tensorflow.org) and Theano. The purpose of Keras was to provide a set of accessible, easy-to-use APIs that developers could use to explore deep learning. When Keras was released in 2015, the deep learning backend libraries that it supported (first Theano and then TensorFlow) provided a broad range of functions but could be challenging for beginners to master. With Keras, developers could get started with deep learning by using familiar syntax and without having to worry about all the details exposed in the backend libraries.

If you were starting a deep learning project back in 2017, your choices included

- Using TensorFlow libraries directly
- Using Keras as a frontend to TensorFlow
- Using Keras with another backend, such as Theano (although by 2017 backends other than TensorFlow were becoming rare)

Although most people who used Keras for deep learning projects exploited Tensor-Flow as the backend, Keras and TensorFlow were distinct, separate projects. All this changed in 2019 with the release of TensorFlow 2:

- Coders using Keras for deep learning are encouraged to use the `tf.keras` package integrated into TensorFlow rather than free-standing Keras.
- TensorFlow users are encouraged to use Keras (via the `tf.keras` package in TensorFlow) as the high-level API for TensorFlow. As of TensorFlow 2, Keras is the official high-level API for TensorFlow (http://mng.bz/xrWY).

In short, Keras and TensorFlow, which had originally been separate but related projects, have come together. In particular, as new TensorFlow point releases come out (such as TensorFlow 2.2.0 [http://mng.bz/yrnJ], released in May 2020), they will include improvements in the backend as well as improvements in the Keras frontend. You can find more details about the relationship between Keras and TensorFlow, particularly the role played by TensorFlow in the overall operation of a deep learning model defined with Keras, in the *Deep Learning with Python* chapter on Keras and TensorFlow (http://mng.bz/AzA7).

5.8 *Migrating from TensorFlow 1.x to TensorFlow 2*

The deep learning model code described in this chapter and chapter 6 was originally written to use self-standing Keras with TensorFlow 1.x as a backend. TensorFlow 2 was released while this book was being written, so I decided to migrate to the integrated Keras environment in TensorFlow 2. Thus, to run the code in streetcar_model_training .ipynb, you need to have TensorFlow 2 installed in your Python environment. If you have other deep learning projects that have not moved to TensorFlow 2, you can create a Python virtual environment specifically for the code example in this book and install TensorFlow 2 there. That way, you will not introduce changes in your other deep learning projects.

This section summarizes the changes that I needed to make to the code in the model training notebook to migrate it from self-standing Keras with TensorFlow 1.x as a backend to Keras in the context of TensorFlow 2. The TensorFlow documentation includes comprehensive migration steps at https://www.tensorflow.org/guide/migrate. Following is a brief summary of the steps I took:

1 Upgraded my existing level of TensorFlow to the latest TensorFlow 1.x level:

```
pip install tensorflow==1.1.5
```

2 Ran the model training notebook end to end to validate that everything worked in the latest level of TensorFlow 1.x.
3 Ran the upgrade script tf_upgrade_v2 on the model training notebook.
4 Changed all Keras import statements to reference the tf.keras package (including changing `from keras import regularizers` to `from tensorflow.keras import regularizers`).

5 Ran the model training notebook end to end with the updated import statements to validate that everything worked.

6 Created a Python virtual environment, following the instructions at https://janakiev.com/blog/jupyter-virtual-envs.

7 Installed TensorFlow 2 in the Python virtual environment. This step was necessary because the Rasa chatbot framework that is part of the Facebook Messenger deployment approach described in chapter 8 requires TensorFlow 1.x. By installing TensorFlow 2 in a virtual environment, we can exploit the virtual environment for the model training steps without breaking the deployment prerequisite for TensorFlow 1.x. Here is the command to install TensorFlow 2:

```
pip install tensorflow==2.0.0
```

The process of migrating to TensorFlow 2 was painless, and thanks to Python virtual environments, I was able to apply this migration where I needed it for the model training without causing any side effects for the rest of my Python projects.

5.9   *TensorFlow vs. PyTorch*

Before exploring Keras in more depth, it's worth quickly discussing the other major library that is currently used for deep learning: PyTorch (https://pytorch.org). PyTorch was developed by Facebook and made available as open source in 2017. The article at http://mng.bz/Moj2 makes a succinct comparison of the two libraries. The community that uses TensorFlow is currently larger than the one that uses PyTorch, although PyTorch is growing quickly. PyTorch has a stronger presence in the academic/research world (and is the basis of the coding aspects of the fast.ai course described in chapter 9), whereas TensorFlow is predominant in industry.

5.10   *The structure of a deep learning model in Keras*

You may recall that chapter 1 described a neural network as a series of nodes organized in layers, each of which has weights associated with it. In simple terms, during the training process these weights get updated repeatedly until the loss function is minimized and the accuracy of the model's predictions is optimized. In this section, we will show how the abstract idea of layers introduced in chapter 1 is manifested in code in Keras by reviewing two simple deep learning models.

There are two ways to define the layers of a Keras model: the sequential API and the functional API. The sequential API is the simpler method but is less flexible; the functional API has more flexibility but is a bit more complex to use.

To illustrate these two APIs, we are going to look at how we would create minimal Keras deep learning models with both approaches for MNIST (https://www.tensorflow.org/datasets/catalog/mnist). If you have not encountered MNIST before, it is a dataset made up of labeled images of handwritten digits. The x values come from the image files, and the labels (y values) are the text representations of the digits. The goal of a model exercising MNIST is to correctly identify the digit for the handwritten images.

MNIST is commonly used as a minimal dataset for exercising deep learning models. If you want more background on MNIST and how it is used to exercise deep learning frameworks, a great article at http://mng.bz/Zr2a provides more details.

It is worth noting that MNIST is not a structured dataset according to the definition of structured data in chapter 1. There are two reasons for choosing MNIST for the examples in this section, even though it's not a structured dataset: the published starter examples of the Keras APIs use MNIST, and there is no recognized structured dataset for exercising deep learning models that is equivalent to MNIST.

With the sequential API, the model definition takes as an argument an ordered list of layers. You can select layers that you want to include in your model from the list of supported Keras layers in TensorFlow 2 (http://mng.bz/awaJ). The code snippet in listing 5.3 comes from keras_sequential _api_mnist.py. It is adapted from the TensorFlow 2 documentation (http://mng.bz/ RMAO) and shows a simple deep learning model for MNIST that uses the Keras sequential API.

Listing 5.3 Code for an MNIST model using the Keras sequential API

```
import tensorflow as tf
import pydotplus
from tensorflow.keras.utils import plot_model

mnist = tf.keras.datasets.mnist

(x_train, y_train), (x_test, y_test) = mnist.load_data()
x_train, x_test = x_train / 255.0, x_test / 255.0

model = tf.keras.models.Sequential([
    tf.keras.layers.Flatten(input_shape=(28, 28)),
    tf.keras.layers.Dense(128, activation='relu'),
    tf.keras.layers.Dropout(0.2),
    tf.keras.layers.Dense(10)
])
model.compile(optimizer='adam',

        loss=tf.keras.losses.SparseCategoricalCrossentropy(from_logits=True),\
                metrics=['accuracy'])

history = model.fit(x_train, y_train, \
                    batch_size=64, \
                    epochs=5, \
                    validation_split=0.2)

test_scores = model.evaluate(x_test,  y_test, verbose=2)
print('Test loss:', test_scores[0])
print('Test accuracy:', test_scores[1])
```

Flatten layer that reshapes the input tensor to a tensor with a shape equal to the number of elements in the input tensor

Dense layer that does the standard operation of getting the dot product of the input to the layer and the weights in the layer, plus the bias

Define Keras sequential model

Output dense layer

Dropout layer that randomly turns off a proportion of the network

Compile the model, specifying the loss function, the optimizer, and the metric to be tracked in the training process.

Fit the model by adjusting the weights to minimize the loss function.

Assess model performance

This simple example of a Keras deep learning model has several characteristics in common with non-deep-learning models that you have already seen:

- The input dataset is split into train and test subsets. The train subset is used in the training process to adjust the weights in the model. The test dataset is applied to the trained model to assess its performance; in this example, according to the accuracy (that is, how closely the predictions for the model match the actual output values).

- Both the training and test datasets are made up of input x values (for MNIST, images of handwritten digits) and labels or y values (for MNIST, the ASCII digits corresponding to the handwritten digits).

- Both non-deep-learning and deep learning models have similar statements to define and fit the model. The code snippets in the next listing contrast the statements to define and fit a logistic regression model and a Keras deep learning model.

Listing 5.4   Code to contrast a logistic regression model and a Keras model

```
from sklearn.linear_model import LogisticRegression

clf_lr = LogisticRegression(solver = 'lbfgs')
model = clf_lr.fit(X_train, y_train)

model = tf.keras.models.Sequential([
  tf.keras.layers.Flatten(input_shape=(28, 28)),
  tf.keras.layers.Dense(128, activation='relu'),
  tf.keras.layers.Dropout(0.2),
  tf.keras.layers.Dense(10)
])
model.compile(optimizer='adam', \
        loss=tf.keras.losses.SparseCategoricalCrossentropy(from_logits=True),\
              metrics=['accuracy'])

history = model.fit(x_train, y_train, \
                    batch_size=64, \
                    epochs=5, \
                    validation_split=0.2)
```

Define the logistic regression model.

Fit the logistic regression model.

First part of defining the Keras deep learning model: defining the layers

Second part of defining the Keras deep learning model: setting the compilation parameters

Fit the Keras deep learning model.

Figure 5.17 shows the output of the `plot_model` function for the MNIST sequential API model.

By contrast with the sequential API, the Keras functional API has a more complex syntax but provides greater flexibility. In particular, the functional API allows you to define a model with multiple inputs. As you will see in section 5.13, the extended example in this book exploits the functional API because it requires multiple inputs.

The code snippet in listing 5.5 comes from keras_functional_api_mnist.py. It is adapted from https://www.tensorflow.org/guide/keras/functional and shows how you would use the Keras functional API to define a simple

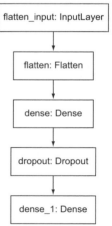

Figure 5.17 `plot_model` output for simple sequential API Keras model

deep learning model for the same MNIST problem for which we showed a sequential API solution.

Listing 5.5 Code for an MNIST model using the Keras functional API

Define layer that flattens the input tensor by reshaping it to a tensor with a shape equal to the number of elements in the input tensor

```
import numpy as np
import tensorflow as tf
from tensorflow import keras
from tensorflow.keras import layers

inputs = keras.Input(shape=(784,))
flatten = layers.Flatten(input_shape=(28, 28))
flattened = flatten(inputs)
dense = layers.Dense(128, activation='relu')(flattened)
dropout = layers.Dropout(0.2) (dense)
outputs = layers.Dense(10) (dropout)
# define model inputs and outputs (taken from layer definition)

model = keras.Model(inputs=inputs, outputs=outputs, \
name='mnist_model')
(x_train, y_train), (x_test, y_test) = keras.datasets.mnist.load_data()

x_train = x_train.reshape(60000, 784).astype('float32') / 255
x_test = x_test.reshape(10000, 784).astype('float32') / 255

# compile model, including specifying the loss function, \
optimizer, and metrics

model.compile(loss=keras.losses.SparseCategoricalCrossentropy( \
from_logits=True), \
    optimizer=keras.optimizers.RMSprop(), \
    metrics=['accuracy'])

# train model

history = model.fit(x_train, y_train, \
                    batch_size=64, \
                    epochs=5, \
                    validation_split=0.2)

# assess model performance

test_scores = model.evaluate(x_test, y_test, verbose=2)
print('Test loss:', test_scores[0])
print('Test accuracy:', test_scores[1])
```

Dense layer that does the standard operation of getting the dot product of the input to the layer and the weights in the layer, plus the bias

Dropout layer that randomly turns off a proportion of the network

Output dense layer

Compile the model, specifying the loss function, the optimizer, and the metric to be tracked in the training process.

Fit the model (with parameters set for the training dataset, batch size, number of epochs, and subset of the training set to reserve for validation) by adjusting the weights to minimize the loss function.

Assess the model performance.

You can see a lot of similarity between the sequential API and functional API approaches to this problem. The `loss` function is defined the same way, for example, and the `compile` and `fit` statements are the same. What is different between the sequential API and the functional API is the definition of the layers. In the sequential API approach, the layers are defined in a single list, whereas in the functional API approach, the layers are recursively defined, with each layer being built on its predecessors.

Figure 5.18 shows the output of `plot_model` for this simple functional API Keras model.

In this section, we have examined a couple of simple Keras models and reviewed the essential characteristics of two approaches offered in Keras: the sequential API and the functional API. In section 5.13, we will see how the streetcar delay prediction model takes advantage of the flexibility of the functional API.

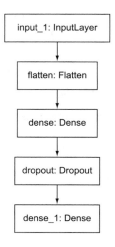

Figure 5.18 `plot_model` output for the simple functional API Keras model

5.11 *How the data structure defines the Keras model*

In chapter 3, you learned that the columns in the structured dataset are categorized as categorical, continuous, or text (figure 5.19).

		Categorical		Categorical		Categorical		Continuous		Categorical	
	Report Date	**Route**	**Time**	**Day**	**Location**	**Incident**	**Min Delay**	**Min Gap**	**Direction**	**Vehicle**
0	2014-01-02	505	06:31:00	Thursday	Dundas and Roncesvalles	Late Leaving Garage	4.0	8.0	E/B	4018.0
1	2014-01-02	504	12:43:00	Thursday	King and Shaw	Utilized Off Route	20.0	22.0	E/B	4128.0
2	2014-01-02	501	14:01:00	Thursday	Kingston road and Bingham	Held By	13.0	19.0	W/B	4016.0
3	2014-01-02	504	14:22:00	Thursday	King St. and Roncesvalles Ave.	Investigation	7.0	11.0	W/B	4175.0
4	2014-01-02	504	16:42:00	Thursday	King and Bathurst	Utilized Off Route	3.0	6.0	E/B	4080.0

Figure 5.19   Column categories in the streetcar dataset

- *Continuous*—These values are numeric. Examples of common continuous values include temperatures, currency values, time spans (such as elapsed hours), and counts of objects or activities. In the streetcar example, Min Delay and Min Gap (the columns containing the number of minutes of delay incurred by the delay and the length in minutes of the resulting gap between streetcars) are continuous columns. The latitude and longitude values derived from the Location column are also treated as continuous columns.
- *Categorical*—These values can be single strings, such as the days of the week, or collections of one or more strings that constitute an identifier, such as the

names of the U.S. states. The number of distinct values in categorical columns can range from two to several thousand. Most of the columns in the streetcar dataset are categorical, including Route, Day, Location, Incident, Direction, and Vehicle.

- *Text*—These values are sets of strings.

It's essential to organize the input dataset into these categories because the categories define how the deep learning model code is assembled in the deep learning approach described in this book. The layers of the Keras model are built up based on these categories, with each category having its own structure of layers.

The following illustrations summarize the layers that are built up for categorical and text columns. Figure 5.20 shows the layers that get built for categorical columns:

- *Embedding*—As explained in section 5.12, embeddings provide a way for the model to learn the relationships between values in categorical categories in the context of the overall prediction the model is making.
- *Batch normalization*—Batch normalization is a method of preventing overfitting (a model working well on the dataset it was trained on, but poorly on other data) by controlling how much weights change in hidden layers.
- *Flatten*—Reshape the input to prepare for subsequent layers.
- *Dropout*—Use this technique to prevent overfitting. With dropout, as the name suggests, rotating, random subsets of nodes in the network are ignored in forward and backward passes through the network.
- *Concatenate*—Join the layers for this input with layers for the other inputs.

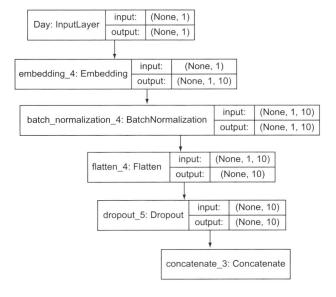

Figure 5.20   Keras layers for categorical inputs

Figure 5.21 shows the layers that get built for text input columns. In addition to the layers for categorical columns, text columns get a GRU layer. A *GRU* (https://keras .io/api/layers/recurrent_layers/gru) is a kind of recurrent neural network (RNN), the class of deep learning models commonly used for text processing. What sets RNNs apart from other neural networks are the gates that control how much previous inputs affect the way that current input changes weights in the model. The interesting point is that the actions of these gates—how much is "remembered" from previous input—is learned in the same way that the generic weights in the network are learned. Adding this layer to the set of layers for text columns means, at a high level, that the order of words in the text column (not the presence of individual words alone) contributes to the training of the model.

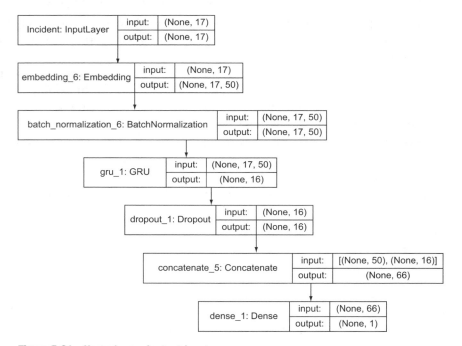

Figure 5.21   Keras layers for text inputs

We've reviewed the layers that are added to the deep learning model for categorical and text columns. What about continuous columns? These columns don't have any special additional layers and are concatenated directly into the overall model.

This section briefly described the layers in the deep learning model that are built up for each of the three column types in a structured dataset: continuous, categorical, and text. In section 5.13, we will go in detail through the code that implements these layers.

5.12 *The power of embeddings*

In section 5.11, you saw the layers that get defined for each type of column in a structured dataset. In particular, you saw that categorical and text columns get embedding layers. In this section, we will examine embeddings and how they are used. We will return to the power of embeddings in chapter 7 in an experiment that demonstrates the effect of categorical column embeddings on the performance of the model.

Embeddings come from the world of natural language processing, in which they are used to map words to a numeric representation. Embeddings are an important topic for this book because they are essential for enabling a deep learning model to exploit categorical and text columns in a structured dataset. This section is not an exhaustive description of embeddings—a topic that deserves a book of its own—but it introduces the concept and describes why embeddings are needed in a deep learning project on structured data. You can find a more detailed description of embeddings in the section on text embeddings in Stephan Raaijmakers's *Deep Learning for Natural Language Processing* (http://mng.bz/2WXm).

The excellent article at http://mng.bz/1gzn states that embeddings are *representations of categorical values as learned, low-dimensional continuous vectors*. That's a lot of information in one sentence. Let's look at it piece by piece:

- *Representations of categorical values*—Recall the definition of categorical values from chapter 3: These values can be "single strings, such as the days of the week, or collections of one or more strings that constitute an identifier, such as the names of the U.S. states. The number of distinct values in categorical columns can range from two to several thousand." The columns in the streetcar dataset that have embeddings associated with them include the categorical columns Route, Day, Location, Incident, Direction, and Vehicle.
- *Learned*—Like the deep learning model weights introduced in chapter 1, the values of embeddings are *learned*. The values of embeddings are initialized before training and then get updated through iterations of the deep learning model. The result is that after the embeddings have been learned, the embeddings for categorical values that tend to produce the same outcome are closer to one another. Consider the context of days of the week (Monday to Sunday) as a derived feature of the streetcar delay dataset. Suppose that delays are less common on weekends. If this is the case, the embeddings learned for Saturday and Sunday will be closer to one another than to the embeddings learned for the weekdays.
- *Low-dimensional*—This term means that the dimension of the embedding vectors is low compared with the number of categorical values. In the model created for the main example in this book, the Route column has more than 1,000 distinct values but has an embedding with a dimension of 10.
- *Continuous*—This term means that the values in the embedding are represented by floating-point values as opposed to the integers that represent the categorical values themselves.

A famous illustration of embeddings (https://arxiv.org/pdf/1711.09160.pdf) demonstrates how they can capture the relationships between the categorical values with which they are associated. This illustration shows the relationship between the vectors associated with four words in Word2Vec (http://mng.bz/ggGR):

`v(`**`king`**`) - v(`**`man`**`) + v(`**`woman`**`) ≈ v(`**`queen`**`)`

This says that the embedding vector for king minus the embedding vector for man plus the embedding vector for woman is close to the embedding vector for queen. In this example, arithmetic on the embeddings matches the semantic relationship between the words associated with the embeddings. This example shows the power of embeddings to map non-numeric, categorical values to a planar space where the values can be manipulated like numbers.

A secondary benefit of embeddings is that they can be used to illustrate implicit relationships among categorical values. You get unsupervised learning analysis of the categories for free as you are solving the supervised learning problem.

A final benefit of embeddings is that they give you a way to incorporate categorical values into a deep learning framework without the drawbacks of one-hot encoding (http://mng.bz/P1Av). In one-hot encoding, if there are seven values (such as for the days of the week), each value is represented by a vector of size 7 with six 0s and a single 1:

- Monday: [1,0,0,0,0,0,0]
- Tuesday: [0,1,0,0,0,0,0,0]
- . . .
- Sunday: [0,0,0,0,0,0,0,1]

In a structured dataset, a one-hot encoding of the days-of-the-week category would require seven columns, which is not too bad for a category with a small number of values. But what about the Vehicle column, which has hundreds of values? You can see how one-hot encoding will quickly explode the number of columns in the dataset and the memory requirements to process the data. By exploiting embeddings in deep learning, we can deal with categorical columns without the poor scaling behavior of one-hot encoding.

This section is a brief introduction to the topic of embeddings. The benefits of using embeddings include the ability to manipulate non-numeric values that are analogous to common numeric operations, the ability to get unsupervised learning-type categorization on values in a categorical range as a byproduct of solving a supervised learning problem, and the ability to train deep learning models with categorical inputs without the drawbacks of one-hot encoding.

5.13   *Code to build a Keras model automatically based on the data structure*

The Keras model is made of up of a sequence of layers through which input columns flow to generate a prediction of a delay in a given route/direction/time-slot combination. Figure 5.22 shows the layers that the input columns flow through, depending on their data category (continuous, categorical, or text), along with examples of the kinds of data in each category. To examine the options you have for exploring these layers, see section 5.14.

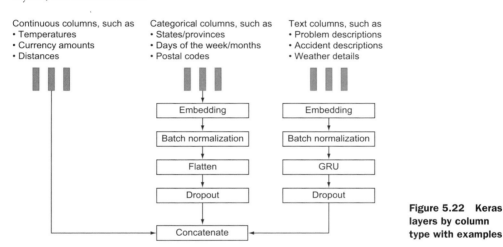

Figure 5.22   Keras layers by column type with examples

The next listing shows the code that assigns each of the columns to one of these categories.

Listing 5.6   Code that assigns columns to categories

The set of text columns in the refactored model is empty.

The set of continuous columns in the refactored model is empty.

```
textcols = []
continuouscols = []
if targetcontinuous:
    excludefromcolist = ['count','Report Date', 'target', \
    ➡ 'count_md','Min Delay']
else:
    excludefromcolist = ['count','Report Date', \
    ➡ 'target','count_md', 'Min Delay']
nontextcols = list(set(allcols) - set(textcols))
collist = list(set(nontextcols) - \
set(excludefromcolist) - set(continuouscols))
```

excludefromcolist is the set of columns that will not train the model.

collist is the list of categorical columns. Here, it is generated by taking the list of columns and removing the text columns, continuous columns, and excluded columns.

These column lists—`textcols`, `continuouscols`, and `collist`—are used throughout the code to determine what actions are taken on the columns, including how the layers of the deep learning model are built up for each column that is being used to train the model. The following sections show the layers added for each column type.

The following listing shows what the training data looks like before it is applied to the model for training. The training data is a list of numpy arrays—one array for each column in the training data.

Listing 5.7   Format of the data before being used to train the model

numpy array for hour.
Values range from 0–23.

numpy array for route.
Values range from 0–14.

numpy array for day of the week. Values range from 0–6.

numpy array for month. Values range from 0–11.

numpy array for year.
Values range from 0–6.

numpy array for direction.
Values range from 0 4.

numpy array for day of the month. Values range from 0–30.

```
X_train_list is
[array([13, 23,  2, ...,  9, 22, 16]),
 array([13, 13,  3, ...,  4, 11,  2]),
 array([1, 6, 5, ..., 5, 3, 2]),
 array([8, 9, 0, ..., 7, 0, 4]),
 array([4, 1, 1, ..., 1, 4, 4]),
 array([10, 10, 23, ..., 21, 17, 15]),
 array([4, 1, 3, ..., 0, 3, 0])]
```

The code that assembles the layers for each type of column is in the streetcar_ model_training notebook in the get_model() function. Following is the code block in get_model() for continuous columns, which simply have the input layer flow through:

```
for col in continuouscols:
        continputs[col] = Input(shape=[1],name=col)
        inputlayerlist.append(continputs[col])
```

In the code block in get_model() for categorical columns, we see that these columns get embeddings and batch normalization layers, as the next listing shows.

Listing 5.8   Code to apply embeddings and batch normalization to categorical columns

Start with the input.

Append the input layer for this column to the list of input layers, which will be used in the model definition statement.

Add the embedding layer.

Add the batch normalization layer.

```
for col in collist:
        catinputs[col] = Input(shape=[1],name=col)
        inputlayerlist.append(catinputs[col])
        embeddings[col] = \
        (Embedding(max_dict[col],catemb)(catinputs[col]))
        embeddings[col] = (BatchNormalization()(embeddings[col]))
```

In the code block in get_model() for text columns, we see that these columns get layers for embeddings, batch normalization, dropout, and a GRU, as shown next.

Listing 5.9 Code to apply the appropriate layers to text columns

Start with the input.

Append the input layer for this column to the list of input layers, which will be used in the model definition statement.

Add the embedding layer.

```
for col in textcols:
    textinputs[col] = \
    Input(shape=[X_train[col].shape[1]], name=col)
    inputlayerlist.append(textinputs[col])
    textembeddings[col] = (Embedding(textmax,textemb)(textinputs[col]))
    textembeddings[col] = (BatchNormalization()(textembeddings[col]))
    textembeddings[col] = \
    Dropout(dropout_rate)( GRU(16,kernel_regularizer=l2(l2_lambda)) \
    (textembeddings[col]))
```

Add the dropout layer and the GRU layer.

Add the batch normalization layer. By default, samples are normalized individually.

In this section, we've gone through the code that makes up the heart of the Keras deep learning model for the streetcar delay prediction problem. We've seen how the `get_model()` function builds up the layers of the model based on the types (continuous, categorical, and text) of the input columns. Because the `get_model()` function does not depend on the tabular structure of any particular input dataset, this function works with a wide variety of input datasets. Like the rest of the code in this example, as long as the columns from the input data set are categorized correctly, the code in the `get_model()` function will generate a Keras model for a wide variety of tabular structured data.

5.14 Exploring your model

The model that we have created to predict streetcar delays is relatively simple but can still be somewhat overwhelming to understand if you have not encountered Keras before. Luckily, you have utilities you can use to examine the model. In this section, we will review three utilities that you can use to explore your model: `model.summary()`, `plot_model`, and TensorBoard.

The `model.summary()` API lists each of the layers in the model, its output shape, the number of parameters, and the layer that is fed into it. The snippet of `model.summary()` output in figure 5.23 shows the input layers daym, year, Route, and hour. You can see how daym is connected to embedding_1, which is in turn connected to batch_normalization_1, which is connected to flatten_1.

When you initially create a Keras model, the output of `model.summary()` can really help you understand how the layers are connected and validate your assumptions about how the layers are related.

If you want a graphical perspective of how the layers of the Keras model are related, you can use the `plot_model` function (https://keras.io/visualization). `model.summary()` produces information about the model in tabular format; the file generated by `plot_model` illustrates the same information graphically. `model.summary()` is easier to use. Because `plot_model` is dependent on the Graphviz package (a Python implementation of the Graphviz [https://www.graphviz.org] visualization software), it

Layer (type)	Output Shape	Param #	Connected to
daym (InputLayer)	(None, 1)	0	
year (InputLayer)	(None, 1)	0	
embedding_1 (Embedding)	(None, 1, 10)	310	daym[0][0]
embedding_2 (Embedding)	(None, 1, 10)	60	year[0][0]
Route (InputLayer)	(None, 1)	0	
batch_normalization_1 (BatchNor	(None, 1, 10)	40	embedding_1[0][0]
batch_normalization_2 (BatchNor	(None, 1, 10)	40	embedding_2[0][0]
embedding_3 (Embedding)	(None, 1, 10)	140	Route[0][0]
hour (InputLayer)	(None, 1)	0	
flatten_1 (Flatten)	(None, 10)	0	batch_normalization_1[0][0]
flatten_2 (Flatten)	(None, 10)	0	batch_normalization_2[0][0]

Figure 5.23 `model.summary()` **output**

can take some work to get `plot_model` working in a new environment, but the effort pays off if you need an accessible way to explain your model to a wider audience.

Here is what I needed to do to get `plot_model` to work in my Windows 10 environment:

```
pip install pydot
pip install pydotplus
conda install python-graphviz
```

When I completed these Python library updates, I downloaded and installed the Graphviz package (https://graphviz.gitlab.io/download) in Windows. Finally, to get `plot_model` to work in Windows, I had to update the PATH environment variable to explicitly include the bin directory in the install path for Graphviz.

The following listing shows the code in the streetcar_model_training notebook that invokes `plot_model`.

Listing 5.10   Code to invoke `plot_model`

Check whether the save_model_plot switch is set in the streetcar model training config file.

If so, set the filename and path where the model plot will be saved.

```
if save_model_plot:
    model_plot_file = "model_plot"+modifier+".png"
    model_plot_path = os.path.join(get_path(),model_plot_file)
    print("model plot path: ",model_plot_path)
    plot_model(model, to_file=model_plot_path)
```

Call plot_model with the model object and the fully qualified filename as parameters.

Figure 5.24 and 5.25 show the output of `plot_model` for the streetcar delay prediction model. The start of the layers for each column is highlighted with a number:

1. Direction
2. Hour
3. Year
4. Route
5. Month
6. Day of month
7. Day

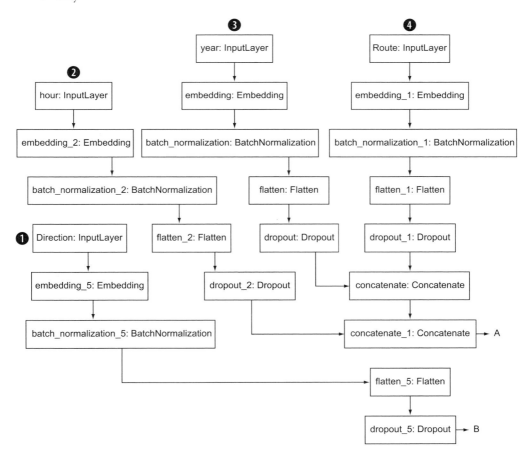

Figure 5.24 **Output of `plot_model` showing the layers in the model (top portion)**

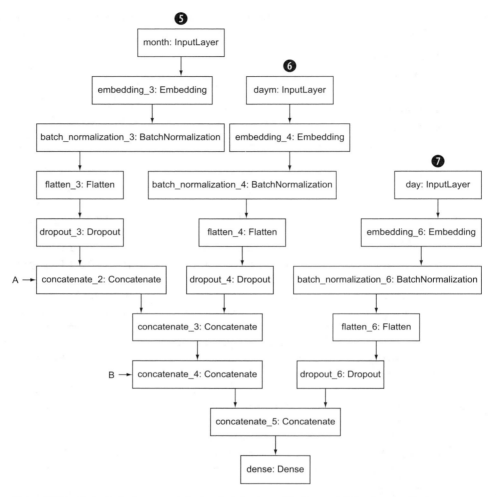

Figure 5.25   Output of `plot_model` showing the layers in the model (bottom portion)

Figure 5.26 shows a closeup of `plot_model` output for the day column.

In addition to `model.summary()` and `plot_model,` you can use the TensorBoard utility to examine the characteristics of a trained model. TensorBoard (https://www.tensorflow.org/tensorboard/get_started) is a tool provided with TensorFlow that allows you to graphically track metrics such as loss and accuracy, and to generate a diagram of the model graph.

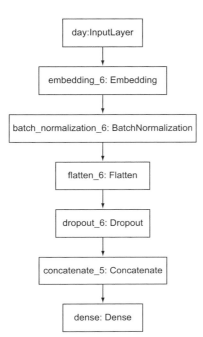

Figure 5.26 Closeup of the layers for the day column

To use TensorBoard with the streetcar delay prediction model, follow these steps:

1 Import the required libraries:

```
from tensorflow.python.keras.callbacks import TensorBoard
```

2 Define a callback for TensorBoard that includes the path for TensorBoard logs, as shown in this snippet from the set_early_stop function in the streetcar_model_training notebook.

Listing 5.11 Code to define callbacks

If the tensorboard_callback parameter is set to True in the streetcar_model_training config file, define a callback for TensorBoard.

Define a log file path, using the current date.

```
if tensorboard_callback:
        tensorboard_log_dir = \
os.path.join(get_path(),"tensorboard_log", \
datetime.now().strftime("%Y%m%d-%H%M%S"))
        tensorboard = TensorBoard(log_dir= tensorboard_log_dir)
    callback_list.append(tensorboard)
```

Define the tensorboard callback with the log directory path as a parameter.

Add the tensorboard callback to the overall list of callbacks. Note that the tensorboard callback will be invoked only if early_stop is True.

3 Train the model with early_stop set to True so that the callback list (including the TensorBoard callback) is included as a parameter.

When you have trained a model with a TensorBoard callback defined, you can start TensorBoard with the following command in the terminal, as the next listing shows.

Listing 5.12   Commands to invoke TensorBoard

Command to start TensorBoard. The logdir value corresponds with the directory set in the definition of the TensorBoard callback.   **The command returns the URL to use to launch TensorBoard for this training run.**

```
tensorboard --logdir="C:\personal\manning\deep_learning_for_structured_data\
  data\tensorboard_log"
Serving TensorBoard on localhost; to expose to the network,
  use a proxy or pass --bind_all
TensorBoard 2.0.2 at http://localhost:6006/ (Press CTRL+C to quit)
```

Now if you open the URL returned by the TensorBoard command in your browser, you will see the TensorBoard interface. Figure 5.27 shows TensorBoard with the accuracy results by epoch for a training run of the streetcar delay prediction model.

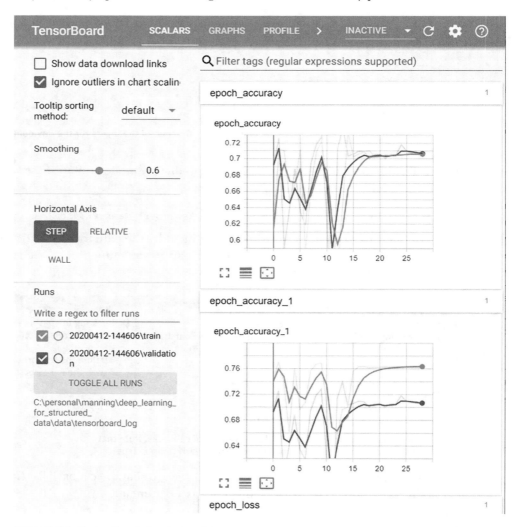

Figure 5.27   TensorBoard showing model accuracy

In this section, you've seen three options for getting information about your model: `model.summary()`, `plot_model`, and TensorBoard. TensorBoard in particular has a rich set of features for exploring your model. You can get a detailed description of the many visualization options for TensorBoard in the TensorFlow documentation (https://www.tensorflow.org/tensorboard/get_started).

5.15 Model parameters

The code includes a set of parameters that control the operation of the model and its training process. Figure 5.28 summarizes the valid values and purposes of these parameters. A detailed description of the standard parameters (including learning rate, loss function, activation function, batch size, and number of epochs) is beyond the scope of this book. You can find a succinct summary of the key hyperparameters at http://mng.bz/Ov8P.

You can use the parameters listed in figure 5.28 to adjust the behavior of the model. If you are adapting this model to a different dataset, you may want to begin with a smaller learning rate until you get an idea of whether the model is converging on a good result. You will also want to reduce the number of epochs for your first few iterations of training the model on a new dataset until you get an idea of how long it takes for an epoch to complete on your dataset in your training environment.

The `output_activation` parameter controls whether the model predicts a category (such as streetcar trip delayed/streetcar trip not delayed) or a continuous value (such as "streetcar trip delayed by 5 minutes"). Given the size of the input dataset for streetcar delays, I chose a category prediction for the model. But if you adapt this model for a different dataset, as described in chapter 9, you may decide to use a continuous prediction, and you can adjust the `output_activation` parameter to a value for a continuous prediction, such as linear.

Parameter	Value	Purpose
learning_rate	Positive floating point value	Control rate of weight changes.
l2_lambda, dropout_rate	Positive floating point value	Control overfitting.
loss_func	Loss function name	Specify function optimized in training.
output_activation	Activation function name	Specify output.
BATCH_SIZE	Positive integer	Control number of records processed per weights update.
epochs	Positive integer	Control number of iterations through the dataset.

Figure 5.28   Parameters you can set in the code to control the model and its training

These parameters are defined in the config file streetcar_model_training_config.yml. Chapter 3 introduced config files with Python as a way to keep hardcoded values out of your code and to make adjusting parameters faster and less error-prone. The excellent article at http://mng.bz/wpBa has a good description of the value of config files.

You would need to change the parameters listed in figure 5.28 rarely, if at all, when you are going through training iterations. Here's what these parameters control:

- *Learning rate* controls the magnitude of changes to the weights per iteration during training of a model. If the learning rate is too high, you can end up skipping the optimal weights, and if it's too low, progress toward the optimal weights can be extremely slow. The learning rate value that is originally set in the code should be adequate, but you can adjust this value to see how it affects the progress of training of the model.

- *Dropout rate* controls the proportion of the network that is omitted in training iterations. As we mentioned in section 5.11, with dropout rotating, random subsets of nodes in the network are ignored in forward and backward passes through the network to reduce overfitting.

- *L2_lambda* controls regularization of the GRU RNN layer. This parameter affects only text input columns. Regularization constrains the weights in the model to reduce overfitting. By forcing down the size of the weights, regularization prevents the model from being influenced too much by particular characteristics of the training set. You can think of regularization as making the model more conservative (https://arxiv.org/ftp/arxiv/papers/2003/2003.05182.pdf) or simpler.

- *Loss function* is the function that is optimized by the model. The goal of the model is to optimize this function to lead to the best predictions from the model. You can see a comprehensive description of the choices for loss functions available with Keras at http://mng.bz/qNM6. The streetcar delay model predicts a binary choice (whether or not there will be a delay on a particular trip), so `binary_crossentropy` is the default choice for the `loss` function.

- *Output activation* is the function in the final layer of the model that generates the final output. The default setting for this value, `hard_sigmoid`, will generate output between `0` and `1`.

- *Batch size* is the number of records processed before the model is updated. You should not need to update this value.

- *Epochs* is the number of complete passes through the training sample. You can adjust this value, starting with a small value to get initial results and then increasing the value if you see better results with a larger number of epochs. Depending on how long it takes to run a single epoch, you may need to balance the additional model performance from more epochs against the time taken to run more epochs.

For the two parameters that define the loss function and the output activation function, *Deep Learning with Python* contains a useful section (http://mng.bz/7GX7) that goes into greater detail on the options for these parameters and the kinds of problems to which you would apply those options.

Summary

- The code that makes up a deep learning model can be deceptively anticlimactic, but it is the heart of a complete solution that has a raw dataset coming in one end and a deployed trained model coming out the other end.

- Before training a deep learning model with a structured dataset, we need to confirm that all the columns on which the model will be trained will be available at scoring time. If we train the model on data that we won't have when we want to make a prediction with the model, we risk getting overly optimistic training performance for the model and ending up with a model that cannot generate useful predictions.

- The Keras deep learning model needs to be trained on the data formatted as a list of numpy arrays, so the dataset needs to be transformed from a Pandas dataframe to a list of numpy arrays.

- TensorFlow and Keras began as separate but related projects. Beginning with TensorFlow 2.0, Keras has become the official high-level API for TensorFlow, and its recommended libraries are packaged as part of TensorFlow.

- The Keras functional API combines ease of use with flexibility and is the Keras API that we use for the streetcar delay prediction model.

- The layers of the streetcar delay prediction model are generated automatically based on the categories of the columns: continuous, categorical, and text.

- Embeddings are a powerful concept adapted from the world of natural language processing. With embeddings, you associate vectors with non-numeric values such as the values in categorical columns. The benefits of using embeddings include the ability to manipulate non-numeric values that are analogous to common numeric operations, the ability to get unsupervised learning-type categorization on values in a categorical range as a byproduct of solving a supervised learning problem, and the ability to avoid the drawbacks of one-hot encoding (the other common approach to assigning numeric values to non-numeric tokens).

- You can use a variety of approaches to explore your Keras deep learning model, including `model.summary()` (for a tabular view), `plot_model` (for a graphical view), and TensorBoard (for an interactive dashboard).

- You control the behavior of the Keras deep learning model and its training process through a set of parameters. For the streetcar delay prediction model, these parameters are defined in the streetcar_model_training_config.yml config file.

Training the model and running experiments

So far in this book, we have prepared the data and examined the code that makes up the model itself. Now we are finally ready to train the model. We'll review some of the basics, including selecting the training, test, and validation dataset. Then we'll go through an initial training run to validate that the code functions without errors and will cover the critical topic of monitoring your model's performance. Next, we'll show how to take advantage of the early stopping facility in Keras to get maximum benefit from your training runs. After that, we will go over how you can use your trained model to score a new record before you have the model fully deployed. Finally, we will run a series of experiments to improve the performance of the deep learning model.

6.1 Code for training the deep learning model

When you have cloned the GitHub repo (http://mng.bz/v95x) associated with this book, you'll find the code related to training the model in the notebooks subdirectory. The following listing shows the files that contain the code described in this chapter.

> **Listing 6.1 Code in the repo related to training the model**

```
                    Directory for pickled intermediate dataset dataframes
├── data  ◁────┘
│                   Directory for saving trained models
├── models  ◁──────────┘
│                                   Contains definitions of pipeline classes
├── notebooks                        ◁─────┐
│   │   custom_classes.py  ◁─────────────┘
│   │   streetcar_model_training.ipynb  ◁──────  Notebook containing dataset
│   └── streetcar_model_training_config.yml  ◁──  refactoring and model training code
│
└── pipelines  ◁────── Directory for saved pipelines
```

Config file for model training: definitions of hyperparameter values, train/validate/test proportions, and other configuration parameters

6.2 Reviewing the process of training a deep learning model

If you have already trained a classic machine learning model, the process for training a deep learning model will be familiar to you. A detailed review of training classic machine learning models is beyond the scope of this book, but Alexey Grigorev's *Machine Learning Bookcamp* (Manning Publications, 2021) has an excellent section on the model training process (http://mng.bz/Qxxm) that covers the topic in more detail.

When a deep learning model is trained, the weights associated with each node are updated iteratively until the loss function is minimized and the model's predictive performance is optimized. Note that by default, the weights are initialized randomly.

Let's consider the high-level steps you would take to train a machine learning model:

- *Define subsets of the dataset for training, validation, and testing.* In addition to the subset of the data used to train the model, reserve a distinct subset for validation (checking the performance of the training process in flight) and testing (checking the performance of the training process when it is complete). It is critical to maintain a subset of the data that was not used in training to check the performance of the model. Suppose that you used all your available data to train your model with no data reserved for testing. After you trained your model, how would you get an idea of its accuracy in making predictions on data it had never seen before? Without a validation dataset to track performance during training and a test dataset to assess performance when training is complete, you would not be able to get an idea of the performance of your model before deployment.

- *Do an initial run to validate the function.* This initial run will ensure that your model code is functionally correct and doesn't cause any immediate errors. The Keras deep learning model described in this book is simple. Even so, it took several iterations to get the model to complete its first run without errors and to clean up issues with how the final stage of the input data was defined and how the layers of the model were assembled. Getting your model to complete a small initial run, perhaps with only one epoch (one iteration through the training data), is a necessary step on the road to training the model.
- *Iterate through training runs.* Check performance and make adjustments (to hyperparameters, including the number of *epochs*, or iterations through the training data) to get the optimal performance for your model. When you have completed an initial run to validate that your model code can run without errors, you need to make repeated experiments to observe your model's behavior and see what you can adjust to improve performance. These iterative experiments (such as the experiments described in section 6.11) involve a certain amount of trial and error.

  When you start training a deep learning model, you may be tempted to start with long runs with many epochs (in the hope that the model will find its way to an optimal state if it's allowed to run long enough) or to change multiple hyperparameters (such as learning rate or batch size) at the same time in the hope that you will find the golden combination of hyperparameter settings that will boost the performance of your model. I strongly recommend starting slowly. Start with a small number of epochs (iterations through the entire training set) and with a subset of the training set so that you can get a decent number of training runs done quickly. Note that in the case of the streetcar delay prediction model, the training set is not huge, so we can train with the whole training set right from the start and still complete a modest run of 20 epochs in less than five minutes in a standard Paperspace Gradient environment.

  As the performance of your model improves, you can do longer runs with more epochs to observe whether additional iterations through the training data improve the performance of your model. I also strongly recommend that you adjust only one hyperparameter at a time.

- *Save the model from your optimal training run.* Section 6.9 describes how you can explicitly save trained models when you complete a training run. As you do longer training runs with more epochs, however, you will probably find that the model reaches its peak performance on an epoch that is not the last epoch. How can you ensure that you save the model on the epoch on which the model has optimal performance? Section 6.7 describes how to use the callback facility in Keras to save the model regularly during the training run and to stop training when the model's performance is no longer improving. With this facility, you can do a long training run and be confident that at the end of the run, you will have saved the model with the best performance, even if that optimal performance was achieved in the middle of the run.

- *Validate your trained model with the test set and score at least one new, single data point.* You want to get an early validation of the deployment process that you will create in chapter 8 by applying your trained model to a data point and examining the result. You can think of this early validation as being a dress rehearsal for your trained model. As a dress rehearsal is a way for the cast and crew of a performance to go through their paces before they need to face a live audience, applying a single data point to your trained model is a way to get a taste of how it will behave before you go through the effort of deployment.

  Section 6.8 describes how you can apply your model to the entire test set and also how you can get an early view of how your model will behave when it is deployed by exercising it on a new data point that is completely outside your original dataset. These two activities are related but have different goals. Applying your trained model to the test set gives you the best possible sense of its performance based on the dataset you have available because you are exercising the model with data that was not involved in the training process.

  By contrast, *one-off scoring*, or scoring on a net new data point not taken from your original dataset, forces you to exercise the trained model as it will be exercised when it is deployed, but without doing all the work required to complete model deployment. One-off scoring gives you a quick glimpse of your model's behavior when it is deployed and helps you anticipate and correct problems (such as a need for data that won't be available when scoring happens) before you deploy the model.

These steps are largely common between deep learning and classic machine learning. The key difference is the number of hyperparameters that need to be tracked and maintained for a deep learning model. Looking at the list of hyperparameters from chapter 5 (figure 6.1), which ones are unique to training deep learning models?

Parameter	Value	Purpose
learning_rate	Positive floating point value	Control Rate of weight changes
l2_lambda, dropout_rate	Positive floating point value	Control overfitting
loss_func	Loss function name	Specify function optimized in training
output_activation	Activation function name	Specify output
BATCH_SIZE	Positive integer	Control number of records processed per weights update
epochs	Positive integer	Control number of iterations through the dataset

Figure 6.1   List of hyperparameters

Of these hyperparameters, the following are specific to deep learning:

- `dropout_rate`—This parameter is related primarily to deep learning because it controls overfitting by turning off random subsets of the network. Other types of models employ dropout to control overfitting. XGBoost (Extreme Gradient Boosting; http://mng.bz/8GnZ) models can incorporate dropout (see parameters for Dart booster at https://xgboost.readthedocs.io/en/latest/parameter .html). But the dropout approach of controlling overfitting is more commonly applied to deep learning models.

- `Output_activation`—This parameter is specific to deep learning because it controls the function that is applied in the final layer of a deep learning model. This parameter is less a tuning parameter (controlling the performance of the model) than a functional parameter because it controls the functional behavior of the model. You can set the output activation function to have your model produce a binary outcome (such as the streetcar delay prediction model, which predicts yes/no on whether a particular streetcar trip will be delayed), a prediction of one of a set of outcomes, or a continuous value.

The other parameters are common to deep learning and at least some classic machine learning approaches. Note that in the training process for this model I adjusted the hyperparameters manually. That is, I ran repeated experiments adjusting one hyperparameter at a time until I got adequate results. This learning process was great because I was able to observe closely the effects of changes such as adjusting the learning rate. But tuning hyperparameters manually is not practical for business-critical models. Here are some great resources that show you how to take a more methodical approach to hyperparameter tuning:

- *Real World Machine Learning* by Henrik Brink, et al. (Manning Publications, 2016) includes a section that describes the basics of grid search (http://mng.bz/X00Y), an approach that searches the possible combinations of values for each hyperparameter and assesses the model performance for each combination to find an optimal combination.

- The article at http://mng.bz/yrrJ recommends an end-to-end approach to hyperparameter tuning for Keras models.

6.3 *Reviewing the overall goal of the streetcar delay prediction model*

Before we jump into the steps involved in training a model, let's review the overall purpose of the streetcar delay prediction model. We want to predict whether a given streetcar trip is going to encounter a delay. Note that for this model, we are not predicting the length of the delay, only whether there is going to be a delay. Here are the reasons for having the model predict a delay only instead of the length of the delay:

- Earlier experiments in getting a prediction of the length of the streetcar delay (that is, a *linear prediction*) from the model were not successful. I suspect that the dataset is too small to give the model a decent chance of picking up a signal this specific.

- From a user's perspective, the chance of a delay can be more significant than the duration of a delay. Any delay longer than five minutes makes it worthwhile to consider an alternative to a streetcar trip, such as walking, taking a taxi, or taking an alternative transit route. Thus, for simplicity, the binary prediction delay/no delay is more useful for the audience for this model than a linear prediction of the length of a delay.

Now that we have reviewed what the model will be predicting, let's look at a specific example of the user's experience. Assume that the user gets the model to predict whether the trip they want to take now, starting westbound on the Queen streetcar route, is going to be delayed. Let's examine the possible outcomes:

- *The model predicts no delay, and no delay happens.* With this outcome, the model's prediction matches what happens in real life. We call this result a *true negative* because the model predicts that the event (a delay on the westbound Queen streetcar) is not going to happen, and the event does not happen: there is no delay.

- *The model predicts no delay, but a delay happens.* With this outcome, the model's prediction does not match what happens in real life. This result is called a *false negative* because the model predicts that the event (a delay on the westbound Queen streetcar) is not going to happen, but the event does happen: the trip is delayed.

- *The model predicts a delay, but no delay happens.* With this outcome, the model's prediction does not match what happens in real life. This result is called a *false positive* because the model predicts that the event (a delay on the westbound Queen streetcar) is going to happen, but the event does not happen: there is no delay.

- *The model predicts a delay, and a delay happens.* With this outcome, the model's prediction matches what happens in real life. This result is called a *true positive* because the model predicts that the event (a delay on the westbound Queen streetcar) is going to happen, and the event does happen: the trip is delayed.

Figure 6.2 summarizes these four outcomes.

True negative:	**False positive:**
• Actual outcome: **no delay**	• Actual outcome: **no delay**
• Predicted outcome: **no delay**	• Predicted outcome: **delay**
False negative:	**True positive:**
• Actual outcome: **delay**	• Actual outcome: **delay**
• Predicted outcome: **no delay**	• Predicted outcome: **delay**

Figure 6.2 Four possible outcomes for streetcar delay predictions

Of the four possible outcomes, we want to get the highest possible proportion of true negatives and true positives. But as we go through the iterative process of training the model, we see a trade-off between the number of false negatives and the number of false positives. Consider experiment 1, described in section 6.10. In this experiment, we do not make any adjustments in the model to account for the training dataset being imbalanced. Delays are rare. Only around 2% of all route/direction/time-slot combinations in the training dataset have delays. If we don't account for this imbalance in the training dataset, the training process (which is optimized for accuracy in experiment 1) will generate weights for the model that result in the trained model's predicting "no delay" all the time. Such a model will have what looks like great accuracy: more than 97%. But this model would be useless for our user because it never predicts a delay. Although delays may be rare, users of the model need to know when delays are likely to happen so that they can make alternative travel arrangements.

Figure 6.3 shows the results of applying the model from experiment 1 to the test dataset: zero true positives and the maximum possible number of false negatives.

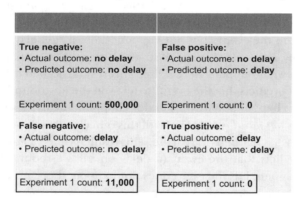

Figure 6.3   Outcomes of applying to test set to the trained model for experiment 1

As we go through the experiments in section 6.10, you will see that there can be a trade-off between false negatives and false positives. As we reduce the false negatives (the number of times the model predicts no delay when there is a delay), the false positives can increase (the number of times the model predicts a delay when there is no delay). Obviously, we want the model to have as low a proportion as possible of both false negatives and false positives, but if we have to make a trade-off between false negatives and false positives, what is the best result for our users? The worst outcome is that the model predicts no delay and then a delay occurs. In other words, the worst outcome for our users is a false negative. With a false positive, if a user takes the model's advice and walks or takes a taxi to avoid a streetcar delay that never happens, they still have a decent chance of arriving at their destination on time. With a false negative, however, if the user follows the model's advice and takes the streetcar, they miss the opportunity to take an alternative form of transit and risk arriving at their destination late.

As you will see in section 6.6, we direct the model training toward our overall goal by monitoring two measurements:

- *Recall*—true positive/(true positive + false negative)
- *Validation accuracy*—The proportion of predictions that the model gets right on the validation dataset

Now that we have reviewed the overall goal of the training process for the streetcar delay prediction model and established which outcomes are most important for the user, let's return to the steps for model training, starting with selecting the subsets of the dataset for training, validation, and testing.

6.4 Selecting the train, validation, and test datasets

The original dataset that we were working with had fewer than 100,000 records. With the refactoring we described in chapter 5, we now have a dataset with more than 2 million records. As described in section 6.2, we need to divide the dataset into the following subsets so we have records from the dataset that we can use to assess the performance of the model:

- *Train*—Subset of the dataset that is used to train the model
- *Validate*—Subset of the dataset that is used to track the performance of the model while it is being trained
- *Test*—Subset of the dataset that is not used during the training itself. The trained model is applied to the test set as a final validation with data the model has never seen.

What proportion of the dataset should we allocate to each of these subsets? I chose a ratio of 60% of the dataset for training and 20% each for validation and testing. This proportion strikes a balance between having a big-enough training set to give the model a decent chance to extract a signal and get decent performance during training with the need to have big-enough validation and test sets to exercise the model on data it did not see during the training process. A ratio of 70/15/15 would have been a reasonable choice as well. For a dataset that is less than millions of records, the proportion of validate and test should not drop below 10% each to ensure that there is a sufficient portion of the dataset to track performance during training iterations (the validation set), as well as a sufficient holdout (the test set) to apply to the trained model to ensure adequate performance on data it has never seen.

6.5 Initial training run

Before making changes to optimize the training runs, we want to do an initial run to ensure that everything works functionally. In this initial run, we are not trying to get great accuracy or minimize false negatives. We will focus on the performance of the model in later runs. For this initial training run, we simply want to confirm that the code works functionally—executes from end to end without generating errors.

For your initial run of the model, you can follow along by using the streetcar_model _training notebook with the default settings in the streetcar model training config file to specify the hyperparameter values and other config settings for the run. The next listing shows the key values in the config file.

Listing 6.2 Key parameters defined in the config file

```
test_parms:
    testproportion: 0.2        <--| The proportion of the dataset
    trainproportion: 0.8          reserved for the test dataset
    current_experiment: 0      <--
hyperparameters:                   The experiment number determines a set of other
    learning_rate: 0.001           parameters, including the number of epochs in the
    dropout_rate: 0.0003           training run and whether early stopping is used.
    l2_lambda: 0.0003
    loss_func: "binary_crossentropy"
    output_activation: "hard_sigmoid"
    batch_size: 1000
    epochs: 50
```

The following listing shows the settings for experiment 0, the initial training run.

Listing 6.3 Settings for experiment 0

Experiment 0 has no early stopping.

```
early_stop = False         Experiment 0 makes no allowance
one_weight = 1.0    <--|    for the dataset's being imbalanced.
epochs = 1          <--
                           Experiment 0 includes a single iteration
                           through the training dataset: 1 epoch.
```

The next listing is the code block that triggers the training of the model.

Listing 6.4 Code that triggers the training of the model

Call the function that builds the model, as described in chapter 5.

Because early_stop is set to False in experiment 0, this fit statement gets invoked.

```
model = get_model()
if early_stop:
modelfit = model.fit(X_train_list, dtrain.target, epochs=epochs, \
    batch_size=batch_size, validation_data=(X_valid_list, \
dvalid.target), class_weight = {0 : zero_weight, 1: one_weight}, \
verbose=1,callbacks=callback_list)
else:
    modelfit = model.fit(X_train_list, dtrain.target, epochs=epochs, \
batch_size=batch_size, validation_data=(X_valid_list, dvalid.target), \
class_weight = {0 : zero_weight, 1: one_weight}, verbose=1)    <--
```

Let's take a closer look at the statement that fits the model, shown in figure 6.4.

Figure 6.4   Key elements of the `fit` statement

- The training set and labels (`target`) for training are identified.
- The validation set and label (`target`) for validation are also identified.
- Because the dataset is skewed (there are many more route/direction/time slots with no delays than there are slots with delays), we use the Keras facility to apply weights to the output classes to account for this imbalance. Note that the use of `weight` here is purely to compensate for the imbalance in the input dataset. It is not related to the weights that are set in the training process as described in chapter 1.

As the `fit` command executes, you will see output like that shown in figure 6.5.

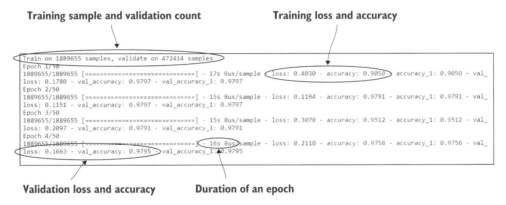

Figure 6.5   Output of the `fit` command

The output begins with a recap of the number of samples available to train and validate the model. Following is a line per epoch (iteration through the training dataset) that shows a variety of measurements. We will focus on these measurements:

- *Loss*—Aggregate delta between the predictions and the actual target values for the training set
- *Accuracy* (`acc`)—Proportion of predictions in this epoch that match the actual target values for the training set

- *Validation loss* (`val_loss`)—Aggregate delta between the predictions and the actual target values for the validation set
- *Validation accuracy* (`val_accuracy`)—Proportion of predictions in this epoch that match the actual target values for the validation set

When the `fit` command has completed, you have a trained model. Values have been assigned to the trainable parameters, and you have a model you can use to score new values:

```
Total params: 1,341
Trainable params: 1,201
Non-trainable params: 140
```

6.6   *Measuring the performance of your model*

The output produced as the training run executes gives you an initial picture of the performance of your model. When the training run is complete, you have two easy ways to examine the performance of the model.

One way to examine the performance of the model is to plot training and validation loss and accuracy. The chart in figure 6.6 shows training and validation accuracy for a 30-epoch training run.

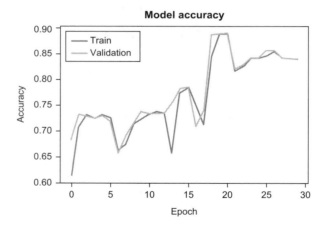

Figure 6.6   Training and validation accuracy graph

The next listing shows the code that generates accuracy and loss graphs.

Listing 6.5   Code to generate the accuracy and loss graphs

Specify the title of the chart.

```
#   acc
plt.plot(modelfit.history['accuracy'])
plt.plot(modelfit.history['val_accuracy'])
plt.title('model accuracy')
plt.ylabel('accuracy')
```

Specify that the chart is tracking accuracy and val_accuracy

Specify the y-axis label.

```
plt.xlabel('epoch')
plt.legend(['train', 'validation'], loc='upper left')
plt.show()
```

Specify the x-axis label.

Specify the labels in the legend.

Display the chart.

Recall the table from section 6.3 that showed the four possible outcomes of a prediction, as shown in figure 6.7.

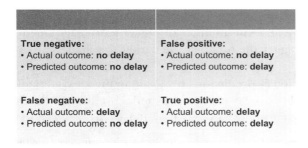

True negative:
• Actual outcome: **no delay**
• Predicted outcome: **no delay**

False positive:
• Actual outcome: **no delay**
• Predicted outcome: **delay**

False negative:
• Actual outcome: **delay**
• Predicted outcome: **no delay**

True positive:
• Actual outcome: **delay**
• Predicted outcome: **delay**

Figure 6.7   The four possible outcomes of the streetcar delay prediction model

The other way to examine the performance of the model is the *confusion matrix,* shown in figure 6.8. The `sklearn.metrics` library includes a feature that lets you generate a table like this one, showing the count of true negative, false positive, false negative, and true positive outcomes for a run of your trained model.

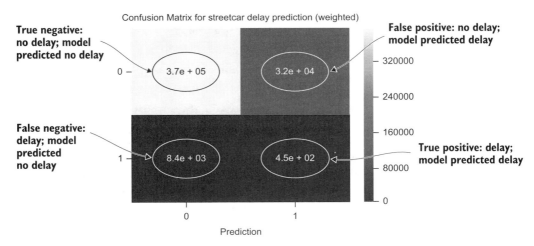

Figure 6.8   Confusion matrix

The confusion matrix has four quadrants:

- *Top left*—There was no delay for this route/direction/time slot, and the model predicted no delay.
- *Bottom left*—There was a delay for this route/direction/time slot, but the model predicted no delay.

- *Top right*—There was no delay for this route/direction/time slot, but the model predicted a delay.
- *Bottom right*—There was a delay for this route/direction/time slot, and the model predicted a delay.

The confusion matrix takes a bit of interpreting:

- The outcome counts in each quadrant are in scientific notation, so there are 370,000 (= 3.7E+05) true negatives.
- The shades indicate the absolute number of outcomes in each quadrant. The lighter the shade, the bigger the number; the darker the shade, the smaller the number.
- The quadrants are labeled as predictions (0/1) along the x axis to indicate that the model did not predict a delay (0) and the model predicted a delay (1).
- The y axis indicates what actually happened: no delay (0) and delay (1).

Despite its drawbacks in terms of visual appeal, the confusion matrix is a useful tool for comparing the results of training runs because it packs a lot of information into one easy-to-generate package.

The following listing shows the code that generates the confusion matrix.

Listing 6.6   Code to generate the confusion matrix

```
cfmap=metrics.confusion_matrix(y_true=test['target'], \
                      y_pred=test["predround"])          ◁——┐ Specify the actual
                                                            │ (y_true) and
label = ["0", "1"]                                          │ prediction (y_pred)
sns.heatmap(cfmap, annot = True, xticklabels = label, \    │ outcomes.
yticklabels = label)
plt.xlabel("Prediction")
plt.title("Confusion Matrix for streetcar delay prediction (weighted)")
plt.show()        ◁——┐
                     │ Show the graph.
```

We will use two measurements in particular to study the performance of the streetcar delay prediction model in several training iterations: validation accuracy and recall. *Validation accuracy* (the proportion of correct predictions on the validation dataset) will give us an indication of the overall accuracy of the model on new data, but it won't tell the whole story. As mentioned in section 6.3, we want to minimize the number of false negatives (the model predicts no delay when there is a delay). That is, we don't want the model to miss predicting delays when a delay is going to happen. To monitor for this outcome, we can track recall:

```
true positive / (true positive + false negative)
```

Let's consider what recall means in terms of the table of outcomes we introduced in section 6.3, using the labels shown in figure 6.9.

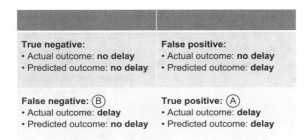

True negative:	False positive:
• Actual outcome: **no delay**	• Actual outcome: **no delay**
• Predicted outcome: **no delay**	• Predicted outcome: **delay**
False negative: (B)	True positive: (A)
• Actual outcome: **delay**	• Actual outcome: **delay**
• Predicted outcome: **no delay**	• Predicted outcome: **delay**

Figure 6.9   Recall = A / (A + B)

Recall is important because it allows us to track the key outcome that we want to avoid: predicting no delay when a delay occurs. By monitoring validation accuracy and recall together, we get a balanced picture of the performance of the model.

6.7   *Keras callbacks: Getting the best out of your training runs*

By default, when you call the `fit` statement to kick off a training run for a Keras model, the training run keeps going for the number of epochs you specify in the `fit` statement, and you will be able to save the weights (a trained model) only after the last epoch has run. With its default behavior, you can think of a Keras training run as being a factory that produces pies on a conveyor belt. With each epoch, a pie (trained model) is baked. Our goal is to get the biggest pie (the optimally trained model), and if the factory has stopped baking bigger pies, we want to shut down the factory rather than waste ingredients making small pies. That is, we don't want to run a bunch of epochs if the model is not improving.

The pie factory bakes a series of pies of different sizes (representing models with different performance characteristics), as shown in figure 6.10.

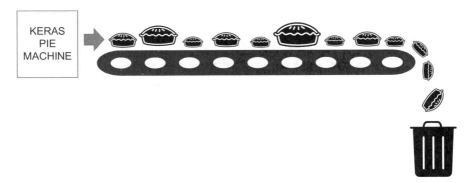

Figure 6.10   A default Keras training run

The problem is that with the default Keras training run behavior, the pie factory keeps baking pies even if it starts to bake smaller pies (the model performance is no longer improving), and the pie that gets saved (the trained model you have available to save at the end of the training run) is the last one, even if it isn't the biggest pie. The result is that the pie factory can end up being wasteful by baking a lot of pies that aren't getting bigger, and the pie that you get at the end can be a small one, as shown in figure 6.11.

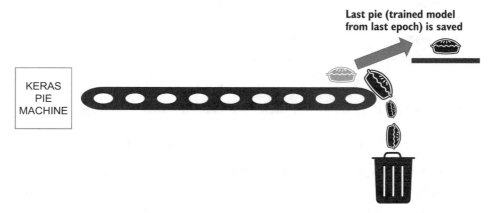

Figure 6.11   After a default training run, you can save only the final model, even if it's not the best model.

Fortunately, Keras provides callback facilities that give you the opportunity to do much more effective training. In the terms of the pie factory, callbacks let you do two things:

- Save the biggest pie (the optimal trained model), even if it's not the last pie, as shown in figure 6.12.

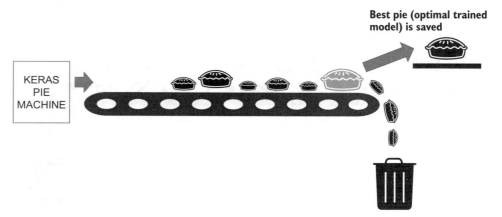

Figure 6.12   Save the biggest pie.

- Stop the pie factory automatically if it is no longer baking bigger pies (generating models with better performance) so you are not wasting resources baking small pies, as shown in figure 6.13.

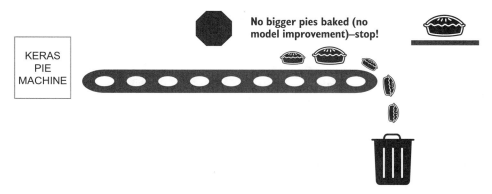

Figure 6.13 Stop the pie factory early if it stops baking bigger pies.

Let's examine how Keras callbacks work for real. Keras callbacks give you the power to control how long your training run goes and stop the training run when it is no longer improving. Keras callbacks also allow you to save models to a file after every epoch in which a given criterion (such as validation accuracy) hits a local maximum. By combining these facilities (early stopping and saving the model that gets the optimal measurement for your key criteria), you can meet the two goals of controlling how long your training runs goes and stopping the training run when it stops improving.

To use early stopping, we first have to define a callback (https://keras.io/callbacks). A *callback* consists of a set of functions that can be applied during the training run to give you insight into the training process. Callbacks allow us to interact with the training process while it is in motion. We can use callbacks to monitor a performance measure epoch by epoch during a training run and take actions based on what happens with this performance measure. We can track validation accuracy, for example, and allow the run to continue as long as validation accuracy continues to increase. When validation accuracy drops, we can get the callback to stop the training run. We can use the `patience` option to delay stopping the training run so that it continues for a given number of epochs when validation accuracy is no longer increasing. This option allows us to avoid missing increases in validation accuracy that occur after a temporary drop or plateau.

The control we get from an early-stopping callback is a big improvement over letting the training run go for the full set of epochs. But what happens if the best result for the performance measure we care about occurs for an epoch other than the last epoch? If we simply save the final model, we could be missing better performance that occurred in an interim epoch. We can address this situation by using another callback that allows us to keep saving through the training run the model that has the best result for the performance measure we are tracking. Using this callback in concert with the early-stopping callback, we know that the last model saved during the training run will have the best performance measure result of all the epochs in the run.

Figure 6.14 shows the snippets of code in the streetcar_model_training notebook where the callbacks are defined.

The performance measure the callback will track: validation loss

```
es_monitor = "val_loss"
es_mode = "min"
```

The objective (mode) of the callback: minimize validation loss

```
patience_threshold = 15
```

Threshold of epochs to keep going once there is no further improvement

**Early stopping callback to minimize validation loss, waiting
15 epochs after no improvement before stopping**

```
def set_early_stop(es_monitor, es_mode):
    es = EarlyStopping(monitor=es_monitor, mode=es_mode, verbose=1,patience = patience_threshold)
    save_model_path = path+'models/'+'scmodel'+modifier+"_"+str(experiment_number)+'.h5'
    mc = ModelCheckpoint (save_model_path, monitor=es_monitor, mode=es_mode, verbose=1, save_best_only=True)
    return(es,mc,save_model_path)
```

Callback to save the model every time validation loss hits a new minimum

Figure 6.14   Defining callbacks to track a performance measure and save the model with the best performance

Now let's look at an example to see the effect of callbacks on a training run. We are going to look at a 20-epoch run, first with no callbacks in place and then when callbacks have been applied. The next listing shows the parameters we need to set before doing this run.

Listing 6.7   Parameters to set to control early stopping and dataset balancing

```
early_stop = False                        ◁──────  Specify no callbacks.
one_weight = (count_no_delay/count_delay) + one_weight_offset      ◁────┐
```
**Take into account the imbalance in the dataset between
records with delays and records with no delays.**

To start, figure 6.15 is the accuracy graph for this 20-epoch run without an early-stopping callback in place.

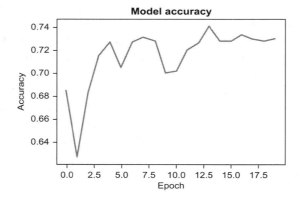

**Figure 6.15   Accuracy graph for a
run of 20 epochs with no callbacks**

After this 20-epoch run, the final `val_accuracy` has a value of `0.73`:

```
val_accuracy: 0.7300
```

Figure 6.16 shows that the `val_accuracy` produced by the final epoch is not the maximum for the training run.

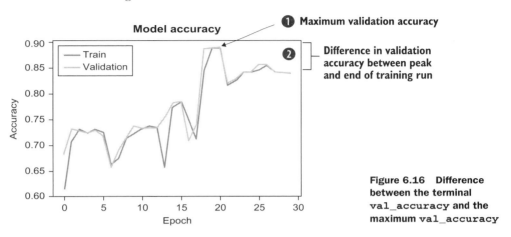

Figure 6.16   Difference between the terminal `val_accuracy` and the maximum `val_accuracy`

Let's see what happens when we add early stopping to this run, using the code shown in the next listing to stop the run when validation accuracy stops increasing.

Listing 6.8   Code to set callbacks

Function to define Keras callbacks. Parameters are es_monitor (the measurement to track in the mc callback) and es_mode (the extreme min or max to track in the es early-stopping callback).

List to contain all the callbacks defined in this function

```
def set_early_stop(es_monitor, es_mode):
    callback_list = []
    es = EarlyStopping(monitor=es_monitor, mode=es_mode, \
        verbose=1,patience = patience_threshold)
    callback_list.append(es)
    model_path = get_model_path()
    save_model_path = os.path.join(model_path, \
        'scmodel'+modifier+"_"+str(experiment_number)+'.h5')
    mc = ModelCheckpoint(save_model_path, monitor=es_monitor, \
        mode=es_mode, verbose=1, save_best_only=True)
    callback_list.append(mc)
    if tensorboard_callback:
        tensorboard_log_dir =
os.path.join(get_path(), \
"tensorboard_log",datetime.now().strftime("%Y%m%d-%H%M%S"))
        tensorboard = TensorBoard(log_dir= tensorboard_log_dir)
        callback_list.append(tensorboard)
    return(callback_list,save_model_path)
```

Define es callback for early stopping based on es_monitor measurement no longer moving in the direction indicated by es_mode, and add it to the list of callbacks

Define mc callback for saving the best mode based on es_monitor measurement getting to the best value defined by es_mode

Define path to save the model during the training process when the measurement es_monitor reaches a new optimal value

If required, define TensorBoard callback. See chapter 5 for details on defining the TensorBoard callback.

```
if early_stop:
    modelfit = model.fit(X_train_list, dtrain.target, epochs=epochs, \
    batch_size=batch_size, validation_data=(X_valid_list, dvalid.target), \
    class_weight = {0 : zero_weight, 1: one_weight}, \
    verbose=1,callbacks=callback_list)
```

If early_stop is set to true, the fit command is called with the callbacks parameter set to the list of callbacks returned by the set_early_stop() function.

To get an early-stopping callback, we set the parameters in the next listing.

Listing 6.9   Parameters to set for an early-stopping callback

Specify that callbacks get included in the invocation of the fit statement.

Specify that val_accuracy is the measurement for controlling the callbacks.

```
early_stop = True
    es_monitor="val_accuracy"
    es_mode = "max"
```

Specify that the max of val_accuracy is tracked by the callbacks.

With these parameters set, we rerun the experiment, and this time, the callbacks are invoked during the training process. You can see the result in figure 6.17.

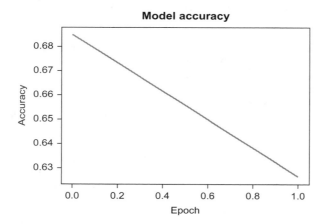

Figure 6.17   Accuracy with an early-stopping callback in place

Instead of running for the full 20 epochs, the training run stops after 2 epochs because the validation accuracy has dropped. This result isn't exactly what we want; we would like to give the model a chance to get better, and we certainly don't want to stop training as soon as accuracy has dropped. To get a better result, we can set the `patience_threshold` parameter to a value other than the default 0 in the model training config file:

```
patience_threshold: 4
```

What happens if we rerun the same training exercise with the `patience_threshold` parameter added to the early-stopping callback? The run stops after 12 epochs instead of 2 and takes three minutes to complete. The terminal validation accuracy is 0.73164, as shown in figure 6.18.

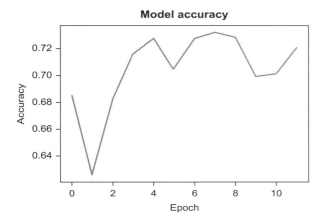

Figure 6.18 Accuracy with a patient early stop

The results of these changes (adding callbacks and setting a nonzero value for the `patience_threshold` parameter) are better validation accuracy with fewer epochs and less time required to complete the training. Figure 6.19 summarizes the results for this set of experiments.

Experiment	Epochs run	Terminal validation accuracy	Run time
No callbacks	20	0.73	6 minutes
Callbacks with patience_threshold = 0	2	0.6264	54 seconds
Callback with patience_threshold = 4	12	0.73164	3 minutes

Figure 6.19 Summary of callback experiments

These experiments show that the callback facility in Keras is a powerful way of making your training runs more efficient by avoiding repeated epochs that aren't providing benefit for your key measurements. The callback facility also allows you to save the model iteration that gives you the optimal value for your key measurement, regardless of where this iteration occurs in your training run. By adjusting the patience parameter, you can balance the cost of running more epochs with the potential benefit of getting better performance after a temporary dip.

6.8   *Getting identical results from multiple training runs*

You may be asking how it was possible for the experiments shown in section 6.7 to get consistent results between training runs. By default, aspects of the training process, including the initial weights assigned to nodes in the network, are set randomly. You will see this effect if you run repeated experiments with the deep learning model with identical inputs and parameter settings; you will get different results (such as validation accuracy per epoch) each time, even if the inputs are identical. If there is an intentional element of randomness in training a deep learning model, how can we control this element so that we can do repeated, controlled experiments to assess the effect of a specific change, such as the callbacks introduced in the example in section 6.7? The key is setting a fixed seed for the random number generator. The random number generator provides the random inputs for the training process (such as initial weights for the model) that result in different results between training runs. When you want to have identical results from multiple training runs, you can explicitly set the seed for the random number generator.

If you look at the config file for the model training notebook, you see a parameter called `repeatable_run` in the `test_parms` section (see the next listing).

> **Listing 6.10 Parameters to control test execution**

```
test_parms:
    testproportion: 0.2 # proportion of data reserved for test set
    trainproportion: 0.8 # proportion of non-test data dedicated \
to training (vs. validation)
    current_experiment: 9
    repeatable_run: True      ◄───┤ Parameter to control whether we want a repeatable
                                    experiment. Do we want to seed the random number
                                    generator with a fixed value to get consistent results
                                    for multiple runs?
```

The model training notebook uses the `repeatable_run` parameter to determine whether to explicitly set the seed for the random number generator and, thus, generate identical results from multiple training runs:

```
if repeatable_run:
    from numpy.random import seed
    seed(1)
    tf.random.set_seed(2)
```

In this section, we've summarized how you can get the same results from multiple training runs. For more details on getting repeatable results with Keras, check out the great article at http://mng.bz/Moo2.

6.9 *Shortcuts to scoring*

When we have a trained model, we want to be able to exercise it. Let's quickly review the high-level steps:

1 *Train the model.* Use the process described in this chapter, in which the weights in the model are iteratively set by the model repeatedly going through the training data set with the goal of minimizing the loss function. In our case, the loss function measures the delta between the predictions that the model makes for delay/no delay and the actual delay/no delay outcome that occurred for each route/direction/time-slot combination in the training dataset.

2 *Score with the model (one-off scoring).* Get the trained model's predictions for new data points: delay/no delay for route/direction/time-slot combinations that the model never saw during the training process. These new datapoints can be from the test subset of the original dataset or net new datapoints.

3 *Deploy the model.* Make the trained model available to provide efficient predictions on net new datapoints. In addition to describing deployment, chapter 8 describes the difference between deployment and one-off scoring.

As you will see in chapter 8, it can take several steps to get the model deployed. Before going through the full deployment process, you want to be able to do some scoring with the model to validate its performance on data that the model did not see during the training process. This section describes shortcuts to scoring that you can take advantage of before full-blown model deployment.

To exercise the model on the entire test set, you can call `predict` on the model with the test set as the input:

```
preds = saved_model.predict(X_test, batch_size=BATCH_SIZE)
```

What if you want to exercise a single new test example? This is the typical use case of the deployed model: a client using the model to determine whether a streetcar trip they want to take is predicted to be delayed.

To score a single datapoint, we first need to examine the structure of the input to the model. What is the structure of `X_test`?

```
print("X_test ", X_test)
X_test  {'hour': array([18,  4, 11, ...,  2, 23, 17]),
'Route': array([ 0, 12,  2, ..., 10, 12,  2]),
'daym': array([21, 16, 10, ..., 12, 26,  6]),
'month': array([0, 1, 0, ..., 6, 2, 1]),
'year': array([5, 2, 3, ..., 1, 4, 3]),
'Direction': array([1, 1, 4, ..., 2, 3, 0]),
'day': array([1, 2, 2, ..., 0, 1, 1])}
```

`X_test` is a dictionary in which each value is a numpy array. If we want to score a single new data point, we can create a dictionary that contains a single entry numpy array for each key in the dictionary:

```
score_sample = {}
score_sample['hour'] = np.array([18])
score_sample['Route'] = np.array([0])
score_sample['daym'] = np.array([21])
score_sample['month'] = np.array([0])
score_sample['year'] = np.array([5])
score_sample['Direction'] = np.array([1])
score_sample['day'] = np.array([1])
```

Now that we have defined a single data point, we can use the trained model to get a prediction for this data point:

```
preds = loaded_model.predict(score_sample, batch_size=BATCH_SIZE)
print("pred is ",preds)
print("preds[0] is ",preds[0])
print("preds[0][0] is ",preds[0][0])
```

For one of the models we've trained, we get the following output:

```
pred is  [[0.35744822]]
preds[0] is  [0.35744822]
preds[0][0] is  0.35744822
```

So for this single data point, the model does not predict a delay. This ability to score a single data point is a good way to validate the model quickly, particularly if you have prepared data points that represent a trip that you consider unlikely to be delayed, as well as data points that represent a trip that you believe will be delayed. By getting the trained model to score these two datapoints, you get validation of whether the trained model makes the predictions that you expect.

Figure 6.20 shows two example trips that could be scored to exercise the trained model. We would expect Trip A (on a less-busy route late on a weekend) to not be delayed, and we would expect Trip B (during rush hour on a busy route) to have a high likelihood of being delayed.

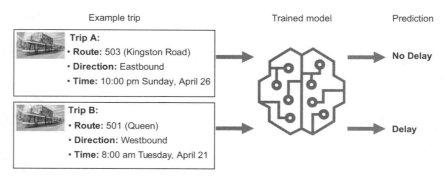

Figure 6.20   Exercising the model by scoring individual trips

6.10 *Explicitly saving trained models*

Like a Pandas dataframe, a trained model exists only for the life of your Python session unless you save it. You need to be able to serialize and save your trained model so that you can load it again later to experiment with it and, ultimately, deploy it so you can conveniently score new data by using your trained model. The model is saved as part of the callbacks if you set the `early_stopping` parameter. If not, the code block in the next listing saves the model.

Listing 6.11   Code to save the model if early stopping is not used

```
if early_stop == False:          ◄────────────┐  Check whether the model has
    model_json = model.to_json()              │  already been saved via callbacks.
    model_path = get_model_path()
    with open(os.path.join(model_path,'model'+modifier+'.json'), \
    ➥ "w") as json_file:
        json_file.write(model_json)          ◄──────┐ Save the model
    model.save_weights(os.path.join(model_path, \    │ to a JSON file.
    ➥ 'scweights'+modifier+'.h5'))
    save_model_path = os.path.join(model_path, \
    ➥ 'scmodel'+modifier+'.h5')              ◄──────┐ Save the weights of the
    model.save(save_model_path,save_format='h5')     │ trained model to an h5 file.
    saved_model = model
```

Save the model and weights to an h5 file.

You can exercise loading a model that you have saved to an h5 file (see the next listing).

Listing 6.12   Code to load a model from an h5 file

```
from keras.models import load_model                  Load your saved model by
loaded_model = load_model(os.path.join(model_path, \ using the same path you
'scmodel'+modifier+'.h5'))          ◄─────────────── used to save the model.
```

Now that you have loaded your saved model, you can apply it to get predictions on the test set:

```
preds = loaded_model.predict(X_test, batch_size=BATCH_SIZE)
```

6.11 *Running a series of training experiments*

Now let's pull everything together by running a series of experiments that build on what we've learned so far in this chapter. You can run these experiments yourself by changing the `current_experiment` parameter in the model training config file (listing 6.13), as shown in the next listing.

Listing 6.13   Parameters to control test execution

```
test_parms:
    testproportion: 0.2 # proportion of data reserved for test set
    trainproportion: 0.8 # proportion of non-test data \
dedicated to training (vs. validation)
    current_experiment: 5          ◄──────────  Set the experiment number.
```

```
    repeatable_run: True # switch to control whether \
runs are repeated identically
    get_test_train_acc: False # switch to control whether \
block to get test and train accuracy is after training)
```

The `current_experiment` parameter in turn is used to set the parameters for the experiment in the call to the `set_experiment_parameters` function:

```
experiment_number = current_experiment
early_stop, one_weight, epochs,es_monitor,es_mode = set_experiment_parameters
➥ (experiment_number, count_no_delay, count_delay)
```

Figure 6.21 summarizes the parameter settings for these experiments along with the key results: validation accuracy, number of false negatives, and recall on the test set.

Experiment	Epochs	Early stop enabled?	Weight for "1" (delay) values	Early stop controls		Terminal validation accuracy	False negatives exercising model on test set	Recall on test set: true positive/(true positive + false negative)
				Monitor	Mode			
1	10	no	1.0	NA	NA	0.98	11,000	0
2	50	no	1.0	NA	NA	0.75	7,700	0.31
3	50	no	No delay/ delay	NA	NA	0.8	4,600	0.59
4	50	yes	No delay/ delay	Validation loss	Min	0.69	2,600	0.76
5	50	yes	No delay/ delay	Validation accuracy	Max	0.72	2,300	0.79

Figure 6.21 Summary of the results of a set of experiments training the model

These experiments layer in various techniques, from adding additional epochs to weighting the less common outcome (delay) to early stopping. These experiments are defined by values set for a series of parameters, as shown in the following listing.

Listing 6.14 Parameters that control numbered experiments

```
    if experiment_number == 1:
        #
        early_stop = False
        #
        one_weight = 1.0
        #
        epochs = 10
    elif experiment_number == 2:
        #
        early_stop = False
        #
        one_weight = 1.0
        #
        epochs = 50
```

```
elif experiment_number == 3:
    #
    early_stop = False
    #
    one_weight = (count_no_delay/count_delay) + one_weight_offset
    #
    epochs = 50
elif experiment_number == 4:
    #
    early_stop = True
    es_monitor = "val_loss"
    es_mode = "min"
    #
    one_weight = (count_no_delay/count_delay) + one_weight_offset
    #
    epochs = 50
elif experiment_number == 5:
    #
    early_stop = True
    es_monitor = "val_accuracy"
    es_mode = "max"
    #
    one_weight = (count_no_delay/count_delay) + one_weight_offset
    #
    epochs = 50
```

In these experiments, we will adjust the number of epochs, the weighting of delay outcomes, and early-stopping callbacks. For each experiment, we will track the following performance measures:

- *Terminal validation accuracy*—The validation accuracy for the last epoch of the run
- *Total number of false negatives*—The number of times the model predicts no delay when there is a delay
- *Recall*—True positives / (true positives + false negatives)

As we make changes in the parameters for the experiments, the performance measures improve. This set of experiments is useful for a problem as simple as the streetcar delay problem, but it is not representative of how much experimentation may be needed in real-world deep learning problems. In an industrial-strength model training situation, you would expect to include a larger variety of experiments that vary the values of a larger number of parameters (such as the learning rate, dropout, and regularization parameters described in chapter 5). It's also possible that you may adjust the number and kind of layers in the model if you don't get the required performance measures from your original model.

When you are beginning with deep learning, it can be tempting to make these kinds of changes in the architecture of the model if you are not seeing adequate performance with your original architecture. I advise you to begin by focusing on understanding the performance characteristics of your original model, starting with test runs with a small number of epochs, methodically adjusting parameters one at a time, and measuring a consistent performance measure (such as validation accuracy or validation loss) throughout the runs. Then, if you exhaust performance improvements for your original architecture and still haven't met your performance goals, consider changing the architecture of the model.

Let's go through each of the five training experiments we defined earlier in this section. Starting with experiment 1, we run for a small number of epochs, don't account for the imbalance in the training data between delays and nondelays, and don't employ callbacks. The accuracy result looks good, but the confusion matrix shown in figure 6.22 reveals what's happening: the model is always predicting no delay.

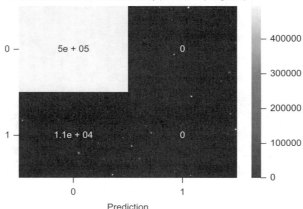

Figure 6.22   Confusion matrix for experiment 1

This model will not be useful for the application to which we want to apply this model because it will never predict a delay. Figure 6.23 shows what happens in experiment 2 when we have five times as many epochs.

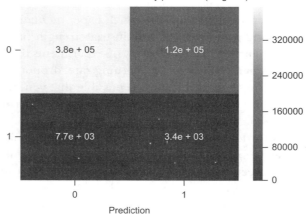

Figure 6.23   Confusion matrix for experiment 2

With more epochs, the model is predicting some delays, but there are twice as many false negatives as true positives, so this model is not meeting the goal of minimizing false negatives.

In experiment 3, we account for the imbalance in the dataset between delays and nondelays by weighting the delays (figure 6.24).

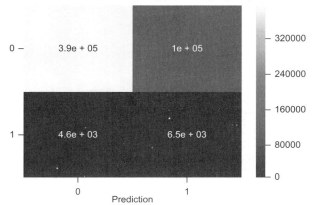

Figure 6.24 Confusion matrix for experiment 3

With this change, we see more true positives than false negatives, so it's a move in the right direction for recall, but we can do better.

In experiment 4, we add callbacks. The training process will be monitored for validation loss: the cumulative difference between the predictions and the actual values for the validation set. The training runs will stop if the validation loss does not decrease for a given number of epochs. Also, the model for the epoch that has the lowest validation loss will be the one saved when the training run ends. Again, with this change the ratio of true positives to false negatives (as indicated in recall) increases, as shown in figure 6.25, but we can still do better.

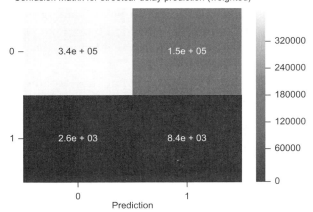

Figure 6.25 Confusion matrix for experiment 4

In experiment 5, we also have callbacks, but instead of monitoring validation loss, we monitor validation accuracy. We stop training if the accuracy does not improve for a given number of epochs. We save the model that has the maximum value for this measurement by the end of the training run. Figure 6.26 shows the confusion matrix for this run.

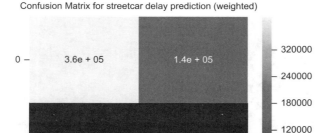

Confusion Matrix for streetcar delay prediction (weighted)

Figure 6.26   Confusion matrix for experiment 5

The ratio of true positives to false negatives (as reflected in recall) is even better in experiment 5, and the validation accuracy is also slightly better.

Note that you may get different results when you run these experiments yourself with the same input. But you should see the same general trend as you layer in the changes shown in these five experiments. Also note that you can take additional steps to get better results: higher accuracy and a better ratio of true positives to false negatives. We will examine some of these steps in chapter 7.

Summary
- Training a deep learning model is an iterative process. By tracking the right performance measurements during and at the conclusion of training runs, you will be able to methodically adjust parameters involved in the training process, see the effect of the changes, and progress toward a trained model that meets your goals for the training process.
- Before starting the training process, you need to define subsets of the dataset for training, validation (tracking the performance of the model during the training process), and testing (assessing the performance of the trained model).
- For your initial training run, pick a simple, single-epoch run to validate that everything is working correctly and you don't have any functional problems. When you have successfully completed this initial run, you can progress to more complex training runs to improve the performance of the model.

- Keras provides a set of measurements that you can use to assess the performance of your model. Which one you pick depends on how your trained model is going to be used. For the streetcar delay prediction model, we assess performance by validation accuracy (how well the trained model's predictions on the validation set match the actual delay/no delay values for the validation set) and recall (how well the model avoids predicting no delay when a delay occurred).

- By default, a Keras training run goes through all the specified epochs, and the trained model you get is whatever was produced in the final epoch. If you want the training process to be efficient by avoiding extraneous epochs and ensuring that you save the best model, you need to take advantage of callbacks. With callbacks, you can stop the training process when the performance measurements you care about stop improving and can ensure that the best model from your training run gets saved.

- When you have a trained model, it's a good idea to experiment with scoring a few data points with it. In the case of the streetcar delay prediction model, you would score some time/route/direction combinations with your trained model. Doing this gives you a way to validate the overall behavior of the trained model before investing effort in the full-blown deployment of the model.

7

More experiments with the trained model

This chapter covers

- Validating whether removing bad values improves the model performance
- Validating whether embeddings for the categorical columns improve the model performance
- Possible approaches to improving the performance of the model
- Comparing the performance of the deep learning model with a non-deep-learning model

In chapter 6, we trained the deep learning model and did a series of experiments to measure and improve its performance. In this chapter, we will go through a set of additional experiments to validate two key aspects of the model: removing bad values (a step that we took as part of the data preparation described in chapters 3 and 4) and including embeddings for the categorical columns (as described in chapter 5). Then we will describe an experiment to compare the deep learning solution using the streetcar delay prediction deep learning model with a solution that uses a non-deep-learning approach called XGBoost.

7.1 Code for more experiments with the model

When you have cloned the GitHub repo (http://mng.bz/v95x) associated with this book, you'll find the code related to the experiments in the notebooks subdirectory. The following listing shows the files used in the experiments described in this chapter.

Listing 7.1 Code in the repo related to the model training experiments

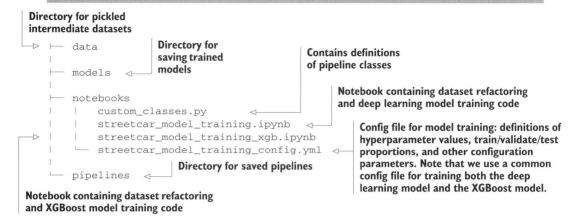

Directory for pickled
intermediate datasets

```
data
Directory for
saving trained
models
models
Contains definitions
of pipeline classes

notebooks
    custom_classes.py
Notebook containing dataset refactoring
and deep learning model training code
    streetcar_model_training.ipynb
    streetcar_model_training_xgb.ipynb
    streetcar_model_training_config.yml
Config file for model training: definitions of
hyperparameter values, train/validate/test
proportions, and other configuration
parameters. Note that we use a common
config file for training both the deep
learning model and the XGBoost model.
Directory for saved pipelines
pipelines
```

Notebook containing dataset refactoring
and XGBoost model training code

7.2 Validating whether removing bad values improves the model

Back in chapter 4, we reviewed the number of records in the dataset with bad values—records with a value in one of the columns that is not valid. The input record may have had a route value that doesn't exist, for example, or a direction value that isn't one of the compass points. By default, we remove these values before saving the output dataframe at the end of the streetcar_data_preparation notebook. We want to do an experiment to validate that this choice is the best one to make for the performance of the model. Following is such an experiment:

1. Rerun the streetcar_data_preparation notebook with the following values set in streetcar_data_preparation_config.yml to save a cleaned output dataframe that includes records with bad values, as shown in the next listing.

Listing 7.2 Parameters in the data preparation config for bad values experiment

```
general:
    load_from_scratch: False
    save_transformed_dataframe: True
    remove_bad_values: False
file_names:
    pickled_input_dataframe: 2014_2019.pkl
    pickled_output_dataframe:
        2014_2019_df_cleaned_no_remove_bad_values_xxx.pkl
```

Specify that the output
dataframe should be saved.

Specify that the bad values should
not be removed from the output
dataframe.

Set a unique filename for
the output dataframe.

2   Rerun the streetcar_model_training notebook with the following values set in streetcar_model_training_config.yml to use a control file for refactoring the dataset that includes route/direction combinations with "bad route" and "bad direction," as the next listing shows.

> **Listing 7.3   Parameter settings for the bad values experiment**

Specify the same filename that you specified for the pickled_output_dataframe in the data preparation config file.

Control file that includes route/direction combinations with "bad route" and "bad direction".

```
pickled_dataframe: \
    '2014_2019_df_cleaned_no_remove_bad_values_xxx.pkl'
route_direction_file: 'routedirection_badvalues.csv'
```

Now when we run experiment 5 from chapter 6 with these changes (to use the input dataset that includes bad values), we get the result shown in figure 7.1. Validation accuracy is not that different, but the model trained with an input dataset that includes bad values has much worse recall.

Experiment	Epochs	Terminal validation accuracy	False negatives exercising model on test set	Recall on test set: true positive/(true positive + false negative)
No bad values	50	0.78	3,500	0.68
Bad values	50	0.79	6,400	0.53

Figure 7.1   Comparison of model performance with and without bad values in the training dataset

Overall, we get better performance from the model trained with a dataset that excludes bad values. This experiment confirms our decision in chapter 4 to exclude by default records with bad values from the model training process.

7.3   *Validating whether embeddings for columns improve the performance of the model*

Embeddings play an important role in the performance of the deep learning model we created in chapter 5 and trained in chapter 6. The model incorporates embedding layers for all the categorical columns. As an experiment, I removed only these layers and trained the model to compare its performance with and without embedding layers for the categorical columns.

To perform this experiment, I replaced these two lines in the model building section in the streetcar_model_training notebook

```
embeddings[col] = (Embedding(max_dict[col],catemb) (catinputs[col]))
embeddings[col] = (BatchNormalization() (embeddings[col]))
```

with the line

```
embeddings[col] = (BatchNormalization() (catinputs[col]))
```

and reran experiment 5, described in chapter 6. This experiment is a 50-epoch training run with early stopping defined based on validation accuracy. Figure 7.2 shows the results of this experiment run with and without embeddings for categorical columns.

Performance on test set	Categorical columns without embedding layer	Categorical columns include embedding layer
Accuracy	59.5%	78.1%
recall: true positive / (true positive + false negative)	0.57	0.68
false negatives	4,700	3,500

Figure 7.2   Comparing performance for the model with categorical columns without and with embedding layers

Every performance measure is much worse when the embedding layers are removed from the model for categorical columns. This example demonstrates the value of embeddings even in a simple deep learning model like the one we have defined for streetcar delay.

7.4   *Comparing the deep learning model with XGBoost*

The thesis of this book is that it's worth considering deep learning to be an option for doing machine learning on structured, tabular data. In chapter 6, we trained a deep learning model on the streetcar delay dataset and examined the model's performance. What if we were to train a non-deep-learning model with the same streetcar delay dataset? In this section, we are going to show the results for such an experiment. We will replace the deep learning model with XGBoost, a gradient-boosting decision-tree algorithm that has gained a reputation as the "go to" machine learning approach for problems involving structured, tabular data. We will compare the results for both models and determine what these results tell us about the viability of deep learning as a solution for problems involving structured data.

In the same way that a book about Batman would not be complete without describing the Joker, a book about using deep learning with structured data would be incomplete if it didn't say something about XGBoost. In terms of dealing with structured, tabular data, XGBoost is the archnemesis of deep learning, and it is the approach most often recommended instead of deep learning for dealing with structured data.

XGBoost is an example of a kind of non-deep-learning machine learning called a gradient-boosting machine. In gradient boosting, predictions from a set of simple models are aggregated to get a consolidated prediction. It is worth noting that XGBoost offers you a set of capabilities that is not identical to those offered by deep learning models. XGBoost has a built-in feature, importance capability (http:// mng.bz/awwJ), that can help you determine how much each feature contributes to the model, although this capability should be used judiciously, as demonstrated by the article at http://mng.bz/5pa8. A detailed description of all the features of XGBoost is beyond the scope of this book, but the XGBoost section in *Machine Learning for Business* (http://mng.bz/EEGo) provides an excellent and accessible description of how XGBoost works.

To get a comparison between the deep learning model and XGBoost, I updated the model training notebook streetcar_model_training to replace the deep learning model with XGBoost. My intention was to make minimal changes to the code. If you think of the entire model training notebook as a car, I wanted to swap out the existing engine (the deep learning model) and put in another engine (XGBoost) without changing the body panels, wheels, tires, interior, or anything else about the car, as shown in figure 7.3.

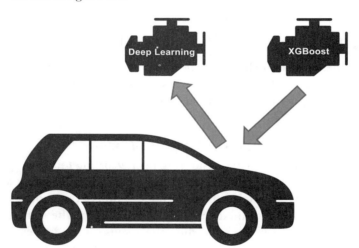

Figure 7.3   Replacing the deep learning engine with the XGBoost engine

When I had the new engine working, I wanted to take the car out on the track to assess what it was like to drive compared with the same car with its original engine. If I keep everything else on the car the same and change only the engine, I can expect to get a fair comparison of what it is like to drive the car with each engine. Similarly, I hoped that by keeping code changes in the notebook to a minimum, I would be able to get a fair comparison between the deep learning model and XGBoost.

You can find the code for training the XGBoost model in the streetcar_model _training_xgb notebook, and if you examine this notebook, you will see that the car analogy holds: I changed engines, but the rest of the car remains the same. The first part of this notebook is identical to the deep learning model training notebook streetcar _model_training, with the exception of including the import statement for the XGBoost model:

```
from xgboost import XGBClassifier
```

The XGBoost-specific content begins after the master block to invoke the pipeline. At this point, the dataset is a list of numpy arrays, with one numpy array for each column in the dataset:

```
[array([ 9, 13,  6, ..., 11,  8,  2]),
array([20, 22, 13, ...,  6, 16, 22], dtype=int64),
array([4, 4, 1, ..., 0, 2, 0]),
array([ 2, 18, 14, ..., 24, 11, 21], dtype=int64),
array([0, 2, 3, ..., 3, 1, 2], dtype=int64),
array([0, 5, 4, ..., 3, 6, 0], dtype=int64),
array([ 2, 10, 11, ...,  4,  6,  7], dtype=int64)]
```

The multi-input Keras model in the deep learning training code expects this format. XGBoost, however, expects the dataset to be a numpy array of lists, so before we can train an XGBoost model with this data, we need to convert it to the format that XGBoost expects. We begin by converting the train and test datasets from lists of numpy arrays to lists of lists, as shown in the following listing.

Listing 7.4 Code to convert the train and test datasets to lists of lists

```
list_of_lists_train = []
list_of_lists_test = []
for i in range(0,7):
    list_of_lists_train.append(X_train_list[i].tolist())
    list_of_lists_test.append(X_test_list[i].tolist())
```

For both the train and test datasets, iterate through the numpy arrays, and convert them to lists so we end up with two lists of lists.

Next, for the test and train datasets, we convert the lists to numpy arrays and transpose the numpy arrays:

```
xgb_X_train = np.array(list_of_lists_train).T
xgb_X_test = np.array(list_of_lists_test).T
```

Here is what the resulting training dataset xgb_X_train looks like:

```
array([[ 9, 20,  4, ...,  0,  0,  2],
       [13, 22,  4, ...,  2,  5, 10],
       [ 6, 13,  1, ...,  3,  4, 11],
       ...,
       [11,  6,  0, ...,  3,  3,  4],
       [ 8, 16,  2, ...,  1,  6,  6],
       [ 2, 22,  0, ...,  2,  0,  7]])
```

The dataset that came out of the pipelines as a list of numpy arrays has been converted to a numpy array of lists with the content transposed—exactly what we need to train the XGBoost model in the next block, as shown in the next listing.

Listing 7.5   Code to train an XGBoost model

**Build the path where the trained
XGBoost model will be saved.**

**Define the XGB model object, using defaults for all
parameters except scale_pos_weight, which is used
to account for the imbalance between positive (delay)
and negative (no delay) targets. This value is identical
to the one used in the deep learning model to
account for the imbalance.**

```
model_path = get_model_path()
xgb_save_model_path = \
os.path.join(model_path, \
'sc_xgbmodel'+modifier+"_"+str(experiment_number)+'.txt')
model = XGBClassifier(scale_pos_weight=one_weight)
model.fit(xgb_X_train, dtrain.target)
model.save_model(xgb_save_model_path)
y_pred = model.predict(xgb_X_test)
xgb_predictions = [round(value) for value in y_pred]
xgb_accuracy = accuracy_score(test.target, xgb_predictions)
print("Accuracy: %.2f%%" % (xgb_accuracy * 100.0))
```

**Save the
trained model.**

**Fit the model, using the training
dataset that we transformed
into a numpy array of lists.**

**Calculate the accuracy
of the model.**

Apply the trained model to the test dataset.

Now that we have seen what changes needed to be made to get the model training notebook to work with XGBoost, what happened when we trained and assessed the XGBoost model? Figure 7.4 summarizes both the results of comparative training and evaluation runs with XGBoost and deep learning, as well as high-level differences between the two approaches.

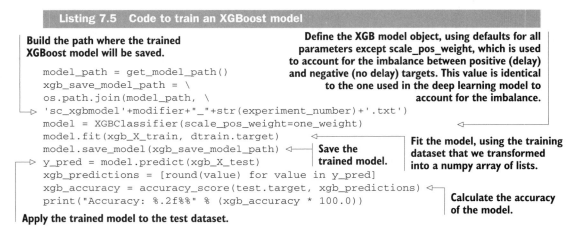

Category	XGBoost	Keras deep learning	Winner?
Performance on test set			
Accuracy	80.1%	78.1%	
recall: true positive/(true positive + false negative)	0.89	0.68	XGBoost
False negatives	1,200	3,500	
Training time	1 minute 24 seconds	2–3 minutes for experiment 5 depending on hw env and patience setting	Inconclusive—deep learning training time varies
Code complexity	• Extra steps required to transform data coming out of pipeline • One line to build model	• Data from pipeline ready to train model • Complex model build	Inconclusive
Flexibility	Handles continuous & categorical columns	Handles continuous, categorical and text columns	Deep learning

Figure 7.4   Comparison of XGBoost and Keras deep learning models

- *Performance*—Right out of the box, with no tuning, the XGBoost model got better performance than deep learning. For accuracy on the test set, the high-water mark was 78.1% for deep learning and 80.1% for XGBoost. For recall and volume of false negatives (as we stated in chapter 6, this factor is key to the performance of the model in terms of the user's final experience), XGBoost was also better. Compare the confusion matrix for XGBoost in figure 7.5 with the confusion matrix in figure 7.6 for a high-accuracy deep learning run, and it's clear that XGBoost is ahead.

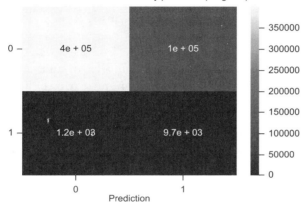

Figure 7.5   XGBoost
confusion matrix

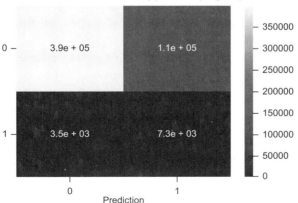

Figure 7.6   Deep learning
confusion matrix

- *Training time*—The deep learning model training time is more hardware-dependent than the training time for XGBoost. On a mediocre Windows system, XGBoost takes in the range of 1.5 minutes to train, and the deep learning model takes in the range of 3 minutes to run experiment 5. But deep learning training time for experiment 5 (50 epochs, with early-stopping patience parameter set at 15) varies widely depending on the patience parameter (how many epochs are run in training when the optimized performance measurement, such as validation accuracy, stops improving before the training run is stopped) and the hardware available in the environment. Although XGBoost has shorter training time, the gap is close enough, and the training performance of the deep learning model is variable enough, that I would call the comparison a draw.

- *Code complexity*—There is little difference in terms of complexity between the fitting code of the deep learning model and XGBoost. The code leading up to the fitting statements is different. Before the fitting code, the deep learning model has complex code in the `get_model()` function to construct the model itself. As described in chapter 5, this function assembles different layers for different types of input columns. XGBoost does not need this complex code block, but it requires additional steps to convert the dataset from a list of numpy arrays (the format required by the deep learning model) to a numpy array of lists (the format required by XGBoost). I would call this category a draw as well, although an argument could be made that XGBoost is simpler because the additional data preparation code it requires is simpler than the model building code. But model building code is a key part of deep learning's rating in the last category.
- *Flexibility*—As described in chapter 5, the deep learning model is built to work with a wide variety of structured datasets. Because of the way that XGBoost was retrofitted into the code, it benefits from this flexibility, and its implementation in the streetcar_model_training_xgb notebook will also work with a variety of structured datasets. There is one important exception: the deep learning model would work with datasets that include freeform text columns. As discussed in chapter 4, the streetcar delay dataset does not have any such columns, but they are common in many structured datasets.

  Consider, for example, a table that tracked items for sale in an online footwear retail site. This table could include continuous columns (like price) and categorical columns (like color and shoe size). It could also include a description of each item in freeform text. The deep learning model would be able to incorporate and get training data from such a text column. XGBoost would need to exclude this column from its analysis. In this important respect, the deep learning model is more flexible than XGBoost.

It's worth noting that I was able to adapt the code in streetcar_model_training to work with XGBoost with minimal extra work. When I began training the XGBoost model, I found that with no tuning other than setting the `scale_pos_weight` parameter to account for the much higher number of "no delay" records than "delay" records in the input dataset, the XGBoost model consistently outperformed the deep learning model.

What's the ultimate conclusion of comparing deep learning and XGBoost for the streetcar delay prediction problem? XGBoost has better performance than the deep learning model, and it was relatively easy to integrate into the existing code structure that I created for the deep learning model. Returning to the car analogy, XGBoost was an easy engine to fit into the car and get running. Does that mean that the conclusion of the comparison has to align with the conventional wisdom that non-deep-learning methods—in particular, XGBoost—are better than deep learning for structured data problems?

If we freeze the streetcar delay prediction problem where it is now, the answer probably is yes, but it would be naïve to expect that in a real-world situation, the model would not change. As you will see in chapter 9, many options are available to extend and improve the streetcar delay prediction model by considering additional datasets, and as soon as we consider these improvements, we run into the limitations of XGBoost. Any dataset that includes freeform text columns (such as the weather dataset described in chapter 9), for example, could be incorporated easily into the deep learning model but could not be incorporated directly into XGBoost. XGBoost would not be suitable for some of the extensions to the streetcar delay prediction problem described in chapter 9; neither would it be suitable for any problem in which the structured data includes columns with any kind of BLOB data (https://techterms .com/definition/blob), such as images, video, or audio. If we want a solution that is generally applicable to a truly wide range of tabular, structured data, XGBoost isn't going to be the solution. Although XGBoost can beat deep learning for performance on a given application, deep learning has the flexibility to exploit the full variety of structured data.

7.5 Possible next steps for improving the deep learning model

After all the experiments described in chapter 6, we end up with a trained model that is a little better than 78% accurate on the test set and has a recall of 0.79. What steps could we take to improve the performance on subsequent iterations? Here are some ideas:

- *Adjust the mix of features.* The set of features used in the deep learning model is relatively limited to keep the training process as simple as possible. One feature that could be added is a geospatial measurement based on the latitude and longitude values generated from the addresses in chapter 4. As described in chapter 9, you could use bounding boxes for each route to divide each route into lateral segments (for example, 10 sections per route) and use these segments as one of the features of the model. Such an approach would isolate delays to specific subsets of each route and could improve the performance of the model.

- *Adjust the threshold for delay.* If the threshold for what constitutes a delay is too small, the model will be less useful, because transitory delays will count as incidents. On the other hand, if the threshold is set too high, the model's predictions would have less value, because delays that would constitute an inconvenience for travelers would not be captured. This boundary is set in the model by the `targetthresh` parameter in the model training config file. Adjusting this threshold could provide improvements in the model's performance, particularly as the input data evolves over time. As noted in chapter 3, over the years there has been an overall trend for delays to be more frequent but shorter, so a smaller value for the `targetthresh` parameter could be worth exploring.

- *Adjust the learning rate.* The learning rate controls how much the weights are adjusted in each training iteration. If it's set too high, the training process could skip right over a minimum loss point. If it's set too low, training progress will be slow, and you'll consume more time and system resources than you need to train the model. In the early stages of the model training process, I adjusted the learning rate and settled on the value that is currently in the model training config file because it produced stable results. Further experiments to fine-tune the learning rate could yield improvements in the model's performance.

The model meets the performance goal we set for it at the outset (at least 70% accuracy), but there is always room for improvement. The preceding list shows some of the potential tweaks that could be made to the deep learning model to improve its performance. If you have worked through the code to this point, I encourage you to try some of the recommendations in this section and run experiments to see whether these tweaks improve the performance of the model.

Summary

- By default, we discard records with bad values from the dataset. You can perform an experiment to validate this choice and demonstrate that a model trained on a dataset with bad values removed has superior performance to a model trained on a dataset that keeps the bad values.
- By default, the model incorporates embeddings for categorical columns. You can perform an experiment to confirm and show that a model that incorporates embeddings for categorical columns has better performance than a model that does not have embeddings for categorical columns.
- XGBoost is currently the default machine learning approach for problems involving tabular, structured data. You can perform a series of experiments on a version of the model training notebook in which the deep learning model has been replaced with XGBoost.
- XGBoost does have somewhat better performance than deep learning on the streetcar delay prediction problem, but performance isn't the only consideration, and deep learning beats XGBoost in the key area of flexibility.

Deploying the model

This chapter covers

- Overview of model deployment
- Deployment versus one-off scoring
- Why deployment is a difficult topic
- Steps for deploying your model
- Introduction to pipelines
- Maintaining a model after it has been deployed

In chapter 6, we went through the process of iteratively training the deep learning model for predicting streetcar delays, and in chapter 7, we went through a further set of experiments to explore the behavior of the model. Now that we have a trained model, we are going to look at two ways to deploy the model or, in other words, make it possible for streetcar users to get predictions about whether their streetcar trips are going to be delayed. First, we'll get an overview of the deployment process. Next, we'll contrast the one-off scoring we introduced in chapter 6 with deployment. Then we will go through the specific steps to deploy the model by using two approaches: a web page and Facebook Messenger. Next, we will describe how to encapsulate the data preparation process by using pipelines and go over the details of implementing pipelines for the streetcar delay prediction model. We will wrap up the chapter with a review of how to maintain a model when it has been deployed.

NOTE   In this chapter, to prevent confusion between the Keras deep learning model that we have trained for streetcar delay prediction and the Rasa chatbot model used in the second deployment approach, we will refer to the former as the Keras model if there is any chance of ambiguity.

8.1 *Overview of model deployment*

Deployment is a critical step in making a deep learning model useful. *Deployment* means making our trained model available to users or other applications outside the context of your development environment. In other words, deployment is everything we need to do to make our trained model useful for the outside world. Deployment could mean making the model available to other applications via a REST API or, as in our case, making it directly accessible to the users, who want to know whether their streetcar trips are going to be delayed.

If we revisit the end-to-end diagram from chapter 4, deployment encompasses the right side of figure 8.1.

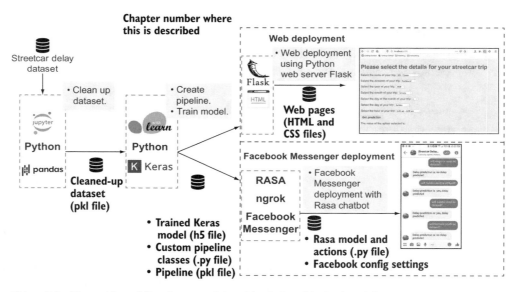

Figure 8.1   The end-to-end flow from raw dataset to deployed trained model

In this chapter, we are going to deploy our trained model by using two techniques:

- *Web deployment*—This minimal deployment uses Flask (https://flask .palletsprojects.com/en/1.1.x), a basic web application framework for Python, to serve web pages where a user can specify the parameters for their trip and see the model's prediction. This solution consists of a Python flask_server.py file for the Flask server and related code, along with two HTML files to get the scoring parameters (home.html) and display the result (show-prediction.html). The HTML page home.html contains JavaScript functions to collect the scoring parameters (such as route, direction, and time). These scoring parameters are passed to the Python code in flask_server.py, which applies the pipelines to the scoring parameters and applies the trained model to the output of the pipelines. By default, Flask serves the web pages at localhost. In chapter 9, we describe how you can use ngrok (https://ngrok.com) to make the web pages served at local-host available to users who don't have access to your development system.

- *Facebook Messenger deployment*—The web deployment is simple, but the user experience is not ideal. To provide a better user experience, we are also going to deploy our model with a Rasa chatbot that is exposed in Facebook Messenger. To deploy our model, we will incorporate the trained model that we completed in chapter 6 and integrate it into the Python layer of Rasa, along with pipelines to prepare new data points to have predictions made on them by the model. The user will enter their requests to determine whether a particular streetcar trip will be delayed via Facebook Messenger. Our Rasa chatbot will parse these requests and pass on the trip information (route, direction, and date/time) to Python code that is associated with the Rasa chatbot. This Python code (the scoring code) will apply the pipelines to the trip information, apply the trained Keras model to the output of the pipelines, and compose a response based on the prediction made by the trained Keras model. Finally, this response will come back to the user in Facebook Messenger.

8.2 *If deployment is so important, why is it so hard?*

Deployment is the difference between a model that's an experiment and a model that can provide benefit. Unfortunately, deployment tends to be glossed over in introductory material about deep learning, and even professional cloud providers have not yet been able to make deployment simple. Why is this the case?

Deployment is hard because it involves a variety of technical topics that go way beyond the deep learning stack that we have covered in this book so far. To deploy a model in an industrial-strength production environment, you have to work with a broad technology stack that could include a cloud platform like Azure or AWS, Docker and Kubernetes for containerization and orchestration, REST APIs to provide a callable interface for your trained model, and web infrastructure to provide a frontend for your model. This stack is complex and technically demanding. To do even a minimal, dead-simple web deployment (as described in sections 8.5 and 8.6), you need to work with a web server, HTML, and JavaScript, all of which are additional to everything you've learned so far about machine learning in general and deep learning in particular.

In this chapter, we present two contrasting deployment approaches: web deployment and Facebook Manager deployment. Web deployment is relatively easy, but the user experience is not ideally suited to the problem of predicting delays for streetcar trips. Real users of the model are not likely to want to go to a separate website to find out whether their streetcars are going to be delayed. But they might very well be happy to have a brief chat in Facebook Messenger to get the same information. Both deployment options are free and use an open-source stack (with the exception of Facebook Messenger itself). Both deployment options also allow you to exercise deployment completely from your own local system while at the same time providing access to other people with whom you want to share the model results.

8.3   *Review of one-off scoring*

In chapter 6, you learned how to take a new data record and apply the trained model to it to get a prediction. We call this quick way of exercising the trained model *one-off scoring*. You can exercise the Python file one_off_scoring.py to see an example of how you can prepare a single data point manually and use the trained model to get a prediction (also called a score) for this data point.

To understand what full deployment means, let's contrast one-off scoring with full deployment. Figure 8.2 summarizes one-off scoring.

One-off scoring of new data points

```
score_sample = {}
score_sample['hour'] = np.array([18])
score_sample['Route'] = np.array([0])         In Python session:
score_sample['daym'] = np.array([21])
score_sample['month'] = np.array([0])         • Hand-craft a single data point
score_sample['year'] = np.array([5])
score_sample['Direction'] = np.array([1])
score_sample['day'] = np.array([1])


loaded_model = load_model(model_path)         • Load trained model

                                                                      Python

preds = loaded_model.predict(score_sample,    • Get prediction for hand-crafted
batch_size=BATCH_SIZE)                          data point

print("prediction is "+str(preds[0][0]))
                                              • Print prediction
prediction is 0.41801068
```

Figure 8.2   Summary of one-off scoring in a Python session

You do one-off scoring in the context of a Python session, and you need to manually prepare the data point that you want to score. Instead of dealing directly with the values that you want to score—such as `route = 501`, `direction = westbound`, and `time = 1:00 pm today`—you need to have a data point that has already been through all the data transformations, such as assigning an integer value to replace `501` as the route value. Further, you have to assemble the data point into the structure that the model expects: a list of numpy arrays. When you have prepared a data point in the required format and applied the trained model to get a prediction for it, you can display the prediction in the Python session. As you can see, one-off scoring is suitable for doing a quick sanity test of the trained model, but because one-off scoring is done in a Python session and requires manual preparation of the input data, it's not a suitable way to test your model at scale or make it available to an end user.

8.4   The user experience with web deployment

For the streetcar delay prediction problem, we need a simple way for the user to specify what trip they want to get a delay prediction for, along with an easy way to show the model's prediction. Web deployment is the easiest way to achieve this goal.

In section 8.5, we will get into the details of setting up web deployment for your trained deep learning model, but first, let's review what the user experience will be with the completed web deployment (as shown in figure 8.3):

1 The user goes to `home.html` (served by Flask at `localhost:5000`) and selects the details of the trip they want a prediction for: route, direction, year, month, day of month, day of the week, and hour.
2 The user clicks the Get Prediction button.
3 The prediction is displayed in show-prediction.html.
4 The user can click Get Another Prediction to return to `home.html` and enter details about another trip.

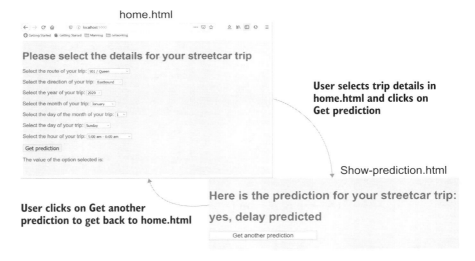

Figure 8.3   The user experience with web deployment

8.5   Steps to deploy your model with web deployment

In section 8.4, we went through the user experience with the web-deployed model. This section leads you through the steps to set up local web deployment of your trained model.

As noted in section 8.4, web deployment depends on Flask to serve the web pages and associated code for the deployment. An end-to-end description of Flask is beyond the scope of this book, but if you want to get more background on this easy-to-use Python web application framework, the tutorial at http://mng.bz/oRPy provides an excellent overview.

Flask is not your only choice for web serving in Python. Django (https://www .djangoproject.com) is another Python web application framework that trades the simplicity of Flask for a richer function set. See http://mng.bz/nzPV for a good comparison of Flask and Django. For the purposes of the streetcar delay prediction project, I chose Flask because we don't need a sophisticated web application to deploy the model and because Flask is easier to get started with.

When you have cloned the GitHub repo (http://mng.bz/v95x) associated with this book, you will see the directory structure in the following listing.

Listing 8.1   Code in the repo related to deployment

```
├── data
├── deploy
│   ├── data
│   ├── input_sample_data
│   ├── keras_models
│   ├── models
│   ├── pipelines
│   ├── test_results
│   └── __pycache__
├── deploy_web
│   ├── static
│   │   └── css
│   ├── templates
│   └── __pycache__
├── models
├── notebooks
│   ├── .ipynb_checkpoints
│   └── __pycache__
├── pipelines
└── sql
```

The files related to web deployment, shown next, are in the deploy_web subdirectory .

Listing 8.2   Code in the repo related to web deployment

Contains definitions
of pipeline classes

Config file for web deployment: pipeline
filenames, model filename, and debug settings

```
    │   custom_classes.py
    │   deploy_web_config.yml
    │   flask_server.py
    │
    ├── static
    │   └── css
    │
    │           main.css
    │           main2.css
    │
    └── templates
            home.html
            show-prediction.html
```

Main Python file for the Flask server and for applying
the pipelines and trained model to the user's input
parameters about their streetcar trip

CSS file for display characteristics of HTML files

Alternate CSS file (used to force
updates during development)

HTML file for entering scoring parameters

HTML file for displaying scoring results

With the files in place, here are the steps to take to get the web deployment working:

1　Go to the deploy_web subdirectory in your local instance of the repo.

2　Edit the deploy_web_config.yml config file to specify which trained model and pipeline files you want to use for the deployment. If you are using model and pipeline files that you created yourself by following the instructions in chapter 6, ensure that you are using pipeline and model files that come from the same run, as shown in the next listing.

Listing 8.3　Parameters to set in the web config file for web deployment

> Replace the values for the parameter pipeline1_filename and pipeline2_filename parameters with the filenames of the pipeline files you want to use—pickle files in the pipelines subdirectory that is a sibling of the deploy_web subdirectory. For the pipeline files and the model file only, specify the filename; the rest of the path will be generated in flask_server.py.

```
general:
    debug_on: False
    logging_level: "WARNING"
    BATCH_SIZE: 1000
file_names:
    pipeline1_filename: sc_delay_pipeline_dec27b.pkl
    pipeline2_filename: sc_delay_pipeline_keras_prep_dec27b.pkl
    model_filename: scmodeldec27b_5.h5
```

Replace the value for the model_filename parameter with the name of the file where you saved the trained model that you want to use—an h5 file in the models subdirectory.

3　If you have not already done so, enter this command to install Flask:

```
pip install flask
```

4　Enter this command to start the Flask server and related code:

```
python flask_server.py
```

5　Enter this URL in a browser to load home.html:

```
localhost:5000
```

6　If everything has worked, you see home.html, as shown in figure 8.4.

7　Do a sanity test. Set scoring parameters by selecting values for route, direction, and the time/date parameters and then clicking Get Prediction. This click kicks off processing (loading the pipelines, loading the trained model, and running the scoring parameters through the pipelines and the trained model) that may take some time, so please be patient if it takes a few seconds for this step to complete.

8　If your web deployment was successful, you see show-prediction.html with the prediction for your trip, as shown in figure 8.5.

9　If you want to try another set of scoring parameters, click Get Another Prediction to get back to home.html, where you can enter scoring parameters for a new trip.

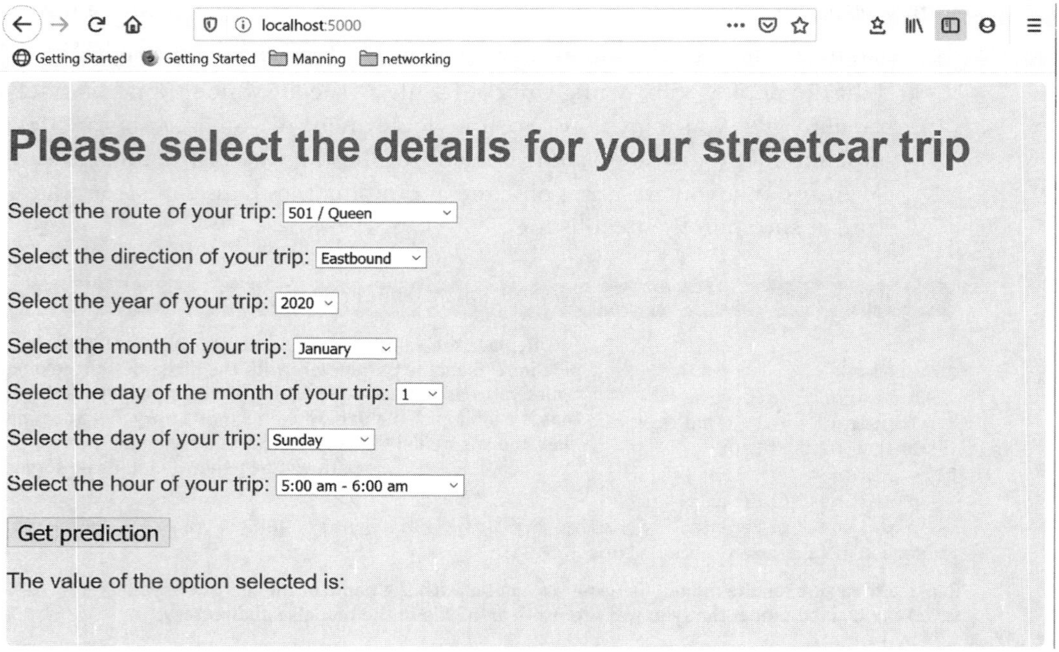

Figure 8.4   home.html displayed when you load localhost:5000 in your browser

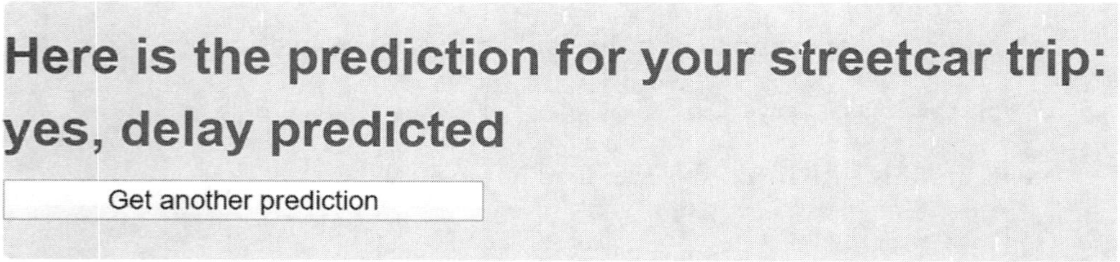

Figure 8.5   Successful sanity test of web deployment

That's it. If you've reached this point, you have done a successful web deployment of a trained deep learning model. As you can see, even this simple deployment required a set of technology that we have not previously needed to use in this book, including Flask, HTML, and JavaScript. As you will see in section 8.8, to get a smoother user experience by deploying the model in Facebook Messenger, we will need an even bigger set of components. This requirement for a set of technical components illustrates the point made in section 8.2: deploying a deep learning model is not easy because deployment currently takes a stack of technology that is distinct from the technology we use to prepare the dataset and train the model.

If you want to share your deployment with others, you can use ngrok to make local-host on your local system available to users outside your local system, as described in chapter 9. Note that if you use the free version of ngrok, you will only be able to have one ngrok server running at a time, so you won't be able to run the web deployment and the Facebook Messenger deployment simultaneously.

8.6   Behind the scenes with web deployment

Let's take a closer look at what's happening behind the scenes with web deployment. Figure 8.6 shows the flow through the stack, from the user entering the details about their intended streetcar trip in home.html to the user getting a response in show-prediction.html. See the following list for more details on the numbered steps in figure 8.6.

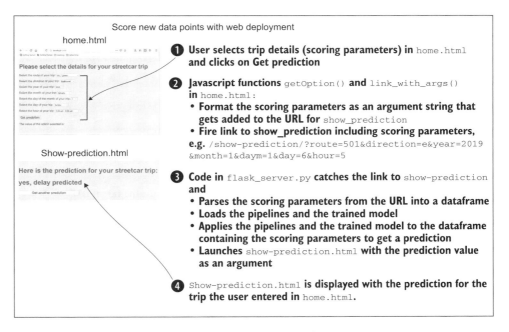

Figure 8.6   The round trip from query to answer with web deployment

1 In the home.html web page served by Flask at localhost:5000, the user selects the details about their streetcar trip by choosing them from drop-down lists for route, direction, and time/date; then the user clicks the Get Prediction button.

2 The JavaScript function getOption()in home.html extracts the scoring parameters that the user selected in the drop-down lists and builds a URL that includes these scoring parameters. The JavaScript function link_with_args() sets the link associated with the Get Prediction button to include the URL that is built in getOption(), as the next listing shows.

Listing 8.4   Code for JavaScript function `getOption()`

Create querySelector objects for each scoring parameter.

```
function getOption() {
    selectElementRoute = document.querySelector('#route');
    selectElementDirection = document.querySelector('#direction');
    selectElementYear = document.querySelector('#year');
    selectElementMonth = document.querySelector('#month');
    selectElementDaym = document.querySelector('#daym');
    selectElementDay = document.querySelector('#day');
    selectElementHour = document.querySelector('#hour');
    route_string = \
    selectElementRoute.options[selectElementRoute.selectedIndex].value
    direction_string = \
    selectElementDirection.options[selectElementDirection.\
    selectedIndex].value
    year_string = \
    selectElementYear.options[selectElementYear.selectedIndex].value
    month_string = \
    selectElementMonth.options[selectElementMonth.selectedIndex].value
    daym_string = \
    selectElementDaym.options[selectElementDaym.selectedIndex].value
    day_string = \
    selectElementDay.options[selectElementDay.selectedIndex].value
    hour_string = \
    selectElementHour.options[selectElementHour.selectedIndex].value
    // build complete URL, including scoring parameters
    prefix = "/show-prediction/?"
    window.output = \
    prefix.concat("route=",route_string,"&direction=",direction_string,\
    "&year=",year_string,"&month=",month_string,"&daym=",daym_string,\
    "&day=",day_string,"&hour=",hour_string)
    document.querySelector('.output').textContent = window.output;
}

function link_with_args(){
    getOption();
    console.log("in link_with_args");
    console.log(window.output);
    window.location.href = window.output;
}
```

Load the values for each scoring parameter into a JS variable.

Set the prefix for the target URL.

Add arguments for each scoring parameter value to the target URL.

Set the target URL as the target of the link associated with the Get Prediction button.

Call getOption() to build the target URL. The target URL will look like this:
/show-prediction/?route=50l&direction=e&year=2019&month=l&daym=l&day=6&hour=5.

3   flask_server.py includes view functions (http://mng.bz/v9xm)—functions in Flask modules that handle different routes/URLs—for each of the HTML files that make up the deployment. The view function for show-prediction contains the scoring code in the next listing.

Listing 8.5 Code for the view function for `show-prediction`

View function for home.html; this is the function that gets executed when the user navigates to localhost:5000.

Load the arguments from the URL— the scoring parameters loaded by the link_with_args() JavaScript function in home.html—into a Python dictionary.

```
@app.route('/')
def home():
    title_text = "Test title"
    title = {'titlename':title_text}
    return render_template('home.html',title=title)

@app.route('/show-prediction/')
def about():
    score_values_dict = {}
    score_values_dict['Route'] = request.args.get('route')
    score_values_dict['Direction'] = request.args.get('direction')
    score_values_dict['year'] = int(request.args.get('year'))
    score_values_dict['month'] = int(request.args.get('month'))
    score_values_dict['daym'] = int(request.args.get('daym'))
    score_values_dict['day'] = int(request.args.get('day'))
    score_values_dict['hour'] = int(request.args.get('hour'))
    loaded_model = load_model(model_path)
    loaded_model._make_predict_function()
    pipeline1 = load(open(pipeline1_path, 'rb'))
    pipeline2 = load(open(pipeline2_path, 'rb'))
    score_df = pd.DataFrame(columns=score_cols)
    for col in score_cols:
        score_df.at[0,col] = score_values_dict[col]
    prepped_xform1 = pipeline1.transform(score_df)
    prepped_xform2 = pipeline2.transform(prepped_xform1)
    pred = loaded_model.predict(prepped_xform2, batch_size=BATCH_SIZE)
    if pred[0][0] >= 0.5:
        predict_string = "yes, delay predicted"
    else:
        predict_string = "no delay predicted"
    prediction = {'prediction_key':predict_string}
    # render the page that will show the prediction
    return(render_template('show-prediction.html', \
        prediction=prediction))
```

The view function for home.html renders the web page.

View function for show-prediction.html; this is the function that gets executed when the user clicks the Get Prediction link in home.html.

Load the pipeline objects.

Create a dataframe to contain the scoring parameters.

Load the scoring parameters into the dataframe.

Load the trained model. Note that model_path is built earlier in flask _server.py, using values loaded from the config file deploy_web_config.yml.

Apply the pipelines to the scoring parameters dataframe.

Convert the prediction to a string.

Apply the trained model to the output of the pipelines to get a prediction.

Create a dictionary for the output prediction string.

Render show-prediction.html with the prediction string as an argument.

4 Flask serves show-prediction.html, showing the prediction string generated by the view function for show-prediction.html in flask_server.py.

This section provided some details on what is happening behind the scenes when you exercise the web deployment. The point of this web deployment was to illustrate a simple yet complete deployment. You can probably see (particularly if you are an experienced web developer) opportunities for improving the web deployment. It would be nice to have the prediction displayed in home.html rather than on a separate page, for example. It would also be good to provide a single button in home.html to let the user specify that they want to take the trip now. To keep the deployment as basic as possible, I erred on the side of simplicity in this web deployment. Sections 8.7–8.10

describe a more elegant deployment that is, in my opinion, much better suited to the streetcar delay prediction problem. Nevertheless, the web deployment described here provides a simple structure that you can adapt (with a few modifications to the HTML and JavaScript) for basic deployment of other machine learning models.

8.7   *The user experience with Facebook Messenger deployment*

The user experience with web deployment is simple, but it has some serious limitations:

- The user has to go to a specific website.
- They have to enter all the information about their trip. Nothing is assumed.
- The entry of the trip parameters and the prediction appear on separate web pages.

We could address all these issues in the web deployment directly by spending more time refining it, but there is a better way to improve the user's experience: deployment in Facebook Messenger. Figure 8.7 shows how simple it is for the user to get a prediction on their trip in the Facebook Messenger deployment.

Contrast the user's scoring experience with Facebook Messenger deployment with their experience with web deployment. Using the model deployed with Facebook Messenger, the user has only to enter an English sentence in Facebook Messenger to get back a prediction. The user can provide minimal information and still get a prediction. Best of all, the user enters the request and gets back the prediction in Facebook Messenger, a natural environment for this kind of lightweight interaction.

Figure 8.7   New data points scored with the deployed model

Another benefit of deploying the model via Facebook Messenger with Rasa is flexibility. In figure 8.8, pairs of queries are labeled with numbers from 1 to 4. Consider the pairs of queries that are tagged with the same number. Each query in these pairs has the same meaning, and the Rasa model is capable of detecting this despite the phrasing differences between each member of the pairs. The Rasa model gets part of this capability from the examples in nlu.md (single-utterance examples) and stories.md (multi-utterance examples) that the Rasa model was trained with. These two sets of training examples give Rasa its ability to parse the aspects of language specific to streetcar trips.

 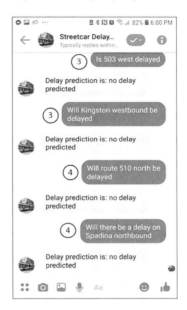

Figure 8.8   The Rasa model correctly assesses pairs of queries as being identical.

A big part of the capability of chatbots written with Rasa comes from exploiting Rasa's default natural language processing (NLP) capability. It's worth mentioning that Rasa's NLP capability is based on deep learning. So deep learning drives two parts of the end-to-end solution (including the Facebook Messenger deployment described in this chapter), as shown in figure 8.9:

- The streetcar delay prediction deep learning model we have been creating throughout this book
- The deep learning that underlies the NLP that we get by using Rasa as part of the deployment of the streetcar delay model

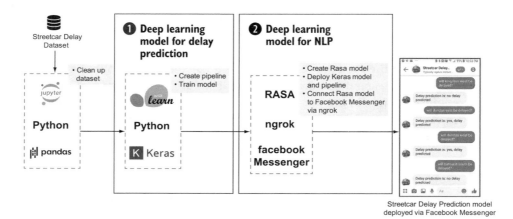

Streetcar Delay Prediction model
deployed via Facebook Messenger

Figure 8.9   Deep learning drives two parts of the end-to-end solution with Facebook Messenger deployment.

8.8   *Behind the scenes with Facebook Messenger deployment*

What is happening behind the scenes when a user enters a question about a streetcar trip in Facebook Messenger? Figure 8.10 shows the flow through the stack from the query entered by the user to the response displayed in Facebook Messenger. See the following list for more details on the numbered steps in figure 8.10:

1 When the user enters a query in English in Facebook Messenger, the query is caught by a simple Rasa chatbot.

2 Rasa applies an NLP model to the query to get the key values (called *slots*) that specify details about the trip for which the user wants a prediction: the route name or number, the direction, and the time.

3 Rasa passes these slot values to a custom action class (part of the scoring code in actions.py) written in Python. The code in that class parses the slot values and sets default values for any slots that are empty. In particular, if the user doesn't specify any time information in their query, the custom action sets the day of the week, month, and year to equal the current date and time.

4 The custom action prepares the trip details, using the same pipelines that were used to prepare the training data. (See sections 8.11–8.13 for more background on pipelines.) Then the custom action scores the prepared trip details by invoking the trained deep learning model on them.

5 Finally, the custom action composes a response that is sent back to the user in Facebook Messenger.

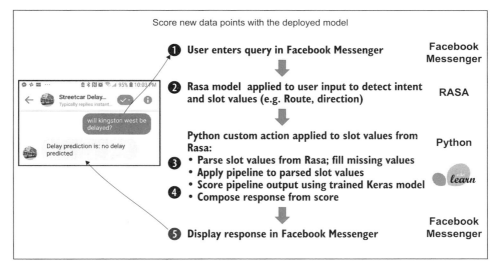

Figure 8.10   The round trip from query to answer with Facebook Messenger deployment

8.9   *More background on Rasa*

A complete review of the Rasa chatbot framework is beyond the scope of this book. Further, the repo contains all the updated Rasa files that you need for the model deployment. When you have followed the steps in section 8.10, you should not need to update any of the Rasa-related files. But if you want some more details about how Rasa works, this section provides some additional background on the essential concepts in Rasa, along with some pointers to more detailed information.

Rasa is an open-source chatbot development framework that lets you create and train chatbots with natural language interfaces. It provides a simple set of interfaces that let you take advantage of its built-in NLP without having to deal with the details of training an NLP model. Rasa connects with Python to let you code sophisticated actions in response to user input. It also supports connections to a variety of messaging platforms, including Facebook Messenger. In sum, the Rasa framework gives us everything we need for a simple deployment, from interpretation of natural language to a connection to Python to an end-user interface with Facebook Messenger.

The Rasa interface is built around a series of chatbot concepts:

- *Intent*—The objective of the user input, such as getting a prediction.
- *Action*—An action that can be performed by the chatbot system. A simple action could be a canned text response (such as returning `hello` in response to a greeting). In the case of our deep learning model deployment, we define an action as the class `ActionPredictDelayComplete` in Python in the actions.py file. This action takes the slot values extracted by Rasa from the user input, fills in values not specified by the slots, runs the values through the pipelines, applies the output of the pipelines to the trained model, and finally composes a response to the user based on the trained model's prediction.

- *Slot*—A set of keys and values that captures essential input from the user. In the case of our deep learning model deployment, slots are defined for all the input columns that the model is expecting (route, direction, hour, month, and so on).
- *Story*—An abstraction of a conversation between a user and the chatbot that can represent multiple back-and-forth exchanges. The main story in our deep learning model deployment is a simple exchange: the user asks whether a trip is going to be delayed, and the bot provides a response to indicate delay or no delay.

Figure 8.11 shows the key files used to train a Rasa model along with the Rasa objects defined in each file. When you train a Rasa model (as you will do in section 8.10), Rasa uses the training data in the nlu.md and stories.md files to train the model.

Figure 8.11   The key Rasa files and objects defined in them

The other key file in the Rasa framework is actions.py, the file that contains the Python custom actions. If Facebook Messenger is the pretty face of the deployment and Rasa's NLP capability is its lovely voice, actions.py is the brains of the deployment. Let's take a closer look at the code in actions.py that gets the slot values that Rasa sets.

The connection between Rasa and actions.py is the tracker structure in the custom class in actions.py. The `tracker.get_slot()` method lets you get the values of slots set by Rasa, or `None` if Rasa did not set a value for a slot. This loop in actions.py iterates through the slot values passed from Rasa and loads the scoring dataframe column that corresponds with the slot value or with the default if the slot value is not set, as shown in the next listing.

Listing 8.6　Code to load slot values from Rasa into a dataframe

```
for col in score_cols:           If the slot is set, use its value.
    if tracker.get_slot(col) != None:
        if tracker.get_slot(col) == "today":
            score_df.at[0,col] = score_default[col]
        else:
            score_df.at[0,col] = tracker.get_slot(col)
    else:
        score_df.at[0,col] = score_default[col]
```

If the date is set by Rasa to today, use the default value, which is the current date.

Otherwise, for the dataframe that will be scored, set the value to be equal to the slot value from Rasa.

If Rasa did not set the value (such as for date and time), use the default, which is the current time/date.

This section provided a brief overview of some of the key concepts in Rasa. For more details, you can get an overview of Rasa and its architecture at https://rasa.com.

8.10　Steps to deploy your model in Facebook Messenger with Rasa

This section describes the steps to deploy your model using Facebook Messenger. When you have completed these steps, you will have a deployed deep learning model that you can query from Facebook Messenger.

　　When you have cloned the GitHub repo (http://mng.bz/v95x) associated with this book, you'll find the files associated with Facebook Messenger deployment in the deploy subdirectory, as shown next.

Listing 8.7　Code in the repo related to Facebook Messenger deployment

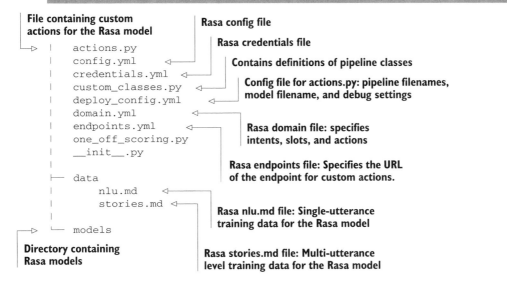

File containing custom actions for the Rasa model

Rasa config file

Rasa credentials file

Contains definitions of pipeline classes

Config file for actions.py: pipeline filenames, model filename, and debug settings

Rasa domain file: specifies intents, slots, and actions

Rasa endpoints file: Specifies the URL of the endpoint for custom actions.

Rasa nlu.md file: Single-utterance training data for the Rasa model

Directory containing Rasa models

Rasa stories.md file: Multi-utterance level training data for the Rasa model

```
    |   actions.py
    |   config.yml
    |   credentials.yml
    |   custom_classes.py
    |   deploy_config.yml
    |   domain.yml
    |   endpoints.yml
    |   one_off_scoring.py
    |   __init__.py
    |
    ├── data
    |       nlu.md
    |       stories.md
    |
    └── models
```

In steps 1 to 4, you will complete the basic setup by installing Python (if you don't already have it installed on your local system) and the Rasa open source chatbot environment:

1 If you don't already have Python 3.7 installed in your local system, install it (https://www.python.org/downloads).

> **NOTE** There is an issue with the TensorFlow dependency with Rasa in Python 3.8, so ensure that you are in Python 3.7 to avoid problems in the Rasa installation step. Also note that Rasa has incompatibilities with TensorFlow 2, so the Python environment that you use for the Facebook Messenger deployment needs to be separate from the Python environment that you use for training the Keras mode.

2 Install the open-source chatbot framework Rasa (https://rasa.com/docs/rasa/user-guide/installation):

```
pip install rasa
```

If you are in Windows, and the Rasa install fails with a message indicating that you need C++, you can download and install Visual C++ Build Tools (http://mng.bz/4BA5). When you have installed the build tools, rerun the Rasa install:

3 Go to the deploy directory in your clone of the repo.
4 Run the following command in the deploy directory to set up a basic Rasa environment:

```
rasa init
```

5 Run the following command in your deploy directory to invoke actions.py in the Python environment for Rasa. If you get any messages about missing libraries, run `pip install` to add missing libraries:

```
rasa run actions
```

In steps 6 to 13, you will set up ngrok (used to connect the deployment environment on your local system with Facebook Messenger) and set up the Facebook app and Facebook page that you need to connect your deployment environment with Facebook Messenger:

6 Install ngrok (https://ngrok.com/download).
7 In the directory where you installed ngrok, invoke ngrok to make your localhost available to Facebook Messenger on port 5005. Here is the command for Windows:

```
.\ngrok http 5005
```

8   Make a note of the https forwarding URL in the ngrok output, as shown in figure 8.12; you will need that URL to complete step 13.

```
ngrok by @inconshreveable

Session Status                  online
Account                         Mark Ryan (Plan: Free)
Update                          update available (version 2.3.35, Ctrl-U to update)
Version                         2.3.34
Region                          United States (us)
Web Interface                   http://127.0.0.1:4040
Forwarding                      http://cbe4bc15.ngrok.io -> http://localhost:5005
Forwarding                      https://cbe4bc15.ngrok.io -> http://localhost:5005

Connections                     ttl     opn     rt1     rt5     p50     p90
                                157     0       0.00    0.00    0.37    3.29
```

Figure 8.12   Output of invoking ngrok

9   Run the following command in the deploy directory to train the Rasa model:

```
rasa train
```

10 Follow the instructions at http://mng.bz/Qxy1 to add a new Facebook app. Make note of the page access token and app secret; you will need to update the credentials.yml file with these values in step 11.

11 Update the credentials.yml file in the deploy directory to set the verify token (a string value you choose) and secret and page-access-token (provided during the Facebook app setup you did in step 10):

```
facebook:
  verify: <verify token that you choose>
  secret: <app secret from Facebook app setup>
  page-access-token: <page access token from Facebook app setup>
```

12 Run the following command in the deploy directory to start the Rasa server, using the credentials you set in credentials.yml in step 11:

```
rasa run --credentials credentials.yml
```

13 In the Facebook app you created in step 10, choose Messenger -> Settings, scroll down to the Webhooks section, and click Edit Callback URL. Replace the initial part of the Callback URL value with the https forwarding URL that you noted when you invoked ngrok in step 7. Enter the verify token that you set in credentials.yml in step 11 in the Verify Token field, and click Verify and Save, as shown in figure 8.13.

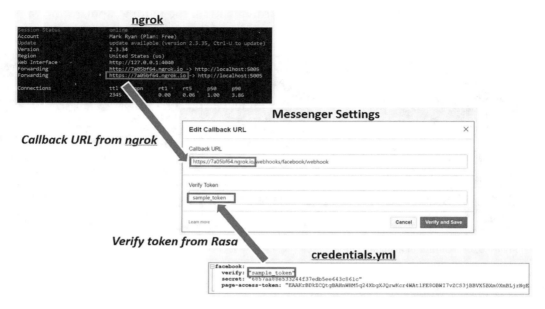

Figure 8.13 Setting the webhook callback URL for Facebook Messenger

Finally, in steps 14 and 15, validate your deployment in Facebook Messenger:

14 In Facebook Messenger (mobile or web application), search for the ID of the Facebook page you created in step 10, and send the following message to that ID:

```
Will Queen west be delayed
```

15 If your deployment was successful, you will see a response like the one shown being served from my local system in figure 8.14. Don't worry about whether the prediction is for a delay; only confirm that you get a response.

8.11 *Introduction to pipelines*

Now that we have gone through the process of deploying the model, we need to review an essential part of the process that makes it possible to prepare user input so that it's ready for the model to generate a prediction on it: pipelines. By using

Figure 8.14 Successful sanity test of model deployment with Facebook Messenger

pipelines, we can apply exactly the same preparation steps (such as assigning numeric identifiers to values in categorical columns) to the streetcar trip details entered by users that we applied to the training data when we were training the Keras model.

Let's look at how the user expects to enter requests for delay predictions on streetcar trips in the Facebook Messenger deployment and compare it with what the trained model expects to get as input for predictions. Figure 8.15 illustrates the gap between the user request and what the model expects as input.

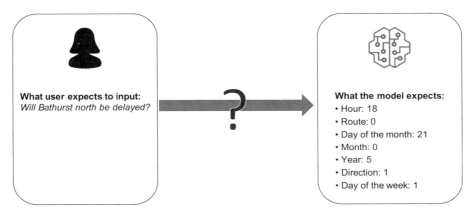

Figure 8.15   How to get from user input to what the model expects

We need to have a way to conveniently prepare data that the user provides for new predictions in the format that the trained model expects. As we saw in section 8.6, Rasa gets us part of the way by extracting the essential information from the user's request and extrapolating missing information, as shown in figure 8.16.

How do we convert the data point that Rasa extracts from the user input to what the model expects? In particular, how do we convert categorical values such as route, month, and day of the week to the integer identifiers that the model expects?

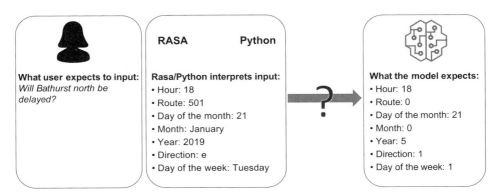

Figure 8.16   How to get from Rasa output to what the model expects

One approach would be to have functions in the training code that encode categorical values available to the scoring code. In the scoring code, we could invoke these same functions to encode the categorical values (such as route and direction) in new data points to which we want to apply the model. The problem is how to ensure that the same mappings are used for new data as we used on the dataset during training. If "2019" was mapped to "5" in the training process, for example, how do we ensure that the identical mapping happens for "2019" in the scoring process? We could pickle the encoder objects we used during the training process, and unpickle and apply these same encoders when we are using the trained model to score new data, but this process would be cumbersome and error-prone. What we need is a convenient way to encapsulate the data preparation process that we used to prepare the training data so that we can apply the same process to new data points that will be scored by the trained model. A proven way to accomplish this goal is to use the pipeline facility (http://mng.bz/X0Pl) provided by scikit-learn.

The pipeline facility in scikit-learn makes it possible to encapsulate all the data transformations (plus the model itself, if you wish) in an object that you can train as one piece. When you have trained a pipeline, you can apply it when you score new data points; the pipeline handles all the data transformations on the new data point and then applies the model to get a result.

The pipeline facility in scikit-learn was designed to be applied with the classic machine learning algorithms included in scikit-learn, including support vector machines, logistic regression, and random forest. It is possible to create a scikit-learn pipeline that incorporates a Keras deep learning model, but I have not been able to create such a pipeline successfully with a multi-input Keras model such as the streetcar delay prediction model. For this reason, when we apply scikit-learn pipelines in this book, they cover only the data preparation steps and do not encapsulate the model itself.

Further, to get around issues with dividing the dataset into train, validate, and test after applying the final data preparation step (converting the dataset from a Pandas dataframe to a dictionary of numpy arrays), we use two pipelines chained together. The first pipeline encodes categorical values (and deals with any remaining missing values), and the second pipeline converts the dataset from a Pandas dataframe to the dictionary of numpy arrays that the model expects. See section 8.12 for the key code elements that make up these two pipelines.

Figure 8.17 shows how new data points to be scored by the trained model get entered by the user, interpreted by Rasa, and then processed by the pipelines so that they are in the correct format for the trained Keras model to make a prediction on.

The pipelines that are applied to new data points entered by the user before the trained model is applied to the new data points are identical to the pipelines that are applied to the dataset before training the model, as shown in figure 8.18.

In this section, we introduced the idea of pipelines and showed at a high level where they fit in the training and deployment processes. In the next section, we will dig into the code that defines the pipelines.

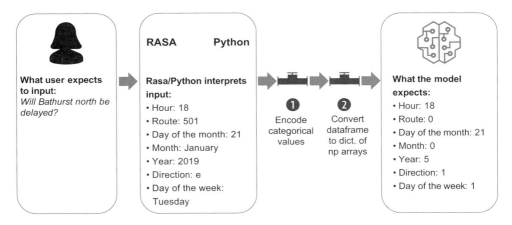

Figure 8.17   The complete flow from user input to what the model expects

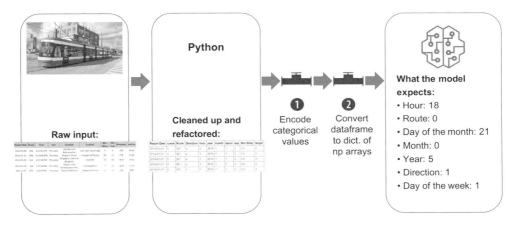

Figure 8.18   Training data flows through the same pipeline as data that is being scored

8.12   *Defining pipelines in the model training phase*

Now that we have looked at the overall purpose of the pipelines, let's go through the details of the code that implements the pipelines used in the streetcar delay prediction project. In this section, we will review how the pipelines get defined in the streetcar_model_training notebook. In section 8.13, we'll review the details of how the pipelines are applied to new data points in the scoring process as part of model deployment.

The pipeline facility in scikit-learn comes with a set of transformation classes that you can use off the shelf, or you can create your own custom transformers by creating new classes as children of the core pipeline classes. For the streetcar delay prediction project, we created custom transformers by deriving new Python classes from the classes provided by scikit-learn. You can find the definitions for these classes in custom_classes.py:

- `encode_categorical`—Encode categorical columns like route, direction, and year.
- `prep_for_keras_input`—Transform the dataset from a Pandas dataframe to the format expected by the Keras model: a dictionary of numpy arrays.
- `fill_empty`—Replace empty values with placeholder values.
- `encode_text`—Encode text columns (not used for the streetcar delay project).

You might wonder why these class definitions are in a separate file from the rest of the code. There are two reasons:

- These classes are needed by the streetcar_model_training notebook, which contains the code for training the model, and by actions.py, which contains the scoring code for the Facebook Messenger deployment. Because both Python programs need access to the same class definitions, it makes sense to put the class definitions in a separate file that both can import.
- The class definitions do not resolve correctly if they are included directly in the scoring code file. Putting the class definitions in a separate file allows them to resolve correctly when the classes are imported into the scoring code actions.py. The import statements are

```
from custom_classes import encode_categorical
from custom_classes import prep_for_keras_input
from custom_classes import fill_empty
from custom_classes import encode_text
```

Let's look at how the pipeline is defined in the training phase in the streetcar_model_training notebook. First, we create instantiations of three of the classes defined in custom_classes.py:

```
fe = fill_empty()
ec = encode_categorical()
pk = prep_for_keras_input()
```

Two things to note:

- If this is your first exposure to the object-oriented aspects of Python, don't worry. You can think of the preceding definitions as creating three objects, each of which has a type equal to the corresponding class. The classes inherit data structures and functions from their parent classes, so with these objects, you can apply both the functions that are explicitly defined in their class as well as the functions that they inherit from their parent classes, `BaseEstimator` and `TransformerMixin`.
- Because there are no text columns in the dataset, we are not creating an object of the `encode_text` class.

Next, we define two pipeline objects, using the class instantiations that we created. The first pipeline incorporates the classes for filling empty values and encoding categorical columns. The second pipeline incorporates the class that converts the dataset from a Pandas dataframe to a list of numpy arrays:

```
sc_delay_pipeline = Pipeline([('fill_empty',fe), \
('encode_categorical',ec)])
sc_delay_pipeline_keras_prep = Pipeline([('prep_for_keras',pk)])
```

Next, we set the parameters for the class instantiations in the pipeline:

```
sc_delay_pipeline.set_params(fill_empty__collist = collist, \
fill_empty__continuouscols = continuouscols, \
     fill_empty__textcols = textcols, \
encode_categorical__col_list = collist)
sc_delay_pipeline_keras_prep.set_params(prep_for_keras__collist = \
collist, prep_for_keras__continuouscols = continuouscols, \
prep_for_keras__textcols = textcols)
```

These statements set the parameters defined in the `set_params` functions in each class. The syntax is the class name followed by two underscores, followed by the parameter name and then the value being assigned to the parameter. In figure 8.19, the top box shows the `set_params` statement with the `col_list` parameter of the `encode_categorical` class highlighted. The bottom box shows where the `col_list` parameter is specified in the `encode_categorical` class definition.

`set_params` statement

```
sc_delay_pipeline.set_params (
                  fill_empty__collist = collist,
                  fill_empty__continuouscols =
continuouscols,
                  fill_empty__textcols = textcols,
                  encode_categorical__col_list = collist)
sc_delay_pipeline_keras_prep.set_params (
                  prep_for_keras_collist = collist,
                  prep_for_keras__continuouscols =
continuouscols,
                  prep_for_keras__textcols = textcols)
```

`encode_categorical` class definition

```
def set_params (self, **kwargs):
       self.col_list = kwargs.get('col_list',
None)
       return self)
```

Figure 8.19 The `set_param` statement sets values for parameters defined in the pipeline classes.

Now that the parameters have been set, let's look at how we apply the first pipeline to encode categorical columns. The first statement in the following code fits the pipeline and transforms the input dataframe, and the second statement saves the fitted pipeline so it can be used when it is time to score new data points:

```
X = sc_delay_pipeline.fit_transform(merged_data)
dump(sc_delay_pipeline, open(pipeline1_file_name,'wb'))
```

The `fit_transform` statement invokes the following methods from the `encode _categorical` customer transformer class, as shown in the next listing.

> **Listing 8.8   Code invoked by the `fit_transform` statement**

```
def fit(self, X, y=None,  **fit_params):
      for col in self.col_list:
          print("col is ",col)
          self.le[col] = LabelEncoder()
          self.le[col].fit(X[col].tolist())
      return self

  def transform(self, X, y=None, **tranform_params):
      for col in self.col_list:
          print("transform col is ",col)
          X[col] = self.le[col].transform(X[col])
          print("after transform col is ",col)
          self.max_dict[col] = X[col].max() +1
      return X
```

In the fit method of the class, the encoder is instantiated.

In the transform method of the class, the encoder that was instantiated in the fit method is applied.

Now that we have reviewed the code that defines the pipelines, it's worth digging deeper to determine what *fitting* means in the context of a pipeline. In this context, *fitting* means that any portions of the pipeline that need to be trained are trained with the input data. For the portion of the pipeline that encodes categorical values, training the pipeline means setting the correspondence between input values in the categorical columns and the integer identifiers that will replace them. To return to the example from section 8.11, if "2019" is mapped to "5" when the model is trained, for new data items that are scored in deployment, "2019" is also mapped to "5." This is exactly what we want, and we have it thanks to pipelines.

8.13 *Applying pipelines in the scoring phase*

In section 8.12, we went through the details of how the pipelines were defined, trained, and saved in the model training phase. In this section, we'll go through how these pipelines are applied in the scoring phase with the deployed Keras model.

The scoring code in actions.py (for Facebook Messenger deployment) or flask_server.py (for web deployment) imports the custom transformer classes from custom_classes.py and loads the trained pipelines that were saved in the streetcar_ model_training notebook. Figure 8.20 summarizes how the pipeline elements are related among these three files.

Let's review the pipeline-related portions of the scoring code. The statements shown here are the same for the web deployment and the Facebook Messenger deployment. First, the scoring code imports the custom transformer class definitions with code that's identical to the code in the model training code:

```
from custom_classes import encode_categorical
from custom_classes import prep_for_keras_input
from custom_classes import fill_empty
from custom_classes import encode_text
```

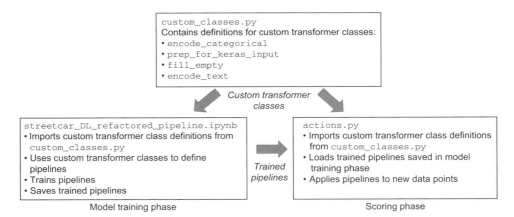

Figure 8.20   Relationships among the files containing pipeline code

The definition for the custom action in the scoring code includes the following statements to load the trained pipelines that were saved in the model training phase:

```
pipeline1 = load(open(pipeline1_path, 'rb'))
pipeline2 = load(open(pipeline2_path, 'rb'))
```

The scoring code loads the data points for the streetcar trip that we want to get a delay prediction for into the Pandas dataframe `score_df`. In the following statements, the pipelines are applied to this dataframe:

```
prepped_xform1 = pipeline1.transform(score_df)
prepped_xform2 = pipeline2.transform(prepped_xform1)
```

Now the output of these pipelines can be applied to the trained model to get a prediction about whether the streetcar trip is going to be delayed:

```
pred = loaded_model.predict(prepped_xform2, batch_size=BATCH_SIZE)
```

We have now been through how pipelines are used in the streetcar delay project, from the definition of the pipelines in the model training phase to the application of pipelines to new data points in the scoring phase with a deployed model. Pipelines are powerful tools that make deployment more straightforward by encapsulating the data transformation steps used in the training process so that they can be used conveniently in the scoring process. In the streetcar delay prediction project, we train pipelines for data preparation in the model training phase and then use the same pipelines to prepare new input data points in the scoring phase for both web deployment and Facebook Messenger deployment.

8.14 *Maintaining a model after deployment*

Deployment is not the end of the road for a trained model. In a full-blown deployment of a deep learning model, it is essential to monitor the model in production to ensure that its performance does not get worse over time. If the performance does get worse (a phenomenon called *model drift* or *concept drift*), it is necessary to retrain the model on fresh data. Figure 8.21 summarizes the cycle of model maintenance. When a model has been trained and deployed, its performance needs to be assessed. If necessary, the model needs to be retrained with data that includes more recent data points. Then the retrained model needs to be deployed.

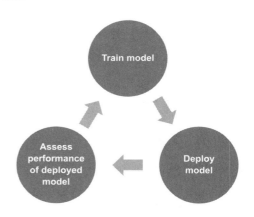

Figure 8.21 Model maintenance cycle

A thorough description of maintaining a deep learning model in an industrial-strength deployment is beyond the scope of this book. (You can find some good advice at http://mng.bz/yry7 and http://mng.bz/ModE, and a great overview that includes deployment options at http://mng.bz/awRx.) But we can look at an example of what happens if the model maintenance cycle is not followed after a model is deployed. Consider the credit card fraud detection example from chapter 1. One of the signals that a credit card fraud prediction model could pick up is two transactions happening on the same day with the same card in physical retail locations that are impossible to travel between in a day. It is currently impossible to get commercial flights to take you between Quebec City and Singapore in less than 24 hours, for example, so if the same card is used in one day to pay for a meal at a high-end restaurant in Quebec City and to pay for a diamond ring at a jewelry store in Singapore, something is wrong. But what happens if an airline starts to offer direct flights between Quebec City and Singapore so it becomes possible to be in both cities in the same day? What if a more drastic change occurs, such as supersonic passenger air travel making a comeback in the early 2030s? Such a change would disrupt any fraud detection model that relied on the signal of same-day purchases in distant cities. The data that feeds machine learning models often comes from the real world, and the real world keeps changing in unpredictable ways. We need to expect that our models will need to be retrained regularly on fresh data.

How often do models need to be retrained? What model performance measurements need to be monitored to determine when retraining is necessary? Can we simply swap the old model out of production and swap in the new model, or do we need to keep both in production and use a blended score (with some proportion from the old model and some from the new model) for a transition period to avoid sudden changes in the end user's experience? See https://mlinproduction.com/model-retraining and http://mng.bz/ggyZ for a more detailed examinations of retraining issues. Here is a brief summary of some best practices for model retraining:

- Save the performance measurements so you can do assessments of performance of the deployed model. To assess the accuracy of your predictions, you will need to have the predictions and the matching real-world outcomes. For the streetcar delay problem, to assess the model performance in production for a month, we need the actual delay data along with predictions that the model would make for the route/direction/time-slot combinations for that month. If we save predictions that are made during a month, we can compare those predictions with the actual delay data when it becomes available for a month.

- Pick a performance measurement that gives you a way to assess how your model is doing without excessive latency. Consider the credit card fraud problem. Suppose that we put a model into production to predict whether transactions are fraudulent, and our performance measurement for the deployed model depends on having a complete report of actual fraudulent transactions for a month. It may take several months to get complete conclusions on all transactions in a given month that are actually fraudulent. In this case, it would be better to have a performance measurement that worked with transactions that were conclusively determined to be fraudulent within the same month. In short, a performance measurement that yields good results soon enough to allow you to make retraining decisions quickly is better than a performance measurement that yields great results but risks having a poorly performing model deployed for many months.

- Do an experiment with historical data to get an idea of how quickly your deployed model's performance will degrade. For the credit card fraud problem, you could train your model with data up to the end of 2018 and then apply the trained model to get predictions on transactions for the first 6 months of 2019. You can compare those predictions with the data you have for actual fraudulent transactions for those 6 months to see whether the accuracy of the model trained on 2018 data gets worse over time on the 2019 data. This process may give you a sense of how quickly your model performance degrades, but it won't be foolproof, because depending on the problem, your data can change in unexpected ways.

- Repeat the data exploration steps you did before training the model on new data. Recall the data exploration that we did in chapter 3. If we were to repeat these steps on new streetcar delay data as it becomes available, we could detect shifts in the characteristics of the data and retrain the model if we find significant shifts.

Let's look at the model retraining question in the context of the streetcar delay prediction model. First, let's look at the raw data. The raw data gets updated monthly with a delay of two to three months. In January, for example, the latest delay data is from the previous October. With a decent development environment, the end-to-end process, from downloading the latest raw data to deploying an updated model, takes less than an hour. With that low a cost, it would be possible to retrain the model every month, but would it be necessary? The data exploration we did in chapter 3 showed that there were some long-term trends (such as delays becoming shorter but more frequent) but no huge oscillations between months. We could probably get away with refreshing the model every quarter, but to be sure, we would want to monitor the model for accuracy by comparing predictions with actual delay data for new months as they become available.

Further, we might want to run some experiments training the model only on more recent data, for example by keeping a three-year rolling window for training data rather than training on the entire dataset since January 2014.

Finally, we would want to provide our users a way to give direct feedback on their experience with the end application. Direct feedback from a subset of users can reveal model problems that monitoring overlooks.

Summary

- A trained deep learning model is not useful by itself. To make it useful, you need to deploy it, making it accessible to other programs or to users who need to take advantage of the model's predictions. Deployment is challenging because it involves a set of technical capabilities that is distinct from the technical approaches that you have learned about in the data preparation and model training chapters of this book.

- You can get a minimal deployment of your model by using Flask, a Python web framework library, along with a set of HTML pages. With this combination of Flask, HTML, and JavaScript, your users can enter the details about their intended streetcar trips in a web page and get predictions on whether the trips will be delayed. Behind the scenes, the trained deep learning model is invoked with the trip details and produces a prediction, which is prepared to be displayed in a web page.

- If you want a smoother user experience, you can deploy your trained deep learning model by using a combination of the Rasa chatbot framework and Facebook Messenger. When you have completed this deployment, your users can message the chatbot in Facebook Messenger with an English-language question such as "Will Route 501 east be delayed?" and get an answer back (delay/no delay) in Facebook Messenger. Behind the scenes, the Rasa chatbot extracts the key details from the question the user entered in Facebook Messenger, invokes a Python module that applies the trained deep learning model to get a prediction for these details, and prepares the prediction for display in Facebook Messenger.

- Pipelines allow you to encapsulate the data preparation steps (including assigning numeric values to categorical column entries and converting the dataset from a Pandas dataframe to the format required by the Keras deep learning model) so that identical transformations can be applied to the data at training time and at scoring time (when the trained model is being applied to new data points, such as the time/route/direction combination for a streetcar trip).

- When you have deployed a trained deep learning model, you need to monitor its performance. If the data changes, the performance of the model may degrade over time, and you may need to retrain the model on more recent data and then replace the currently deployed model with the retrained model.

Recommended next steps

This chapter covers

- A review of what we have covered so far in this book
- Additional enhancements you could make to the streetcar delay prediction project
- How you can apply what you have learned to other real-world projects
- Criteria to use to select a deep learning project that uses structured data
- Resources for additional learning

We have almost reached the end of the book. In this chapter, we'll look back and look forward. First, we'll review what we have learned in the previous chapters, from cleaning up a real-world dataset to deploying a trained deep learning model. Next, we'll go over the steps you can take to enhance the streetcar delay prediction project with new data sources. Then we'll talk about how you can apply what you have learned to other real-world projects, including how to determine whether a given problem involving structured data is a good candidate for a deep learning project. Finally, we'll review some resources for additional learning about deep learning.

9.1 Reviewing what we have covered so far

To review what we have learned so far in this book, let's return to the end-to-end diagram introduced in chapter 2, shown in figure 9.1.

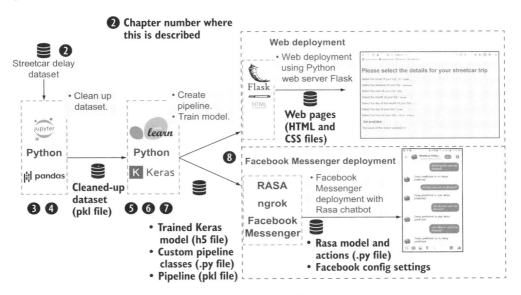

Figure 9.1 The end-to-end view of the streetcar delay prediction project

In chapter 2, we learned how to ingest a tabular structured dataset into Python by using Pandas. In chapters 3 and 4, we went through the process of fixing problems with the dataset, including ill-formed entries, errors, and missing values. In chapter 5, we refactored the dataset to account for the fact that it included information about streetcar delays but no explicit information about situations when there was no delay. We used this refactored dataset to create a simple Keras model whose layers were automatically generated based on the column structure of the dataset. In chapter 6, we iteratively trained this model using the prepared dataset and took advantage of Keras facilities to control the training process and save the model that had the best performance characteristics. In chapter 7, we conducted a set of experiments on the trained model to validate the impact of removing bad records and using embeddings. We also ran an experiment to compare the deep learning model with a key competitor, XGBoost. In chapter 8, we deployed the trained model with a simple web deployment and with a more sophisticated Facebook Messenger deployment. With these deployments, we completed the journey from raw dataset to a working system that a user could use to get predictions on streetcar delays.

9.2   *What we could do next with the streetcar delay prediction project*

We have covered a lot of ground in this book so far, but we could take several other paths with the streetcar prediction project. We could augment the training dataset to include additional data sources, for example.

Why would we want to train the model with additional sources of data? The first reason would be to try to improve the accuracy of the model. It is possible that a model trained with additional data sources would make more accurate predictions than the model we trained in chapter 6. Adding data from other sources (such as historical weather data or traffic data) or making use of more data from the original dataset (such as delay locations) could provide a stronger signal for the model to detect as it tries to predict delays.

Do we know ahead of time whether training the model with additional data sources will make the model's delay predictions more accurate? In short, no, but making the model more accurate isn't the only goal of augmenting the training dataset. The second reason to train the model with additional data sources is that doing so is a great learning exercise. As you go through the process of training the model with additional data sources, you will learn more about the code and prepare yourself for the next step: adapting the deep learning with structured data approach to entirely new datasets, as introduced in section 9.8.

In the following sections, we will briefly review some additional data that you could add to the dataset that is used to train the model. Section 9.4 reviews how you could take advantage of the delay location data that is in the original dataset but not used in the model training we did in chapter 6. It shows you how you could train the model with a dataset that includes a net new data source: historical weather information. Section 9.5 gives you some ideas on how you could augment the training data by deriving new columns from the dataset used to train the model in chapter 6. When you have reviewed these sections, you will be ready for the sections 9.8–9.11 where you will learn how to adapt the approach taken with the streetcar delay prediction problem to new problems involving structured data. In section 9.12 you will see the approach applied to a specific new problem, predicting the price of Airbnb listings in New York City.

9.3   *Adding location details to the streetcar delay prediction project*

In chapter 4, we explained how you can use Google's geocoding API (http:// mng.bz/X06Y) to replace the location data in the streetcar delay dataset with latitude and longitude values. We did not end up using this approach in the rest of the extended example, but you could revisit it to see whether adding geospatial data to the refactored dataset could yield a model with improved performance. You would expect to get higher-fidelity predictions because, as the delay heat map in figure 9.2 shows, delays are clustered in the center of the city. A trip that starts and ends outside the city center should be less likely to be delayed, even if it is on a route/direction/time combination that is likely to encounter delays.

Figure 9.2   Delays are clustered in the central part of the city.

One way that you could take advantage of latitude and longitude values derived from locations in the original dataset is to divide each route into subroutes. Here is an approach you could take to automatically divide each route into subsections based on the latitude and longitude values for the route:

  1 Define a bounding box around the entire route, defined by the maximum and minimum longitude and latitude values for the route. You can use the latitude and longitude values for delays on the route as a proxy for the entire route to get the maximum and minimum values. The streetcar_data_geocode_get_boundaries notebook includes code you can use, including the def_min_max() function, which creates a dataframe with minimum and maximum latitude and longitude values for each route, as the following listing shows.

Listing 9.1   Code to define a dataframe with route boundaries

```
def def_min_max(df):
    # define dataframes with the maxes and mins for each route
    df_max_lat = \
df.sort_values('latitude',ascending=False).drop_duplicates(['Route'])
    df_max_long = \
df.sort_values('longitude',ascending=False).drop_duplicates(['Route'])
    df_min_lat = \
df.sort_values('latitude',ascending=True).drop_duplicates(['Route'])
    df_min_long = \
```

```
df.sort_values('longitude',ascending=True).drop_duplicates(['Route'])
    # rename column names for final dataframe
    df_max_lat = df_max_lat.rename(columns = {'latitude':'max_lat'})
    df_max_long = df_max_long.rename(columns = {'longitude':'max_long'})
    df_min_lat = df_min_lat.rename(columns = {'latitude':'min_lat'})
    df_min_long = df_min_long.rename(columns = {'longitude':'min_long'})
    # join the max dataframes
    df_max = pd.merge(df_max_lat,df_max_long, on='Route', how='left')
    df_max = df_max.drop(['longitude','latitude'],1)
    # join the min dataframes
    df_min = pd.merge(df_min_lat,df_min_long, on='Route', how='left')
    df_min = df_min.drop(['longitude','latitude'],1)
    # join the intermediate dataframes to get the df with the bounding boxes
    df_bounding_box = pd.merge(df_min,df_max, on='Route', how='left')
    return(df_bounding_box)
```

Figure 9.3 shows the resulting minimum and maximum latitude and longitude values for a subset of routes.

	Route	min_lat	min_long	max_lat	max_long
0	501	43.588204	-79.546264	43.687095	-79.281350
1	301	43.591972	-79.544865	43.680364	-79.281542
2	bad route	43.591972	-79.543895	43.684692	-79.281542
3	504	43.591972	-79.543895	43.686952	-79.281542
4	502	43.591972	-79.543895	43.686952	-79.281542

Figure 9.3   Minimum and maximum latitude and longitude values for a subset of routes

2 Now that you have bounding boxes for each route defined as the maximum and minimum latitude and longitude values for each route, you can divide the bounding box into a number (say, 10) of equal-size rectangles along its main axis. For most routes, this axis would be the east–west axis. For the Spadina and Bathurst routes, it would be the north–south axis. The result would be sub-routes for each route defined by minimum and maximum longitude and latitude values. Figure 9.4 shows what the bounding boxes for the subroutes might look like for the St. Clair route.

3 With these subroutes defined for each route, you could add a column in the refactored dataset so that each row of the revised refactored dataset represented a route/subroute/direction/date and time combination. Using the latitude and longitude values for delay locations, for each delay you could identify the subroute where the delay occurred. Figure 9.5 shows a snippet of the original refactored dataset, and figure 9.6 shows what the refactored dataset would look like after a subroute column was added to it.

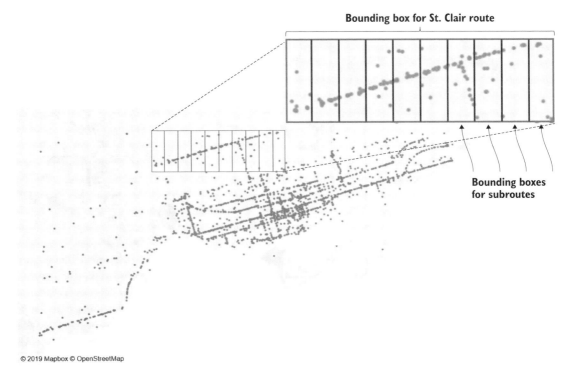

Figure 9.4 Subroute bounding boxes for the St Clair route

	Report Date	Count	Route	Direction	Hour	Year	Month	Daym	Day	Min Delay	Target
0	2014-01-01	0	301	e	0	2014	1	1	2	0.0	0
1	2014-01-01	0	301	e	1	2014	1	1	2	0.0	0
2	2014-01-01	0	301	e	2	2014	1	1	2	0.0	0
3	2014-01-01	0	301	e	3	2014	1	1	2	0.0	0
4	2014-01-01	0	301	e	4	2014	1	1	2	0.0	0

Figure 9.5 Original refactored dataset

**New column
for subroutes**

	Report Date	Count	Route	Sub Route	Direction	Hour	Year	Month	Daym	Day	Min Delay	Target
0	2014-01-01	0	301	0	e	0	2014	1	1	2	0.0	0
1	2014-01-01	0	301	1	e	1	2014	1	1	2	0.0	0
2	2014-01-01	0	301	2	e	2	2014	1	1	2	0.0	0
3	2014-01-01	0	301	3	e	3	2014	1	1	2	0.0	0
4	2014-01-01	0	301	4	e	4	2014	1	1	2	0.0	0

Figure 9.6   Refactored dataset with subroute column added

When you have added subroutes to the refactored dataset and retrained the model with this augmented dataset, you face the challenge of how to enable the user to define what subroutes of a given route they are traveling through. To score with the revised model, you would need to get start and end locations from the user for their trip. For the web deployment, you could add a new control in home.html to allow the user to select the subroute for their trip. The user experience would not be ideal with web deployment, so what about enhancing the Facebook Messenger deployment to allow the user to specify a subroute? You could take two approaches:

- Enhance the Rasa model to allow the user to enter major cross-street names and then use the geocode API to translate the intersections of these streets with the streetcar route into latitude and longitude values.
- Use Facebook Messenger's webview feature (http://mng.bz/xmB6) to display an interactive map widget in a web page that allows the user to select route points.

Overall, adding subroutes to the streetcar delay prediction model would likely improve performance, but it would be nontrivial work to adapt the web deployment or the Facebook Messenger deployment to allow the user to specify the start and end points of their trip.

9.4   *Training our deep learning model with weather data*

Toronto has four distinct seasons, with extremes of weather in the winter and summer. These extremes can have an impact on streetcar delays. Even a modest snowfall, for example, can cause gridlock that delays streetcars across the network. Suppose that we want to harness weather data to see whether it yields better predictions of streetcar delays. Where do we start? This section summarizes what you need to do to add weather data to the streetcar delay prediction model.

The first challenge is finding a source for weather data to incorporate into the training dataset. There are several open source data sources (http://mng.bz/5pp4) for weather information. Figure 9.7 shows the interface for exercising endpoints for one such source: Dark Sky (http://mng.bz/A0DQ). You will need to provide credentials (such as your GitHub ID and password) to access this interface, and although you get a free allocation of API calls, you will need to provide payment information to run a test exercise of the API.

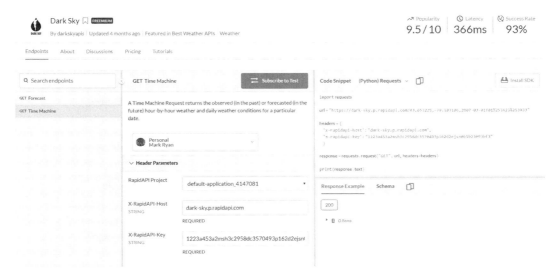

Figure 9.7 Exercising a weather information API

Suppose that we want to see what the weather was like early in the morning of March 3, 2007, at Toronto City Hall. Here are the parameters that the API requires:

- Date time: 2007-03-01T01:32:33
- Longitude: -79.383186
- Latitude: 43.653225

The API interface shows you what the Python API call looks like for this request, as shown in the next listing.

Listing 9.2 Sample code produced by the Dark Sky API interface

```
import requests

url = https://dark-sky.p.rapidapi.com/\
43.653225,-79.383186,2007-03-01T01%253A32%253A33

headers = {
    'x-rapidapi-host': "dark-sky.p.rapidapi.com",
```

URL built with the date/time, latitude, and longitude input

```
        'x-rapidapi-key': <API KEY>
        }

response = requests.request("GET", url, headers=headers)

print(response.text)
```

To run this call, you need to get an API key for Dark Sky and paste it here.

Figure 9.8 shows the results returned by this API call. How could we use this weather data? To begin with, we want to control the number of API calls we need to make to minimize the overall cost. The cost per Dark Sky call is a fraction of a cent, but the overall cost could add up if we aren't careful. Consider the following approach to getting weather data that is specific in location and time:

1 Use the subroutes introduced in section 9.3, and get distinct weather data points for each subroute by using the mean latitude and longitude value for each subroute bounding box.
2 For each subroute, get four weather data points per hour.

With this approach, we would need more than 31 million weather data points to cover the training data starting in January 2014. The cost of all these API calls would be more than $40,000 US—a huge cost for an experiment. How can we still get useful weather data without needing so many data points?

We are lucky that the streetcar delay problem is limited to a relatively small geographic area with predictable weather patterns, so we can make some simplifying assumptions to control the number of weather data points we need. The following simplifying assumptions will let us add weather data to the refactored dataset with a minimal number of API calls:

∨ Response Body

```
▼ {   8 items
      "latitude" : 43.653225
      "longitude" : -79.383186
      "timezone" : "America/Toronto"
    ▼ "currently" : {   16 items
          "time" : 1172730753
          "summary" : "Partly Cloudy"
          "icon" : "partly-cloudy-night"
          "precipIntensity" : 0
          "precipProbability" : 0
          "temperature" : 26.55
          "apparentTemperature" : 24.36
          "dewPoint" : 10.83
          "humidity" : 0.51
          "pressure" : 1022.5
          "windSpeed" : 2.89
          "windGust" : 4.2
          "windBearing" : 15
          "cloudCover" : 0.35
          "uvIndex" : 0
          "visibility" : 10
   }
```

Figure 9.8   Response to weather API call with weather details for Toronto City Hall early on March 3, 2007

- *Weather conditions are consistent for a particular hour.* We get only 24 weather data points for a day, rather than multiple data points per hour. Weather can certainly change within an hour, but the kind of weather that contributes to streetcar delays (such as downpours of rain or major snowfalls) rarely starts and stops in Toronto in the course of a single hour. We can safely take a single weather reading per hour.

- *Weather conditions are consistent throughout the streetcar network.* The entire streetcar network is contained in an area 26 km from east to west and 11 km from north to south, as shown by the bounding box in figure 9.9, so it's a reasonable assumption to say that the kind of weather that would cause streetcar delays is consistent at any time across the entire network. That is, if it's snowing heavily at Long Branch, at the western end of the network, there is probably snow in The Beach, at the eastern end of the network. With this assumption, we can use (43.653225, -79.383186), the latitude and longitude of Toronto's City Hall, for all calls to the weather API.

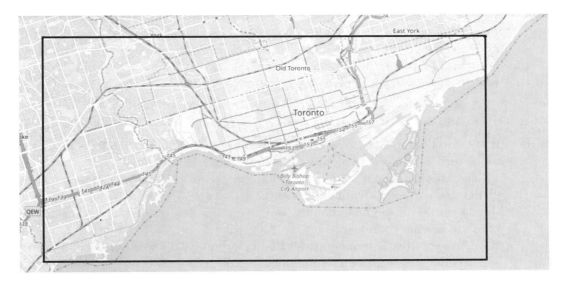

Figure 9.9   Bounding box for the streetcar network

Here are the extremes of the streetcar network as latitudes and longitudes:

```
min_lat = 43.58735
max_lat = 43.687840
min_long = -79.547860
max_long = -79.280260
```

With these simplifying assumptions, we need weather data for every hour since January 1, 2014, or about 52,500 data points. Given what Dark Sky charges per API call, it would cost about $60 US to generate the required weather datapoints.

Now that we've established the volume of historical weather data that we need, which weather features do we want to incorporate into the dataset? Here are some obvious weather dataset fields that could be relevant for predicting streetcar delays:

- *Temperature*—In the absence of active precipitation, temperature extremes could have a correlation with delays. Temperature would be a continuous column in the dataset.
- *Icon*—Values in this field, such as "snow" or "rain," neatly encapsulate the weather conditions. Icon would be a categorical column in the dataset.
- *Summary*—Values in this field, such as "Rain throughout the day" and "Light snow starting in the morning," provide extra context about the overall weather condition captured in the icon column. The summary column could be a text column. Recall that the refactored dataset used to train the deep learning model in chapter 6 did not contain any text columns. It would be interesting to add summary as a text column because it would exercise an aspect of the deep learning model code that the core streetcar delay dataset didn't exploit.

Assuming that you get the weather datapoints described in the preceding list, you will need to update the dataset refactoring code in the streetcar_model_training notebook to incorporate the weather fields. In particular, you need to add the column names for the weather fields to the appropriate lists in def_col_lists():

- Add the temperature column name to continuouscols.
- Add the summary column name to textcols.

If you don't put the icon column name in any other list, it will be added automatically to the list for categorical columns, which is exactly what we want.

The training code is written to work for any set of columns as long as the column names are correctly identified in def_col_lists(). The rest of the training code should work with the new columns and give you a new trained model that incorporates the weather columns.

When you have a trained model that incorporates the weather columns, how do you account for the weather conditions at scoring time when a user wants to know whether their streetcar trip will be delayed? First, you add the new weather columns to the score_cols list in the scoring code. This list is the list of columns that get scored and is used to define score_df, the dataframe that contains the values that are run through the pipelines in the scoring code. You can call the Dark Sky API in the scoring code to get the current weather conditions, using the Toronto City Hall latitude and longitude noted earlier, and build a string for the current time in the format required by Dark Sky: [YYYY]-[MM]-[DD]T[HH]:[MM]:[SS]. So if the current date is May 24, 2021, and the time is noon, the date time string for the Dark Sky API is 2020-05-24T12:00:00. When you get the required weather fields returned from the API call, you can use these values to set the weather columns in score_df. The scoring code runs score_df through the pipelines and applies the output of the pipelines to the trained model, and you get a delay prediction. Because of the simplifying assumptions stated earlier, you don't need any information from the user at scoring time to get the weather data needed for scoring.

Figure 9.10 summarizes the changes required to incorporate weather data into the streetcar delay prediction deep learning project via Facebook Messenger deployment. To adapt the web deployment, you would make similar changes to the scoring code in the main Python program for web deployment, flask_server.py, as specified in figure 9.10 for actions.py, the main Python program for Facebook Messenger deployment.

Changes to model training code
`streetcar_DL_refactored_pipeline.ipynb`

- Call Dark Sky API to get weather data for period covered by training dataset
- Update `prep_merged_data ()` to incorporate weather data
- Update `def_col_lists ()` to include weather columns

Changes to scoring code `actions.py`

- Call Dark Sky API with Torono City Hall latitude/longitude and current date/time to get current weather data
- Update `score_cols` to include weather column names

Figure 9.10   Summary of changes required to add weather data to the streetcar delay model

This exercise of adding weather data to your deep learning model not only gives you the opportunity to improve the performance of the model, but also shows the steps you need to take to add other data sources to the streetcar delay deep learning model. You can extrapolate from the steps described in this section to create a deep learning model on a new dataset. Section 9.8 introduces the additional steps you need to take to apply the approach described in this book to a new structured dataset. But before we look at a new project, in section 9.5 we are going to look at two simple options to augment the training dataset for the streetcar delay prediction project.

9.5   Adding season or time of day to the streetcar delay prediction project

In sections 9.3 and 9.4, we reviewed two additional data sources that we could add to the training data for the model: delay location data and weather data. Both of these data sources are relatively challenging to add to the training process. If you want to take a simpler approach to adding data to the training dataset, you can try to derive new columns from columns in the dataset we used to train the model in chapter 6. A season column derived from the month column, with values 0–3 for the four seasons, is a relatively simple addition, for example.

As you can derive a season column from the month column, you can derive a time-of-day column from the hour column. The interesting aspect of this column is that you could control the boundaries of each time of day. Suppose that you define a time-of-day column with five values:

- Overnight
- Morning rush hour
- Midday
- Afternoon rush hour
- Evening

You could experiment with different start and end times for each category to see the impact on the model's performance. Would it make a difference in the model's performance if you defined a morning rush hour from 5:30 to 10 a.m. versus 6:30 to 9:00 a.m.?

9.6   Imputation: An alternative to removing records with bad values

In chapter 7, we did an experiment to compare the model's performance with two forms of the training dataset:

- Excluding records with bad values (such as records with invalid routes)
- Including records with bad values

The conclusion of this experiment was that the model has better performance when the bad values are removed. Despite this conclusion, we pay a price for removing the records with bad values. For a given run on the data preparation notebook using delay data up until the end of 2019, there are about 78,500 delay records in the input dataset, but only about 61,500 records after the records with bad values have been removed. In this case, we lose around 20% of the records when we remove the bad records. It's important to remember that we remove the whole record when it is has a bad value in one field, so we could be losing a useful portion of the signal when we throw out all the records with bad values. Are there any alternatives that would allow us to preserve some of this lost signal?

As it turns out, an approach called *imputation,* which replaces missing values with another value, could help. In the case of structured, tabular data, the kind of imputation that is available depends on the type of the column:

- *Continuous*—You can replace missing values with a fixed value (such as zero) or a computed value (such as the average of all the values in the column).
- *Categorical*—You can replace missing values with the most common value in the column or take a more sophisticated approach to apply a model (such as the 1,000 nearest neighbors) to find a replacement for missing values.

If you want to experiment with imputation for the streetcar delay prediction model, you can find a more complete discussion of imputation approaches in an article on dealing with missing values (http://mng.bz/6AAG).

9.7   Making the web deployment of the streetcar delay prediction model generally available

In chapter 8, we described how to create a simple web deployment of the trained model. The web deployment described in chapter 8 is entirely local; you can access it only on the system where the deployment is done. What if you want to share this deployment with your friends on other systems?

The simplest way to open the web deployment is to use ngrok, the utility we used in chapter 8 for the Facebook Messenger deployment. In that chapter, we used ngrok to externalize localhost so that your Facebook app could communicate with the Rasa chatbot server running on your local system.

To use ngrok to make your web deployment accessible outside your local system, follow these steps:

1 If you haven't already done so, follow the installation instructions at https://ngrok.com/download to install ngrok.

2 In the directory where you installed ngrok, invoke ngrok to make local-host:5000 on your system externally available. Here is the command for Windows:

```
.\ngrok http 5000
```

3 Copy the https forwarding URL in the ngrok output, highlighted in figure 9.11.

```
ngrok by @inconshreveable

Session Status              online
Account                     Mark Ryan (Plan: Business)
Update                      update available (version 2.3.35, Ctrl-U to update)
Version                     2.3.34
Region                      United States (us)
Web Interface               http://127.0.0.1:4040
Forwarding                  http://1bf6f9dd.ngrok.io -> http://localhost:5000
Forwarding                  https://1bf6f9dd.ngrok.io -> http://localhost:5000

Connections                 ttl     opn     rt1     rt5     p50     p90
                            0       0       0.00    0.00    0.00    0.00
```

Figure 9.11   ngrok output with forwarding URL highlighted

4 Start the web deployment by running this command in the deploy_web directory:

```
python flask_server.py
```

Now that you have ngrok running to externalize localhost:5000, the web deployment will be available to other users at the forwarding URL provided by ngrok. If other users open the ngrok forwarding URL in a browser, they will see home.html, as shown in figure 9.12.

When a user on another system has opened home.html at the ngrok forwarding URL, they can select scoring parameters and click Get Prediction to show a delay prediction for their streetcar trip. Note that this deployment will be available to other users only when your local system is connected to the internet and flask_server.py is

Figure 9.12   home.html served via ngrok with an externally accessible URL

running. Also note that with the free ngrok plan, you get a different forwarding URL each time you invoke ngrok. If you need a fixed URL for your web deployment with ngrok, you need to get one of the ngrok paid subscription options.

In sections 9.3–9.5, we introduced some ideas for additional data sources that could improve the performance of the streetcar delay prediction model. In section 9.8, we'll outline how you could apply the approach used for the streetcar delay problem to a new problem.

9.8   *Adapting the streetcar delay prediction model to a new dataset*

The previous sections outlined how you could augment the streetcar delay prediction model by incorporating additional data in the training set for the model. What if you wanted to adapt the model for a different dataset? This section summarizes the steps to adapt the approach described in this book to a new structured dataset.

The code examples in this book can be applied to other tabular structured datasets, but you need to take some steps, summarized in figure 9.13, to adapt the streetcar delay prediction code.

When you consider applying the approach described in this book to a new dataset, the first challenge is whether the dataset meets the minimum requirements to be

---

Data cleaning code

- Write code to remove errors, rationalize duplicates and deal with missing values
- Adapt code to explore dataset

Model training code

- Update `def_col_lists()` to include columns from your dataset
- Adapt `prep_merged_data`, master prep calls code block and related code for your dataset

---

Scoring code in web deployment

- Update `score_cols` to include the columns from your dataset that are required for scoring
- Adapt `home.html` to display the scoring parameters for your problem and update the JavaScript function `getOption()` to handle the scoring parameters for your problem
- Adapt the view function for `show_prediction` in `flask_server.py` to include the scoring parameters for your problem

Scoring code in Facebook Messenger deployment

- Update `score_cols` to include the columns from your dataset that are required for scoring
- Adapt custom action class code in `actions.py` to include setting default values for scoring columns that you want to be optional for the user
- Adapt Rasa control (`domain.yml`) and training (`nlu.md`, `stories.md`) file for your problem set and retrain Rasa model

Figure 9.13   Summary of changes required to create a model for new dataset

applicable to deep learning. Here are some of the characteristics of a structured dataset that could be considered for deep learning:

- *Big enough*—Recall the discussion in chapter 3 about how big a structured dataset needed to be for deep learning to have a chance of success. A dataset that doesn't have at least tens of thousands of records is too small. On the other side, unless you have the experience and resources to add big data approaches to your toolkit, a dataset with tens of millions of records will be a challenge. A dataset with more than 70,000 records and fewer than 10,000,000 records is a good place to start.

- *Heterogenous*—If your dataset is made up entirely of continuous columns, you will get a better return on your investment from using a non-deep-learning approach, such as XGBoost, to make predictions on it. But if you have a dataset that includes a variety of column types, including categorical and especially text columns, it could be a good candidate for deep learning. If your dataset contains columns with nontext BLOB data, such as images, you could get many benefits from applying deep learning to the whole dataset instead of taking the more conventional approach of applying deep learning only to the BLOB data.

- *Not too imbalanced*—In the refactored streetcar delay dataset, about 2% of the records indicated a delay for the route/direction/time slot of the record. As described in chapter 6, Keras has parameters for the `fit` command that take imbalanced datasets into account. But if the dataset is extremely imbalanced, with only a small fraction of a percent belonging to one of the outcomes, it may not be possible for the deep learning model to pick up the signal of what characterizes the minority outcome.

Let's consider a couple of open datasets and apply these guidelines to them to get a quick assessment of whether problems associated with these datasets could be amenable to a deep learning approach:

- *Traffic signal vehicle and pedestrian volumes* (http://mng.bz/ZPw9)—This dataset comes from the same curated collection as the streetcar delay dataset. It contains traffic volume information for a set of intersections in Toronto. It would be interesting to use this dataset to predict traffic volume in the future. Does this problem lend itself to a deep learning project? Figure 9.14 shows that the dataset has a variety of columns, including continuous, categorical, and geospatial columns.

TCS #	Main	Midblock Route	Side 1 Route	Side 2 Route	Activation Date	Latitude	Longitude	Count Date	8 Peak Hr Vehicle Volume	8 Peak Hr Pedestrian Volume
2	JARVIS ST		FRONT ST E		11/15/1948	43.649418000	-79.371446000	06-21-2017	15662	13535
3	KING ST E		JARVIS ST		08/23/1950	43.650460600	-79.371923900	09-17-2016	12960	7333
4	JARVIS ST		ADELAIDE ST E		09/12/1958	43.651533700	-79.372360000	11-08-2016	17770	7083
5	JARVIS ST		RICHMOND ST E		04/21/1962	43.652717600	-79.372824000	12-08-2015	19678	4369
6	JARVIS ST		QUEEN ST E		08/24/1928	43.653704000	-79.373238000	09-17-2016	14487	3368
7	JARVIS ST		SHUTER ST		11/18/1948	43.655357000	-79.373862000	11-08-2016	15846	3747

Figure 9.14   Columns in the traffic signal vehicle and pedestrian volumes dataset

Figure 9.15 shows that the distribution of traffic volumes is not too imbalanced.

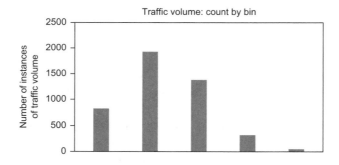

Figure 9.15   Distribution of traffic volumes in the traffic signal vehicle and pedestrian volumes dataset

The problem with this dataset is that it is too small—only 2,300 records—so despite having an interesting set of columns and decent balance, this dataset is not a good candidate for a deep learning project. What about a dataset that covers a similar but distinct problem to streetcar delays?

- *Toronto subway delay dataset* (https://open.toronto.ca/dataset/ttc-subway-delay-data)—As you can see in figure 9.16, the subway delay dataset includes a range of column types, including categorical, continuous, and geospatial. The whole dataset has about half a million records, so it is big enough to be interesting without being unwieldly.

Compared with the streetcar delay dataset, this dataset is a bit more balanced, because there are about seven times as many delays reported on the subway

Date	Time	Day	Station	Code	Min Delay	Min Gap	Bound	Line	Vehicle
2019-12-01	00:23	Sunday	WARDEN STATION	MUSAN	5	10	E	BD	5117
2019-12-01	00:59	Sunday	OLD MILL STATION	MUSAN	5	10	E	BD	5293
2019-12-01	01:13	Sunday	BROADVIEW STATION	TUMVS	0	0	W	BD	5221
2019-12-01	08:00	Sunday	BLOOR DANFORTH SUBWAY	MUO	0	0		BD	0
2019-12-01	08:00	Sunday	BLOOR DANFORTH SUBWAY	MUO	0	0		BD	0
2019-12-01	08:45	Sunday	BLOOR DANFORTH SUBWAY	TUST	0	0	E	BD	5091
2019-12-01	09:00	Sunday	ST PATRICK STATION	TUSC	0	0	S	YU	6051
2019-12-01	09:05	Sunday	VICTORIA PARK STATION	TUOS	0	0	W	BD	5368
2019-12-01	09:15	Sunday	KIPLING STATION	EULT	3	8	E	BD	5009

Figure 9.16 Subway delay dataset

compared with the streetcar system. The interesting aspect of the location data for this dataset is that it is exact. Every delay is identified with one of 75 stations in the Toronto subway, and the spatial relationship between any two stations is easy to encode without needing to use latitude and longitude. Also, at scoring time the user could specify the start and end of a trip exactly by selecting subway stations from a picklist. Accordingly, it would be easier to incorporate location in the training data for a subway delay prediction model than to add location data to the streetcar delay model. Overall, the subway delay prediction project would be a decent candidate for deep learning.

Now that we have looked at a couple of structured datasets that could be candidates for deep learning, section 9.9 provides an overview of the steps required to prepare a new dataset for training a deep learning model.

9.9   *Preparing the dataset and training the model*

When you have picked a dataset that you want to build a deep learning project around, the next challenge is cleaning up the dataset. The examples that you saw in chapters 3 and 4 should guide you in dealing with errors and missing values in your dataset, although the required cleanup steps will vary depending on the dataset and how messy it is.

On the subject of cleaning up data, you may ask why cleaning the data was not a consideration for the weather data described in section 9.4. To answer this question, I'd like to return to an example from chapter 2: creating a Blu-ray disc from an assortment of media (figure 9.17).

The point of this example was to demonstrate that as the various bits of media were not initially recorded with Blu-ray in mind, datasets that are interesting to explore with deep learning were not collected with the intention of applying them to machine learning or deep learning. These messy, real-world datasets must be cleaned up before they can be used to train a deep learning model. A data source like Dark Sky's weather data or the geocoding data available from the Google API, on the other hand, is designed to provide a clean, coherent stream of data that does not require cleaning. These data sources are to deep learning what high-definition digital video clips are to the Blu-ray disc problem: ready to be incorporated without cleanup.

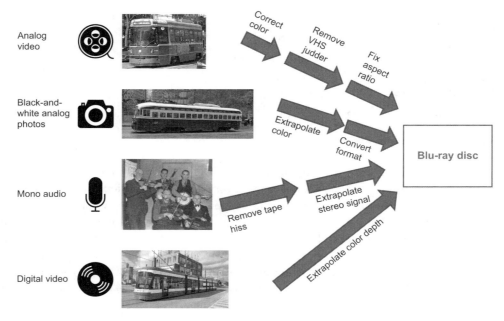

Figure 9.17   Creating a Blu-ray disc from an assortment of media

When you have your new dataset cleaned up, the next step is replacing any non-numeric values, such as by replacing categorical values with integer identifiers. You can adapt the training code to create a dataframe for your new dataset. As in the example of adding weather data, you need to associate the columns you will use to train the model to the correct category in the `def_col_lists()` function. In addition, you need to identify which column contains the target in your dataset. With these changes, you should be able to train a model to make predictions on your new dataset and end up with a trained model along with trained pipelines for preparing data.

Before we go into more detail about how to adapt the code for the streetcar delay problem to another subject area, it's worth revisiting an idea introduced in chapter 4: the critical importance of domain knowledge in a machine learning project. In chapter 4, I explained that one of the reasons I chose the streetcar delay problem as the extended example in this book is that it's a topic about which I happen to have knowledge. As you consider applying deep learning to new subject areas, keep this in mind: if you want to have a successful project, whether it's a modest side project done to hone your own skills or a major project that your organization is betting its future on, you need to have access to domain expertise about the subject area.

9.10 *Deploying the model with web deployment*

Now that you have a trained deep learning model and pipelines for your new dataset, it's time to consider how you will deploy the model. If you choose to use the web deployment option described in chapter 8 to deploy your new model, you will need to make the following updates to the code in the deploy_web directory:

- Update the drop-down lists in home.html (as shown in the following code snippet) to reflect the scoring parameters that you want the user to be able to select to send to the trained model for scoring. In the streetcar delay prediction web deployment, all the scoring parameters are categorical (that is, they can be selected from elements in a list). If your model includes continuous scoring parameters you will need to add controls in home.html where the user can enter continuous values:

```
<select id="route">
    <option value="501">501 / Queen</option>
    <option value="502">502 / Downtowner</option>
    <option value="503">503 / Kingston Rd</option>
    <option value="504">504 / King</option>
    <option value="505">505 / Dundas</option>
    <option value="506">506 / Carlton</option>
    <option value="510">510 / Spadina</option>
    <option value="511">511 / Bathurst</option>
    <option value="512">512 / St Clair</option>
    <option value="301">301 / Queen (night)</option>
    <option value="304">304 / King (night)</option>
    <option value="306">306 / Carlton (night)</option>
    <option value="310">310 / Spadina (night)</option>
</select>
```

- Update the getOption() JavaScript functions in home.html to load the scoring parameters for your model into JavaScript variables. The following snippet shows the code block in getOption() that loads the scoring parameters for the streetcar delay prediction model into JavaScript variables:

```
selectElementRoute = document.querySelector('#route');
selectElementDirection = document.querySelector('#direction');
selectElementYear = document.querySelector('#year');
selectElementMonth = document.querySelector('#month');
selectElementDaym = document.querySelector('#daym');
selectElementDay = document.querySelector('#day');
selectElementHour = document.querySelector('#hour');
route_string = \
 selectElementRoute.options\
[selectElementRoute.selectedIndex].value
direction_string = \
selectElementDirection.options\
[selectElementDirection.selectedIndex].value
year_string = \
selectElementYear.options\
```

```
[selectElementYear.selectedIndex].value
month_string = \
selectElementMonth.options\
[selectElementMonth.selectedIndex].value
daym_string = \
selectElementDaym.options\
[selectElementDaym.selectedIndex].value
day_string = \
selectElementDay.options\
[selectElementDay.selectedIndex].value
hour_string = \
 selectElementHour.options\
[selectElementHour.selectedIndex].value
```

- Update the getOption() JavaScript functions in home.html to build a target URL with the scoring parameters for your model. The following code snippet shows the statement in getOption() that defines the target URL for the street-car delay prediction deployment:

```
window.output = \
prefix.concat("route=",route_string,"&direction=",\
direction_string,"&year=",year_string,"&month=",\
month_string,"&daym=",daym_string,"&day=",\
day_string,"&hour=",hour_string)
```

- Update the view function for show_prediction.html in flask_server.py to build the strings that you want displayed in show_prediction.html for each prediction outcome:

```
if pred[0][0] >= 0.5:
    predict_string = "yes, delay predicted"
else:
    predict_string = "no delay predicted"
```

With these changes, you should be able to use the web deployment from chapter 8 to do a simple deployment of your new model.

9.11 *Deploying the model with Facebook Messenger*

If you choose to use the Facebook Messenger deployment approach described in chapter 8 for your new problem, you will need to make updates to the scoring code in actions.py, including setting score_cols to the names of the columns used to train your model. You will also need to update the code that sets defaults for any values that may not be provided by the user at scoring time. With these changes, you have Python code ready for scoring new data points with your trained model.

The Python code isn't the whole story for deployment using Rasa with Facebook Messenger. You also want to have a natural interface in Facebook Messenger, and to accomplish this task, you will need to create a simple Rasa model. You can use the examples from the streetcar delay deployment to see how to specify sentence-level Rasa training examples in the nlu.md file and multisentence Rasa examples in the stories.md file. Defining the correct set of slots is more challenging. I recommend that you create a slot to correspond with each column name in score_cols. You define these slots in the domain.yml file. For the sake of simplicity, you can set the type of each slot to text. It's best to avoid extraneous slots, so if you are copying the domain.yml file from the streetcar delay example as a starting point, clear out the existing slot values before defining new slot values.

To complete the rest of the deployment of your new model, you will be going through the following subset of the steps you followed in chapter 8 to deploy the streetcar delay prediction model:

1 Create a directory called new_deploy.
2 Run the following command in the deploy directory to set up a basic Rasa environment:

```
rasa init
```

3 Copy the h5 file for your trained model and the pkl files for your pipelines, respectively, into the models and pipelines directories.
4 Replace the actions.py file in the new_deploy directory with the actions.py file that you updated for your new deployment.
5 Replace the nlu.md and stories.md files in the data subdirectory with the nlu.md and stories.md files that you created for your new deployment.
6 Replace the domain.yml file in the new_deploy directory with the domain.yml file for your new deployment.
7 Copy the custom_classes.py and endpoints.yml files from the repo to the new_deploy directory.
8 Copy the deploy_config.yml config file to the new_deploy directory, and update the pipeline and model filename parameters to match the files you copied to the pipelines and models directories in step 3, as shown in the next listing.

Listing 9.3 Parameters that need to be updated in the deploy config file

```
general:
  debug_on: False
  logging_level: "WARNING" # switch to control logging - WARNING for full
  ⇒ logging; ERROR to minimize logging
  BATCH_SIZE: 1000
file_names:
  pipeline1_filename: <your pipeline1 pkl file>    ⊲┘ Replace with the filenames of the
  pipeline2_filename: <your pipeline2 pkl file>       pipeline files you copied to the
  model_filename: <your trained model file>    ⊲┐   pipelines directory in step 3.
```

Replace with the name of the trained model h5 file you copied to the models directory in step 3.

9   Run the following command in your new_deploy directory to invoke actions.py in the Python environment for Rasa:

```
rasa run actions
```

10 In the directory where you installed ngrok, invoke ngrok to make your localhost available to Facebook Messenger on port 5005. Here is the command for Windows; make a note of the HTTPS forwarding URL in the ngrok output:

```
.\ngrok http 5005
```

11 Run the following command in the new_deploy directory to train the Rasa model:

```
rasa train
```

12 Follow the instructions at http://mng.bz/oRRN to add a new Facebook page. You can keep using the same Facebook app you created in chapter 8 for this new deployment. Make note of the page access token and app secret; you will need to update the credentials.yml file with these values in step 13.

13 Update the credentials.yml file in the new_deploy directory to set the verify token (a string value you choose) and secret and page-access-token (provided during the Facebook setup you did in step 12):

```
facebook:
  verify: <verify token that you choose>
  secret: <app secret from Facebook app setup>
  page-access-token: <page access token from Facebook app setup>
```

14 Run the following command in the new_deploy directory to start the Rasa server, using the credentials you set in credentials.yml in step 13:

```
rasa run --credentials credentials.yml
```

15 In the Facebook app you created in chapter 8, choose Messenger -> Settings, scroll down to the Webhooks section, and click Edit Callback URL. Replace the initial part of the Callback URL value with the HTTPS forwarding URL that you noted when you invoked ngrok in step 10. Enter the verify token that you set in credentials.yml in step 13 in the Verify Token field, and click Verify and Save.

16 In Facebook Messenger (mobile or web application), search for the ID of the Facebook page you created in step 12, and enter a query to confirm that your deployed model is accessible.

We have reviewed the steps required to adapt the approach used for the streetcar delay problem to a new structured dataset. Now you have what you need to apply the code samples from this book to new problems when you want to apply deep learning to structured data.

9.12 Adapting the approach in this book to a different dataset

To make it easier to apply the approach in this book to a new problem area, we are going to go through the process of adapting the code that we used for the streetcar delay prediction problem to a new dataset. We aren't going to work through the entire end-to-end problem—only from the initial dataset to a minimal trained deep learning model.

We want to find a dataset that is big enough to give deep learning a fighting chance (a dataset with a record count at least in the tens of thousands), but not so big that the data volume will become the main focus of the exercise. I examined the popular machine learning competition site Kaggle to find a problem with tabular structured data that would be a good fit. I found that the problem of predicting prices for Airbnb properties in New York City (https://www.kaggle.com/dgomonov/new-york-city-airbnb-open-data) had a dataset that was interesting and might be a decent candidate for adapting the methodology described in this book. Figure 9.18 shows a snippet of data from this dataset.

id	name	host_id	host_name	neighbourhood _group	neighbourhood	latitude	longitude	room_type
2539	Clean & quiet apt h	2787	John	Brooklyn	Kensington	40.64749	-73.9724	Private room
2595	Skylit Midtown Cast	2845	Jennifer	Manhattan	Midtown	40.75362	-73.9838	Entire home/apt
3647	THE VILLAGE OF HA	4632	Elisabeth	Manhattan	Harlem	40.80902	-73.9419	Private room
3831	Cozy Entire Floor of	4869	LisaRoxanne	Brooklyn	Clinton Hill	40.68514	-73.9598	Entire home/apt

price	minimum _nights	number_of _reviews	last_review	reviews_per _month	calculated _host_listi ngs_count	availability _365
149	1	9	2018-10-19	0.21	6	365
225	1	45	2019-05-21	0.38	2	355
150	3	0			1	365
89	1	270	2019-07-05	4.64	1	194

Figure 9.18 Example records in the Airbnb NYC dataset

The dataset has slightly fewer than 89,000 records across 16 columns, so the size and complexity of the dataset are in the right ballpark. Let's examine what's in each of the columns:

- id—Numeric identifier for the listing
- name—Description of the listing
- host_id—Numeric identifier for the host associated with the listing
- host_name—Name of the host associated with the listing

- neighbourhood_group—New York borough of the listing: Manhattan, Brooklyn, Queens, Bronx, or Staten Island
- neighbourhood—Neighborhood of the listing
- latitude—Latitude of the listing
- longitude—Longitude of the listing
- room_type—Room type of the listing: entire dwelling, private room, or shared room
- price—Price of the listing (the target of the deep learning model)
- minimum_nights—Minimum number of nights for which the listing can be booked
- number_of_reviews—Number of reviews available for the listing on the Airbnb site
- last_review—Date of the most recent review for the listing
- reviews_per_month—Average number or reviews per month for the listing
- calculated_host_listings_count—Number of listings associated with the host for this listing
- availability_365—Proportion of the year that the listing is available for rental

We get an interesting mix of types with these columns:

- *Continuous*—price, minimum_nights, number_of_reviews, reviews_per_month, calculated_host_listings_count, availability_365
- *Categorical*—neighbourhood_group, neighbourhood, room_type, host_id
- *Text*—name and maybe host_name

In addition to these easily categorized columns, there are id (not interesting from a model training perspective), longitude and latitude (for the purposes of this exercise, we will depend on neighborhood for location), and last_review (for the purposes of this exercise, we won't use this column).

Compared with the streetcar delay dataset, the Airbnb NYC dataset is much less messy. First, let's look at the count of missing values and unique values in each column (figure 9.19).

Compared with the streetcar delay dataset, the Airbnb NYC dataset has fewer columns with missing values. Further, all the categorical columns (neighbourhood_group, neighbourhood, and host_name) seem to have legitimate numbers of values. By comparison, the direction, location, and route columns in the streetcar delay dataset all had extraneous values. The direction column in the raw streetcar delay dataset has 15 distinct values but only 5 valid values, for example.

The relative lack of messiness in the Airbnb NYC dataset highlights one of the problems with the datasets available from Kaggle. Although these datasets are useful for exercising aspects of machine learning, and although participating in competitions on Kaggle is a great way to learn, the curated and sanitized datasets used for the

Column	Missing values	Unique value count
id	0	48895
name	16	47905
host_id	0	37457
host_name	21	11452
neighbourhood_group	0	5
neighbourhood	0	221
latitude	0	19048
longitude	0	14718
room_type	0	3
price	0	674
minimum_nights	0	109
number_of_reviews	0	394
last_review	10052	1764
reviews_per_month	10052	937
calculated_host_listings_count	0	47
availability_365	0	366

Figure 9.19 Column characteristics for the Airbnb NYC dataset

competitions are no substitute for real-world datasets. As you saw in chapters 3 and 4, a real-world dataset is messy in unexpected ways and can take nontrivial work to prepare for training a deep learning model. The limited amount of data preparation that is necessary for the Airbnb dataset (ingesting the CSV file into a Pandas dataframe and replacing missing values with defaults) is contained in the airbnb_data_preparation notebook.

The next listing shows the files from the repo that are related to this example.

Listing 9.4   Code in the repo related to the Airbnb pricing prediction example

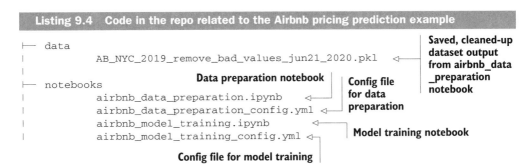

The airbnb_data_preparation notebook saves a pickled version of the cleaned-up dataframe that can be used as input to the deep learning model training notebook, airbnb_model_training. This notebook is a simplified version of the model training notebook for the streetcar delay prediction problem. The target for this simple model is whether the price for an Airbnb property is going to be below (0) or above (1) the average price. The key changes in this notebook from the version used in the main example in this book include the following:

- Membership in the column lists for categorical, continuous, and text columns is set in the config file airbnb_model_training_config.yml rather than in the note-book itself (see the next listing).

> **Listing 9.5   Parameters for column categories for the Airbnb price prediction model**

```
categorical:                         ◁──────  List of categorical
    - 'neighbourhood_group'                    columns
    - 'neighbourhood'
    - 'room_type'
continuous:                          ◁──────  List of continuous
    - 'minimum_nights'                         columns
    - 'number_of_reviews'
    - 'reviews_per_month'
    - 'calculated_host_listings_count'
text: []
excluded:                            ◁──────  List of columns excluded
    - 'price'                                  from training the model
    - 'id'
    - 'latitude'
    - 'longitude'
    - 'host_name'
    - 'last_review'
    - 'name'
    - 'host_name'
    - 'availability_365'
```

List of text columns

- The dataset is read in directly from the pickle file produced by the airbnb_data _preparation notebook and fed into the pipeline. By contrast, the model train-ing notebook for the streetcar delay prediction model contains extensive code to refactor the dataset.

To examine how the model training works with the Airbnb NYC dataset, we'll run the same series of experiments we ran for the streetcar delay prediction model in chapter 6, using the following columns to train the model:

- *Continuous*—minimum_nights, number_of_reviews, reviews_per_month, calculated_host_listings_count
- *Categorical*—neighbourhood_group, neighbourhood, room_type

You can see the results of these experiments on the Airbnb NYC model in figure 9.20.

As you can see, with a minimal amount of code changes, we were able to get rea-sonable results with the Airbnb NYC dataset. The adaptation described in this section is by no means complete, but it demonstrates how you can adapt the approach described in this book to train a deep learning model for a new dataset.

Experiment	Epochs	Early stop enabled?	Weight for "1" (delay) values	Early stop controls		Terminal validation accuracy	Precision on test set: true positive/(true positive + false positive)	Recall on test set: true positive/(true positive + false negative)
				Monitor	Mode			
1	10	no	1.0	NA	NA	0.73	0.6	0.25
2	50	no	1.0	NA	NA	0.75	0.57	0.8
3	50	no	Price ≤ mean/ price > mean	NA	NA	0.55	0.4	0.9
4	50	yes	Price ≤ mean/ price > mean	Validation loss	Min	0.74	0.53	0.86
5	50	yes	Price ≤ mean/ price > mean	Validation accuracy	Max	0.73	0.58	0.78

Figure 9.20   Airbnb NYC model experiment summary

9.13   *Resources for additional learning*

We have covered a broad range of technical issues in this book to build an end-to-end deep learning solution to the streetcar delay prediction problem. But we have only scratched the surface when it comes to the incredibly rich and fast-moving world of deep learning. Here are some additional resources that I recommend if you want to get a deeper background in deep learning:

- *Online deep learning overview courses*—The fast.ai Practical Deep Learning for Coders course (https://course.fast.ai/) is an accessible introduction to deep learning that focuses on learning by doing. It covers classic deep learning applications like image classification as well as recommender systems and other applications of deep learning. I credit this course with sparking my interest in applying deep learning to structured data. You can follow along with the course online for free while using the course forum to connect with other learners. The instructor, Jeremy Howard, is incredibly clear and passionate.

  A contrasting approach to learning about deep learning is the deeplearning.ai Deep Learning Specialization (http://mng.bz/PPm5). This series of online courses, taught by deep learning legend Andrew Ng, starts with the theoretical basics of deep learning and grows from there to cover coding topics. You can audit the deeplearning.ai course for free, but there is a charge to get your coursework marked and to get a certificate on completion of the courses. The specialization is split into five topics that cover technical and practical problems related to deep learning. The coding work in fast.ai is more interesting, but deeplearning.ai does a better job on the math behind deep learning. If you have the time and energy, doing both of these programs will give you a well-rounded grounding in deep learning.

- *Books*—I introduced Francois Chollet's *Deep Learning with Python* in chapter 1 as a great overview of applying deep learning with Python. If you want to get more experience with the PyTorch library that the fast.ai course uses, *Deep Learning with PyTorch* by Eli Stevens et al. is a great resource. *Deep Learning for Natural Language Processing* by Stephan Raaijmakers is a good example of a book that focuses on a particular application of deep learning, as does *Deep Learning for Vision Systems* by Mohamed Elgendy. If you want to examine deep learning in languages other than Python, *Deep Learning with R*, by François Chollet with J. J. Allaire, provides an exploration of deep learning with the other classic machine learning language, and *Deep Learning with JavaScript* by Shanqing Cai et al. shows you how to take advantage of TensorFlow.js to create deep learning models entirely in the lingua franca of web development, JavaScript. Finally, the main instructor for the fast.ai course, Jeremy Howard, is co-author of *Deep Learning for Coders with Fastai & PyTorch* (O'Reilly Media, 2020), which not only expands on the fast.ai course material, but also contains a section on deep learning with structured data.

- *Other resources*—In addition to online courses and books, there are many sources for learning more about deep learning. In fact, there is such a huge amount of material being produced about deep learning that it's hard to identify the best sources. To see what is happening on the cutting edge, the arXiv moderated list for recent machine learning submissions (https://arxiv.org/list/cs.LG/recent) is a good starting point, although the volume and challenging nature of the material can be daunting. I depend on Medium, especially the *Towards Data Science* publication (https://towardsdatascience.com), for a regular stream of accessible, bite-size articles on deep learning topics. Medium is also a friendly place to write articles to share your technical accomplishments with other people who are interested in machine learning.

In addition to these resources for deep learning, there are some interesting developments in the area of applying deep learning to structured data. Google's TabNet, for example (https://arxiv.org/abs/1908.07442), is aimed squarely at the problem of applying deep learning to structured data. The article at http://mng.bz/v99x provides a great summary of the TabNet approach as well as a useful guide to applying TabNet to new problems. The article explains that TabNet implements an attention mechanism (http://mng.bz/JDmQ), which allows the network to learn which subset of the input to apply focus to and facilitates explainability (identifying which inputs are significant for the output).

Summary

- You can add additional data sources to the dataset used to train the streetcar delay prediction model. For example, you can add information about subsets of the streetcar routes to allow your users to get predictions that are focused on a specific part of a streetcar route. You can also incorporate weather data to account for the impact that extreme weather can have on streetcar delays.

- The approach described in this book can be applied to other datasets. With some minor modifications, you can adapt the streetcar delay data preparation and model training notebooks to train a basic model to predict the prices of Airbnb properties in New York City.
- When you are assessing whether a particular structured data problem is a good candidate for deep learning, you should confirm that the dataset is large enough (at least tens of thousands of records), varied enough (a variety of types of columns), and balanced enough (enough examples for the deep learning model to pick up a signal) to be applicable to deep learning.
- You can use ngrok to make the web deployment from chapter 8 available to users outside your local system.
- The body of information about deep learning keeps growing all the time. You can take advantage of books that explore deep learning from different perspectives, such as other programming languages (such as JavaScript) or other application areas (such as natural language processing). In addition to books, there are excellent online resources, including courses, blogs, and scholarly articles.

appendix
Using Google Colaboratory

In chapter 2, we introduced the development environments available for creating and training your deep learning model. In that chapter, I recommended Paperspace Gradient as an optimal cloud-based, deep learning development environment because it balances cost and features. Gradient is not free, but it is much easier to keep track of the cost of Gradient than to control the cost of the machine learning environments in Google Cloud Platform, AWS, or Azure. If your primary concern is cost, however, Google's Colaboratory (referred to as *Colab* through the remainder of this appendix) offers an entirely free environment that is more than adequate for basic deep learning projects. In this appendix, we will go over the key points that you need to know to exercise the code examples with Colab and contrast its advantages with those of Paperspace Gradient.

A.1 Introduction to Colab

Colab is a free, cloud-based Jupyter Notebooks environment that you can use to develop your deep learning projects. Google provides a comprehensive introduction to using Colab (http://mng.bz/w92g) that covers everything that you need to get started. An article at http://mng.bz/VdBG also contains a wealth of helpful tips.

Here is a quick summary of some key characteristics of Colab:

- Colab offers a variety of hardware configurations, including access to GPUs and TPUs (Google's hardware accelerator specifically designed for use with TensorFlow).
- To use Colab, you need a Google ID (http://mng.bz/7VY4).
- If you don't already have Google Drive set up for your Google account, set up Drive by following the instructions at http://mng.bz/4BBB.

- Colab has an interface that incorporates some aspects of JupyterLab (a web-based interface for Jupyter). Although this interface is not identical to the familiar Jupyter Notebooks interface, it takes only a few minutes to get used to it, and it has some useful features that aren't in standard notebooks, including a table of contents and a gallery of code snippets that you can easily copy into your Colab notebook. Figure A.1 shows the Colab interface.

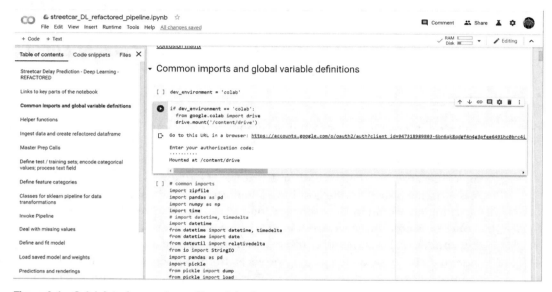

Figure A.1   Colab interface: not a vanilla notebook

- By default, when you save a notebook in Colab, it is saved to a special directory in Drive, so you have access to your work outside the context of Colab (figure A.2).

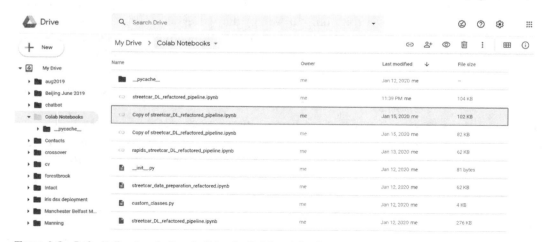

Figure A.2   Default directory in Google Drive for Colab notebooks

This section covered some of the key things you need to know to use Colab. You can refer to the Google documentation (http://mng.bz/mgE0) for complete details on how to use Colab, but we will cover one essential feature in the next section: how to make Google Drive available in Colab.

A.2 *Making Google Drive available in your Colab session*

To get the most out of Colab, you need to mount your Google Drive so that it is accessible in your Colab session. When you have set up access to Drive, your Colab notebooks are accessible at the path /content/drive/My Drive. You can read files from directories in your Drive and write files to Drive as you would to a local filesystem.

To get access to files on Drive from within your notebook, follow these steps:

1 Run the following statements in your notebook:

```
from google.colab import drive
drive.mount('/content/drive')
```

When you run these statements, you get the result shown in figure A.3.

Go to this URL in a browser: https://accounts.google.com/o/oauth2/auth?client_id=947318989803-6bn6qk8qdgf4n4g3pfee

Enter your authorization code:

Figure A.3 **Prompt to enter your authorization code**

2 Click the link to select an account (figure A.4).

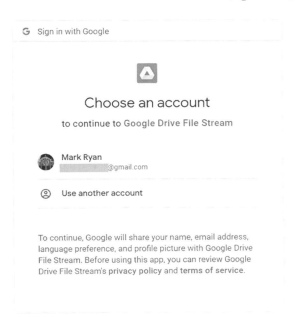

Figure A.4 **Selecting an account**

3 In the screen for Google Drive File Stream access, click Allow (figure A.5).

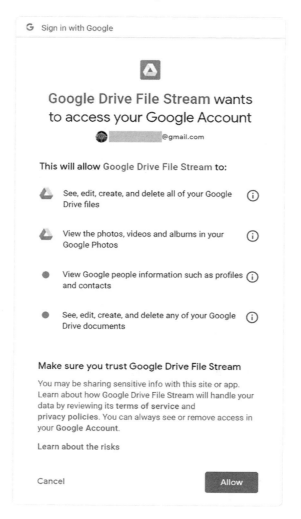

Figure A.5   Allowing Google Drive File Stream access

4 In the Sign In screen, click the Copy icon to copy your access code (figure A.6).

Figure A.6   Copying the access code

5 Return to Colab, paste in the authorization code field, and press Enter (figure A.7).

```
from google.colab import drive
drive.mount('/content/drive')

Go to this URL in a browser: https://accounts.google.com/o/oauth2/auth?client_id=947318989803-6bn6qk8qdgf4n4g3pfee6491hc0brc4i

Enter your authorization code:
[•••••••••••••••••••••••••••••••••••••••••••••••••••••••                    ]
```

Figure A.7   Pasting the access code in your Colab notebook

The cell runs and produces the mounted message shown in figure A.8 to confirm that your Google Drive has been mounted and is available to your Colab notebook.

```
from google.colab import drive
drive.mount('/content/drive')

Go to this URL in a browser: https://accounts.google.com/o/oauth2/auth?client_id=947318989803-6bn6qk8qdgf4n4g3pfee6491hc0brc4i

Enter your authorization code:
..........
Mounted at /content/drive
```

Figure A.8   Confirmation that Google Drive is successfully mounted

By following the steps in this section, you have made your Google Drive available in your Colab notebook. In section A.3, we'll contrast the strengths of Colab and Paperspace Gradient.

A.3   *Making the repo available in Colab and running notebooks*

If you are using Colab to run through the code examples in this book, you need to be aware of some quirks in the way that Colab and Drive work together. In addition to following the instructions in section A.2 to make Drive accessible in Colab, you need to

- Clone the repo (http://mng.bz/xmXX) to a new folder in Drive.
- Ensure that the current directory when you run one of the notebooks is the notebooks directory of your clone of the repo.

First, clone the repo by following these steps:

1 In Drive, create a new folder in the root folder.
    For this exercise, call the new folder dl_june_17.
2 Access the new folder, right-click the background, and choose More -> Google Colaboratory from the contextual menu (figure A.9).
    Colab opens in a new tab.

Figure A.9   Starting Colab from a new folder in Drive

3 Choose Connect -> Connect to hosted runtime (figure A.10).

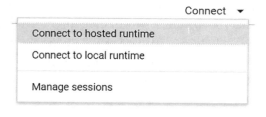

Figure A.10   Connect to a hosted runtime in Colab

4 Follow the steps in section A.2 to make Drive accessible in Colab.

5 To access the dl_june_17 folder you created in step 1, create a new cell in your notebook by clicking +code; then copy and paste the following code into the new cell and run it:

```
%cd /content/drive/My Drive/dl_june_17
```

6 Create another new cell in your notebook in Colab, and run the following as a single line in the new cell to clone the repo:

```
! git clone https://github.com/ryanmark1867/\
deep_learning_for_structured_data.git
```

Now that you have cloned the repo to Drive, you are ready to open one of the notebooks in Colab. The following steps show how to open the model training notebook from the repo and make it ready to run:

1 In Colab, choose File -> Locate in Drive (figure A.11).

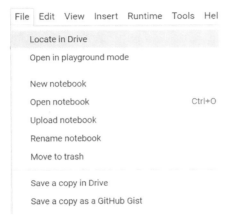

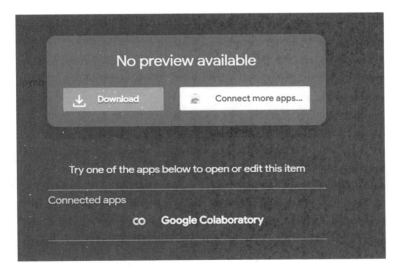

Figure A.11   **Locate in Drive menu selection**

2 Navigate to the notebooks directory where you cloned the repo.
3 Double click streetcar_model_training.ipynb, and select Google Colaboratory in the screen that appears (figure A.12).

The notebook streetcar_model_training.ipynb opens in Colab.

Figure A.12   **Screen that appears when you double-click a notebook file in Drive**

4   Choose Connect -> Connect to Hosted Runtime.

5   Follow the instructions in section A.2 to ensure that Drive is accessible in this notebook.

6   Add a new cell to the notebook, and run the following to make the notebooks directory in the cloned repo your current directory:

```
%cd /content/drive/My Drive/dl_june_17/deep_learning_for_structured_data
```

Now you have completed the steps to make the repo accessible in Colab and to make the notebooks runnable. Note that every time you start a new Colab session, after you have opened one of the notebooks, you will need to follow the steps to make Drive accessible in the notebook and to make the notebooks directory in the cloned repo your current directory.

A.4   *Pros and cons of Colab and Paperspace*

Whether you choose Colab or Paperspace Gradient for your deep learning project will depend on your needs. For most people, cost is the deciding factor in choosing Colab. In my opinion, Paperspace Gradient's advantages in terms of convenience and predictability justify its cost. But Colab is a great option if you want a choice with zero cost. This section contrasts the advantages of Colab (including cost) with the strong points of Paperspace Gradient.

Here are some of the advantages of Colab:

- *Free*—Paperspace Gradient has a modest hourly cost and a completely transparent billing model, but you still pay for every hour that your Paperspace Gradient notebook is active. Further, with a basic subscription, a Gradient notebook gets shut down automatically after 12 hours (figure A.13). If you have an active Gradient session and forget to shut it down, you will be paying for it for 12 hours. I know from experience the sinking feeling that comes from waking up and realizing that I wasted some money because I forgot to shut down Gradient, and my notebook ran all night.

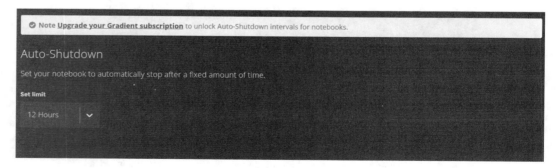

Figure A.13   **With a basic subscription, Gradient notebooks get shut down automatically after 12 hours.**

- *Integrated with Google Drive*—If you already take advantage of Google Drive, you will appreciate the slick integration of Drive with Colab. Google has done a really good job with this integration.
- *Large user community*—Colab has a big user community, with many questions about it answered in Stack Overflow (http://mng.bz/6gO5). Paperspace states that more than 100,000 developers use Gradient (https://paperspace.com/gradient). I have not been able to find a similar estimate for Colab users, but the amount of Stack Overflow traffic for Colab suggests that it has a bigger user community.

Here are some of the advantages of Paperspace Gradient:

- *Completely integrated environment*—Paperspace Gradient is completely tuned for deep learning and uses a standard Jupyter environment. By contrast, Colab has some esoteric aspects that take some getting used to if you're used to vanilla Jupyter notebooks.
- *Independence from the Google infrastructure*—Colab is deeply integrated with the Google infrastructure; you need a Google ID and Google Drive to use Colab. If you are working in a jurisdiction that limits access to the Google infrastructure, this requirement could prevent you from using Colab. Where you do your daily work isn't the only consideration; ask yourself whether you will ever have to do a demo or a conference presentation on your deep learning work in a jurisdiction where access to the Google infrastructure is limited.
- *Dedicated resources*—Your Paperspace Gradient virtual environment is yours, and after an instance has been started, you have access to all its resources. Colab resources are not guaranteed, and it's possible that you will not be able to get the resources you need for a deep learning project at a particular time. If you are flexible about when you do your work, this situation should not be a problem. I have never had a problem getting resources in Colab, but it is theoretically possible that you wouldn't be able to get GPU or TPU resources in Colab when you need them.
- *Support*—When you set up a Paperspace Gradient environment, you pay for every hour that the environment is active. Part of what you get from this cost is support. I have had to contact Paperspace support three times over the past two years, and each time, I received a quick initial response from Paperspace and quick resolution of the issue. Colab is free, so you will not get this kind of personalized support.
- *Faster model training*—Comparing the training runs of experiment 1 (10 epochs, no early stopping, default weighting of 0 and 1 results) in chapter 7, Paperspace is around 30 percent faster than Colab (1 minute, 49 seconds for Paperspace and 2 minutes, 32 seconds for Colab). My experience was that I got the best results by selecting None or TPU in the Hardware Accelerator field of Notebook Settings (displayed by choosing Runtime -> Change Runtime Type).

Selecting GPU as the hardware accelerator yielded worse results for this test (figure A.14).

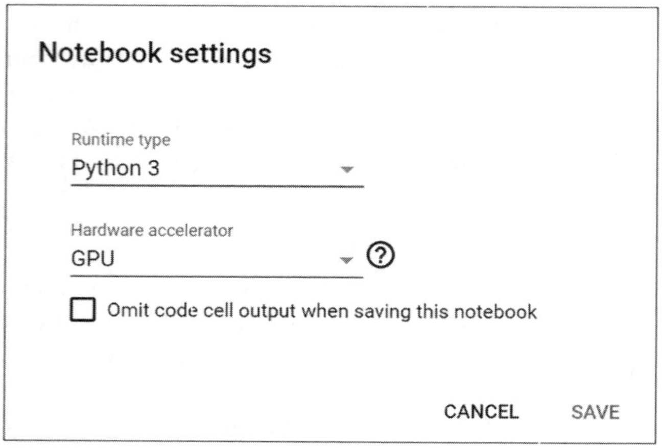

Figure A.14   Setting the hardware accelerator

- *Consistent times for training runs*—Running the same training experiment multiple times on Paperspace took about the same amount of time each time, whereas the time to run identical training experiments on Colab varied considerably.

In this section, we've reviewed the pros and cons of Colab and Paperspace Gradient. Both are great environments for a deep learning project; which one you choose depends on your own requirements.

index